WHO KNEW

BARRY DILLER

Simon & Schuster

New York   Amsterdam/Antwerp   London
Toronto   Sydney/Melbourne   New Delhi

Simon & Schuster
1230 Avenue of the Americas
New York, NY 10020

Copyright © 2025 by Barry Diller

First Simon & Schuster hardcover edition May 2025

Book text design by Paul Dippolito

Manufactured in the United States of America

1   3   5   7   9   10   8   6   4   2

Library of Congress Cataloging-in-Publication Data has been applied for.

ISBN 978-1-6680-9687-1
ISBN 978-1-6680-9689-5 (ebook)

For Diane . . . and Our Family

CONTENTS

ACT THREE

WHO KNEW

PREFACE

I did not set out to write a book about business, nor did I think I was qualified to write a teaching book. I've always thought my life was just a good story, and—if I was going to tell it, there was only one way—tell it personal and tell it true. Maybe that will be too personal for some, as my life has been so much about business, and while I've led a relatively public life, I've lived a selectively private one as well. I've never posed as something I wasn't, but I've long thought it all too complicated to explain or make declarations. And, when I was young, in the United States of the 1960s, I was far too afraid. I'm no longer that and too old to care, so let the story begin.

ACT ONE

loving, that I ached for a family just like that. One of the most paradigmatic shows of glorious family life, *Make Room for Daddy* mirrored what actually went on every day in the Thomas household, which was also so Catholic that a wood carving of *The Last Supper* took up a whole wall in their dining room.

Danny Thomas was that rare public man who was as loved and revered by his family as he was by his adoring fans. I admired everything about them—how they supported one another, the discipline and rules of the household, and the glamour that swirled around them.

One of my magical fantasies was that I would someday marry Terre, one of my first teenage kissing partners, but in the middle of my fateful nineteenth year, I left a party at the Thomases' and got in my car to drive home. Before I got very far, just a few blocks from their house, I ran out of gas. It was late and I didn't want to bother them, so I walked to the nearest gas station to get a can of gas. On the way back, walking up the dead quiet of Elm Drive, I passed the Thomas house and thought of Terre and my daydream. With the gas can in my hand, the actual truth of my situation flashed into my brain. *No, wait a minute, I can't do that. I'm abnormal. I'm not entitled to have a family and children and a life.*

But as quickly as that terrible thought came, it whooshed away, like the vapors from the gas I was pouring into my car. The car coughed to life and I drove home, crawled into my bed, and was quickly asleep.

I woke at three a.m. with a sharp cramp in my left leg, and I became convinced I was paralyzed. I felt pure unrelenting fear. Of course, the leg was not paralyzed, but I couldn't shake the thought.

I was having my first anxiety attack.

I'd never felt any kind of anxiety before; it was all kept in check by the magic boxes I'd so carefully and compulsively built. I didn't know why the magic had stopped working, but it surely had, because all I felt was panic. I couldn't sleep, and I couldn't think it away as the hours wore on. Finally, quavering, I managed to get up and go to my mother's room. I woke her up and said, "I don't know why, but I can't fall asleep." She shrugged and gave me one of her sleeping pills, and that put me out for a few hours.

CHAPTER 1

The household I grew up in was perfectly dysfunctional. My parents separated often and came a day short of divorce several times before I was ten; my brother was a drug addict by age thirteen; and I was a sexually confused holder of secrets from the age of eleven.

We lived in the pocket square of Beverly Hills, where I was cosseted from the realities of life outside its tiny, manicured borders. My early connection to that outer world, primarily through television, was dominated by shows about the American family of the 1950s that were as unreal as the blonde of my mother's hair. I didn't know anything about grit and grime or much of anything else outside that palm-treed cocoon of wealth and superficiality.

The first years of my life were spent bouncing by plane or train up and down the California coast, going from San Francisco, where I was born, to Beverly Hills, where my father had moved to join his brother in the family construction business. My parents' geographical separation was a good cover for the ever-impending end of their marriage. So, down and back I would go for occasional weekends with my father. In San Francisco, I would wait each night for my mother to return from her dates with rich furriers, nervously scurrying from my bed to the living room's huge front window, watching each car come down the street, hoping she would be in one of them. By day I dodged the nanny she left me with, who repeatedly threatened to boil me in a pot on the nearby stove, and tried to avoid my brother, who, like a cat with a mouse, terrorized me for his pleasure.

When we finally moved back together as a family, my generally non-communicative father would take us on Sunday nights to Restaurant Row on La Cienega for silent dinners. I thought then he simply just didn't much want to talk with us. Later, after reading his eloquent and loving letters to my mother while they were separated, I came to see just how much was buried under his grumpy surface—how much she wanted the marriage to end, and how earnestly he wanted it to continue.

My father was Jewish, but he spurned any religiosity because his family had been so oppressively observant. He was the neglected youngest from a very religious family of fourteen, and his parents seemed to stop caring or paying attention to the children after the tenth or eleventh came along. They lived over their delicatessen on McAllister Street in San Francisco, and all the children wanted out as soon as possible. They also all prospered—but had no great fraternity with or for each other. My father and one of his brothers were in business together for thirty years, and we lived two blocks from him and his family, but they were never in our house nor were we in theirs. I also never met my paternal grandparents, or most of my aunts, uncles, and cousins. Relations with relatives were never of interest to the Diller family. Whatever happened growing up in that apartment above that delicatessen must have seared them all.

What took my father from his San Francisco–based construction-supply business to Los Angeles was the postwar housing boom in Southern California, where servicemen coming back from World War II were starting families and looking to use their government loans to buy homes in that sunny land of plenty. Back then, the great valley basin was mostly endless citrus orchards and thousands of acres of undeveloped land. My father, his brother, and three entrepreneurial colleagues essentially bought and built entire sections of Southern California—the San Fernando Valley, Palos Verdes, West Covina—replacing vast orange orchards with hundreds of thousands of tract homes, sometimes in ten-thousand-unit parcels divided into four basic models, mostly indistinguishable from each other. Men like my father made fortunes delivering the American dream to young couples in cookie-cutter houses in made-from-scratch communities. My father was far from the dominating force, that was his brilliant elder brother, and he always felt in his shadow.

When I went down to Los Angeles for weekends, he would take me on Sundays to the openings of these tracts, where streams of veterans and their young families lined up to view the model homes. There was great excitement and a carnival atmosphere around the housing, which was still in short supply. Banners flew in the breeze at the entrance to the office, where the families queued for hours to sign up for as-yet-unbuilt houses.

My father always seemed contained and worried, without ever disclosing why. During the time I was growing up, he built houses, but never bought one. He had a generally cranky glass-half-empty outlook on most things. I don't think he took pleasure in making money, and the only extravagances he displayed were buying the occasional Patek Philippe watch and his yearly trip to the Cadillac showroom to get the latest-model convertible. It was so rare to see his exuberance that I remember clearly his unrestrained smile when, in 1959, he roared up our driveway in a flashy, fire-engine-red Cadillac with exaggerated tail fins and white leather interior. Once he'd obtained some wealth, he mostly floated along, only worrying it might disappear.

He wasn't particularly ambitious or charged up about life and its possibilities. Work for him wasn't an avocation. I never understood exactly what he did. He'd go to his modernist office building on Wilshire Boulevard in the mornings for a few hours and leave in the early afternoon for his club. Day after day, no highs or lows, no business intrigues or stories about accomplishments or setbacks were ever discussed with the family. The only "business" I ever remember hearing about was my father showing me a copy of the $6 million check he'd just signed in 1950 to buy the Platt Ranch, the last remaining large open field in the San Fernando Valley. I had never seen or even heard of such a mind-boggling figure, though the riches it was to bring us didn't mean we were living any better or worse than all our neighbors in the Beverly Hills Flats. "Better" and "worse" are relative terms; there wasn't really an actual worse there.

Beverly Hills was then and is still now divided to the north and south by Santa Monica Boulevard. The south was the "poor" section, and the farther north you went was the wealthier. Relatively again, ridiculously so, since no one was anything close to "poor." We were three-fourths north, on Bedford Drive, the endlessly photographed street with the tall palms that personified the city to the world; at that time, especially compared to now, there was very little outré display. The houses were all nice, but rarely extravagant, and no one talked much of money. Yes, we knew we were privileged, but nothing like the one-percenters of today. It was more balanced in the 1950s, with fewer extremes at the higher end, and there was a pervasive sense of optimism. In Beverly Hills, there were no gates in front of houses, and no one kept their doors locked; there were no fears about safety, other than economic ones, and those fears mostly belonged to the movie folk, who worried they might lose the jobs for which they knew they were overcompensated. Our values were much the same as any small town—and we did call it a town. The two streets of commercial activity we called "the Village," as in "Let's go down to the Village and see a movie." Little thought was given to those living just a few miles away in greater Los Angeles. Ours was a very prosaic and cloistered town with our blinders firmly in place until the Watts Riots in 1965 jarred us into awareness.

This unsettled life of mine continued, with my mother filing and un-filing for divorce, my parents seesawing back and forth from breakup to tentative reconciliation. I never heard any brawling—I think they were just mildly, chronically aggravated with each other. My mother wanted something more, though I never heard her put it into words. During their last separation, the divorce papers stayed in effect for almost the entire year it took to get a final decree in California. On the last day, after my father wrote a tenderhearted plea for my mother to reconsider, they reunited, this time for the rest of their lives, and we settled into a sweet little house with a white picket fence. That house was the first of four, none separated by more than a mile, that we more or less inhabited during the next twenty years. I say "more or less" because all the houses were remarkably underfurnished, reflecting in some unconscious way the impermanence and instability of the life within. There were entire rooms that seemed forgotten, bereft of any attempt at decoration or design. This was counter to my parents' growing affluence, something that seemed to me a kind of old-world Jewish shibboleth, as in "The Cossacks might be coming at any time, so make nothing permanent." There was also something else going on directly threatening me: my dread brother was becoming ever more sadistic to me, and causing my parents much worry about his emerging drug use. As a result, they hadn't the time or interest in either decoration or me. I was also beginning to learn that the exteriors of many of those picture-perfect Beverly Hills homes contrasted sharply with the roiling lives inside.

My brother was almost four years older than me. He was extraordinarily intelligent, physically beautiful, and artistically talented; when he took up the piano at ten he was a genuine prodigy. Until his adolescence we were on the pleasant and light side of kindred spirits. But around puberty he became nasty and cruel to me and increasingly silent with our parents. I have mostly submerged all the grisly details, but later in life family friends recounted how gruesomely and violently abusive he was toward me. They remembered that once he took one of those old heavy Bakelite telephones and twirled it around like a lariat, finally landing it on the side of my head, knocking me out cold. At thirteen, he started hanging out with the few rough kids at Beverly Hills High (there were no more than that out of two thousand). Shortly afterward he started smoking marijuana and very quickly advanced to heroin. By the age of sixteen he was hooked for life.

It was our closely guarded secret; having a drug addict in the family wasn't a topic to be shared in the mid-1950s. And he seemed to be about the only child with this affliction; Beverly Hills wasn't some bebop den of iniquities. All I knew then was that drug abuse existed in the squalid parts of cities. There was not a single student I was aware of at Beverly High who took anything harder than an aspirin. Without anyone to go to for advice, all my parents could do was clumsily hunt and peck their way through in search of a solution. They believed his behavior was somehow their fault, and they had the money, so money was thrown every which way to try and help him. They sent him to a series of psychiatrists, one of whom was the first doctor to use LSD therapeutically. For a summer they shipped him off to a kibbutz in Israel, then to the severe Black-Foxe Military Institute, but he only lasted there one semester before being asked to leave.

Maybe the airlessness or lack of parenting affected him more than me, or maybe it's just a mystery that so many affected families are never able to solve.

My mother always tried to have a cheery good time, signing her letters her entire life with a hand-drawn smiley face. She had endless friends and an active social life, but there were also migraines, which belied the happy face she showed to everyone. She was never a deep thinker, and her problems went mostly unexamined. In our surface lives, nothing of any substance was ever discussed. Monosyllables ruled.

I knew almost nothing of the life she had before I was born. She said her mother was Jewish, but I hardly ever saw her, and my mother rarely spoke of her father. He had been run over by a trolley car in San Francisco when she was three years old. If he was ever mentioned at all, she simply called him by his surname, "Mr. Addison." My grandmother quickly remarried a well-off walnut merchant and with monstrous selfishness put her only daughter in an orphanage. She was five years old. My mother remained locked away there until she was sixteen. She never forgave her mother and never discussed with me her time in the orphanage. I often wondered if she'd been molested there; the surface gaiety, niceness, and kindness she displayed toward others seemed to hide a basic lack of emotional plumbing, as if it had been soldered shut.

My mother was not unloving—when I was a toddler she babied me like the best of them, but had no idea how to be a mother. She had never had one herself.

She sent me to sleepaway camp for the first time when I was four. Yes, four. I was a few years below the minimum-age requirement, but she bribed the people who owned the camp, and I stayed not with the campers but with the camp owners in their house. For six wonderful weeks I cozied into the structure of a real family unit. Three years later, I went back to the same camp, but I was old enough to be in the general population. I was miserable. I felt isolated and alone. In desperation I called my mother and begged her to come and pick me up. I remember waiting at the camp's entrance—sitting on a tree stump alone for hours. She'd assured me she would come straightaway. As each car approached, I peered up expectantly, then resumed my vigil when it wasn't her inside. I stayed there all day. The head of the camp suggested several times that I should come back inside, but I refused. Then it got dark and I knew she wasn't going to come.

I gave up on my mother that night. There would be no rescue. There was no one to protect me. I knew then that I was on my own. A very scary thing for this seven-year-old. As I walked down that driveway back to the life of the camp, I buried that fear and resolved never to trust anyone other than myself again. My mother, Reva Addison Diller, was the only member of my family I had dared depend on, and now I knew for certain that had been a mistake. My father never fathered me, and my brother didn't brother me, so losing my mother shattered my universe. That summer at camp, I cemented myself shut. I became cold and pragmatic and skeptical of all humans on all human affairs. I saw it very clearly. My parents and brother would not have a role in my development. There was never going to be any discussion about my hopes or dreams or worries. We were not going to engage about ideas or books or world affairs. All the rangy discussions overheard at friends' dinner tables with their parents only reinforced that I lived in an alternate universe. I accepted without anger or malice (*at least on the surface*) that this was what my family was like. While always polite and proper with my parents, I held out no hope it would change.

The reserved atmosphere that deeply permeated our family has made it forever hard for me to break out of it with anyone else. We were the deformed results of generations of emotionally stunted families, from my grandparents to my parents and from them to me. It wasn't until late in life that those barriers would be torn down and a new family would form around me.

I have no memory of the bad years with my brother, so deeply did I bury my emotions. I think it was my first act of compartmentalization. As a child I didn't know it had a name, but I discovered I could separate myself from anything painful or terrifying by just locking it away, putting it into a distant box, and having to deal with it hopefully never. This prevented any tidal waves of fear and anxiety from overwhelming me. Compartmentalizing these unwanted feelings became so successful that it has both ruled and riled my life ever since.

There was one other, more fantastical method I began to embrace to control my thoughts and keep my worries aloft. It was off-the-rack obsessive-compulsive behavior, though I wasn't able to name it, either, until I was older. That's where, at nineteen, the dam broke and I had an actual heart- and mind-racing nervous breakdown. All I was certain of then was that if I repeated the same action, a very specific action, in exactly the same way, I would be safe. Like never stepping on a line in the pavement, like never passing the salt. Those are prosaic and bromidic examples, but mine were epic: If I moved an object on a shelf, I'd have to be sure that it remained exactly there or was returned to that exact spot when it was moved again. I couldn't let it deviate a millimeter. That began as a minute (*min*-it) or so rearrangement, but by my mid-teens it took half an hour of minute (my-*noot*) readjustment to get it exactly right. Otherwise I would be in danger.

As my fear of the consequences from my incipient homosexuality mounted—*from the age of eight I knew and didn't know and didn't know and knew*—this compulsion grew to alarming proportions; I spent many hours making absolutely certain I was obeying my increasingly exacting rules. I thought I was the only human behaving in this obsessively delusional way. The word picture I conjured was an anvil hanging by the most tenuous wire over my head and the discovery of my sexuality would snap that wire and the anvil would come crashing down. In the context of the fantasy, it was perfectly symmetrical. A perfectly crazy symmetry, perhaps, but there it is.

If I looked at actual real life around me at all, I looked at it through the lens of my mother's moods. I believed my essential purpose was to make her feel as good as she could and to explain away and rationalize anything that might demoralize her. I intuitively knew when she was unhappy despite her bright exterior. Infusing her with optimism became my mission, my reason for being. Whenever something unpleasant or depressing came up in her life I'd find a way to turn it positive, to distract her with what seemed my native optimism. This started simply as a departure from reality to placate my mother, but, despite everything about my surroundings, it evolved into a bedrock trait, one of my few and very cherished natural buoyancies. While I was sure we had to be the only family on the planet with both a drug addict and a sexually deviant child, I also knew that I was the only one who could pacify my mother's anxieties. If I could do that, then the world—especially my internal world—would be safer. A by-product of this was that I learned early on how to please others better than almost anyone. It eventually became a superpower of sorts, and explains, if anything does, my surprising early-career success. Its corollary was the ability to talk myself out of and around any trouble I got in. Whatever pranks at school I was nailed for, I could always come up with the most imaginative and novel excuses to extricate myself from the punishments I surely deserved.

I developed the ability to say the right thing in order to make a situation better, whether or not it was anchored to any moral belief. I had no core at all, other than to please those who needed pleasing. And except for the self-sufficient few, everyone needs pleasing. This discovery was particularly valuable when applied to those who had power over me or who could further my ambitions. Because of this early training with my mother, I learned to seduce people, especially those much older than I was, and I could accomplish it on demand in any setting. All these ingredients of my botched childhood mixed together to make my early-adult behavior remarkably effective. I could please; I could subordinate myself effortlessly. I had the ability to keep secrets (no surprise there), and even after great success I could never allow any sign of arrogant behavior for fear that the ever-present anvil would drop full force on my exposed head.

I began gradually to gain some confidence in my ability to function on my own. My body was strong. I was never sick. I was discovering odd powers of concentration. I was able to intuit how things (certainly not people) worked. If you put something complex or mechanical in my hands, I could figure out how it worked just by touching and feeling it. Once, at age seven or eight, I fixed a motor simply by staring at it and fooling with its parts long enough to put them back together in the right place. I also began to be unafraid on my own. I was a walker in the city. Around that time, I'd set off alone from our house in San Francisco, trusting my navigating abilities more and more with each step.

My parents' eccentricities were in contrast with their best friends, a dentist and his wife, who had three dutiful and serious children. They had all the best values of a liberal Jewish intellectual family. They lived in a nice and neat house; there were rules and discipline and order. Their kids were about my age, and all their report cards—unlike mine—were looked over and discussed in depth. They were what I imagined a family was supposed to be, so far from what mine was. I yearned for what they had and would later learn that my father looked more than longingly at them, too.

By the time I was nine we had stopped our yo-yoing and moved permanently to Los Angeles, where I could stay out all night without any repercussions like a search or a frantic call to the police. I never had a curfew. My friends all had allowances and chores, but I was just given whatever money I needed, and there were never any disciplinary actions to deprive me of it if I went astray. I felt as if I were being raised in an overly plush forest. I watched my friends' characters grow as their parents gave them responsibilities. I figured I wasn't worth my parents bothering with any character building. They were decent people with solid basic values— kind, politically liberal, and good citizens. But there was never any conversation about anything concerning the lives of their children: no "How was school?"; no "Who are your friends?"; no "Where are you going?"; no celebrations of birthdays or holidays. A complete absence of celebrating anything.

I was a stranger in what seemed like a very well-ordered land, but I wasn't suffering, wasn't depressed or anxious about any of this—yet.

My friends and I were caricatures of our entitled environment. We got into the kinds of mischief only mindless kids living in Beverly Hills were capable of. It was tame even for that tame time. Like when we raided each of our houses for all their cleaning products, took them to the famous fountain at the corner of Santa Monica and Wilshire Boulevards, and dumped them into it at five in the morning. We gleefully watched the busiest intersection in Beverly Hills close down as the authorities tried to clean up the enormous mountain of suds.

There wasn't much physical fighting in our town. The only fight I was ever involved in happened when my friends and I were having a late-night snack at Biff's, the one local restaurant open after eleven. A group of kids from "out of town" (from Fairfax High, all of eight miles away) started razzing us as we were getting into Cary Goddard's father's flame-red Cadillac, so we turned around and followed them to their hangout—the famous Canter's deli on Fairfax—and began our no-dance version of *West Side Story*. It started when Cary took a tennis racket out of his trunk and bashed the window of their less snazzy car. Thus began our two-minute rumble, fists punching wildly every which way, a few bloodied body parts, and for me a run for my life back into the red Caddy and the safe borders of the Beverly Hills city limits. I mean, a tennis racket as a weapon . . .

School wasn't particularly competitive, and there was little anxiety about any future real-life complexities that might have worried less advantaged households. My group wasn't the smartest, we weren't the dumbest, we weren't the nerds or the outcasts or the neurotics; we were the popular, seemingly carefree kids who floated easily from moment to moment. If we had secrets, and I had a few whoppers, they weren't shared.

At fourteen we had been practicing a particularly cruel and painful rite of passage. The eight of us would choose one person and ditch them, meaning walk or ride away (on our bikes). A really mean spurning. After several months of not speaking to them, we'd let the ostracized one back into the group. Grateful, they'd help us find the next victim.

My day finally came. We were all hanging out at an overlook above Beverly Hills when they neatly choreographed stranding me while they whoopily rode off on their bikes. I biked home with the sadness of knowing the next months would be a lonely torture. I couldn't let that stand, and an hour later I got back on my bike and rode over the hill to a distant friend's house, and started a new circle of friends with a vow we'd never turn on each other. Probably for a lot of less-than-altruistic reasons, I didn't like the kid cruelty. And it was the first sign that I had resilience when adversity came my way.

My brother was one of the few bad boys in our little city. Once he got on hard drugs, life was a roller coaster. He'd go on and off heroin with regularity, and when he was off my parents were so relieved they'd get him a new car. Once he was using again, he would inevitably sell it or crash it. Then he'd get clean again, and he would be given another new car. He went through about ten cars by his early twenties. Amazing but true.

I wasn't jealous, but I knew that whatever had rotted my brother's brain wasn't going to be fixed with bribes. I hated how he dominated and subverted their lives, and I sensed all the attempts to help him would fail. My brother was their life burden, and the source of their guilt, but no matter what he did, they couldn't or wouldn't let go; they always held on to hope.

I did not. I knew who my brother was from the time I was nine years old, and I never changed my mind. He never changed his attitude toward me, either: he was disdainful of my very being. To him I was dumb and clunky, and probably homosexual. All this planted a corrosive and deep seed in me that there absolutely shouldn't—there *couldn't*—be two "bad" sons. One a drug addict and the other a sexual outcast. I thought that would be celestially unfair to my parents. Since one part of me was clearly bad, I had to try even harder to repress it, so that in every outward respect I could be the "good" son.

No one came into our little Beverly Hills enclave who didn't live there. There wasn't tourism in those days. We would go down to the Village— what is now the overdusted and glamorous shopping district of Rodeo Drive—to wander around or eat in the Hawaiian restaurant, the Luau, which was run by the movie star Lana Turner's ex-husband. We little rats didn't range outside our territory, other than on weekends, when we'd go to beach houses in Malibu. On winter Friday nights we'd go watch a brand-new movie at the home of the legendary Hollywood producer and studio head Pandro Berman or at the house of Lew Wasserman, the equally legendary head of MCA and Universal. They were always either out for the night or out of town, so their houses were our playhouses. They were always stocked with anything a kid would want—as in alcohol and food—and no one was ever home to supervise or prevent us fourteen-year-olds from taking their cars out for a midnight drive. It is no great thing to be as unaware as I was about life outside our borders; I wish I could say I was curious about lives less privileged, but I just wasn't, a permanent knock on my spoiled, know-nothing self.

It was at Pandro Berman's that I first met Nora Ephron, who would become one of the great chroniclers of late twentieth-century life. She was about a year older than me, and we became friends. I would walk her home along the Santa Monica paths, and we would have long emotional talks about the flirtations she was having and I was not. What I was having weren't the normal flirtations of postadolescence.

I was sixteen, driving my red Thunderbird down Sunset Boulevard on a hot July night. At a stoplight in West Hollywood, I caught the eye of a shaggy blond guy standing on his terrace. He motioned to the parking space below his apartment. Like a tractor beam and without conscious thought, I turned left and parked. Up the stairs and into his apartment. It was tame and fairly uneventful, and that was an underwhelming that.

I drove away, firmly thinking, *Well, okay—did that—but I'll never have to do it again.*

About a month later, though, as I sat in an overstuffed chair at a friend's house, I realized with dread that, like a serial killer, I had an overpowering urge to go back. I picked myself up and, while my four friends kept on trash-talking with each other, silently headed out the door.

I drove back to the building, ran up the stairs, knocked on his door, and . . . did it again. It was then I knew this wasn't a meaningless childhood experiment. It's what I would want to do forever.

From that point on, my sexual excursions increased at exactly the same velocity as my obsessive-compulsive ministrations, without my ever relating them to each other.

Even Inspector Clouseau couldn't be that clueless. But I was.

These brief, mostly one-off encounters began with street cruising in West Hollywood. Some were in bars along Melrose Avenue, where I'd dart in and out through a side door, wary of anyone seeing me. I was so afraid of everything, other than the actual sex of it. My fears were rarely realized, except for one traumatizing experience when I was eighteen. I had my own phone line that rang late one night—the caller said that unless I paid him $10,000 he would expose me to my parents. I hung up, shivered for days, but he never called back. What a terror those times brought to these otherwise healthy pursuits.

I wasn't able to get interested in school. I wasn't diligent, I wasn't competitive, nor was I much involved or engaged. I had no ambition and no expectations or enough of a sense of self to think I qualified for anything other than slogging through the day. I worked a little on the school newspaper until Nora, who was the editor, told me I wasn't serious and fired me.

I wasn't very coordinated, but played sports because it was expected. I looked much like my father—stocky and strong-featured, rather than how my brother looked, dazzlingly beautiful like my mother. I was on the football team for two years and hated every second of it. In my last season, somebody tackled me and dislocated my shoulder. The coach told me to grit my teeth and go back in and play. I refused. He pulled up one pant leg and showed me a huge scar. "UCLA, 1924," he said. "I got that and I still played the whole game."

I said, "So that's why your leg looks like that," and I walked to the showers and never went back. They flunked me in sports.

A lot of the time I just skipped school; I believed I could get away with anything. I refused to do homework, I hated then and still do the idea I had to study something I had no interest in. I excelled at nothing other than being able to find shortcuts around any hard work. But what really educated me, what saved me, I think, is that I read everything in sight. I loved reading because it was something I could do on my own. Everything from Archie comics and Scrooge McDuck and *Mary Poppins* to John O'Hara and Edith Wharton. Simply from my voracious early reading, I had a vastly better vocabulary than anyone around me. There was one English teacher in the tenth grade, Lucy Helgesson, who told me I was a good writer. It was the first encouragement I had from a teacher. The idea that anybody thought I could do anything well was so novel that I remember her name to this day.

Finally, the Beverly High authorities caught on to me and my louche ways, and they called my mother to come for a conference. Later that day I walked into my house and my mother confronted me, something that probably hadn't happened since I was two. No preamble, just a furious "You cannot do this to me."

I said, "What can I not do?"

She said, "I arrive at the principal's office to be told you've been skipping school, and when they go get you to join the meeting, you're nowhere to be found. You cannot embarrass me."

She did not ask me where I went.

As high school ended, despite the plans my friends were making about their future—what schools to go to, what fraternities to join—I had absolutely no thought of going anywhere, much less to college. I was hibernating because just keeping the fear at bay shut everything else down. And my parents never bothered to ask what my plans might be, nor did they attend my graduation. In the months after, I continued meandering through the days, waking up at noon, staying out until four or five in the morning, dodging my father as we passed silently in the hallways. He'd come back in the afternoon from his club just as I was starting my aimless day. I did keep up my reading, though, and was drawn to tales of aspirational lives—not that I thought I would ever achieve anything. I felt disqualified from being able to lay claim to an actual life.

Whatever low-lit life I was leading in my teens would soon end. And so, too, the dead calm before the storm that was soon to overwhelm me and end my sleepwalking, my years of evasion and avoidance.

CHAPTER 2

All my teenage sexual encounters were responses to biological urges; my specific homosexual experiences weren't fraught with any conscious trauma or guilt. Nor with much emotion or romance. But revealing that behavior to anyone was too frightening to contemplate. Growing up in the 1950s, any mentions of homosexuality I recall were either a scathing insult, a disparaging joke, or a hushed reference. There were no support groups, no one to talk to or get any guidance from; you were on your own with your shameful nature. There was no "coming out," only the tearing away of exposure and ensuing scandal. To my confused adolescent brain, being exposed as a homosexual meant the end of life as I knew it.

You'd think there'd be more empathy for those who carry the burden of this self-knowledge at such a young age. You'd think heterosexuals would understand what an awfully cruel thing it is for anyone to be tortured for something that is in no way an elective choice. The stunting of normal growth at the beginning of adolescence is a heinous crime to commit against a child. It extinguishes the general effervescence of adolescence. Part of that development, when a child frequently shifts from exuberance to misery, is coming to know that you can survive those extremes.

But in those days, with the prospect of exposure always present, all other development was stilled. For me, and I think for my entire generation growing up in the two decades before Stonewall, the potential revelation of those secrets was like an incriminating document in the hands of a blackmailer.

When I was eleven and could no longer ignore my feelings, I was so bothered by not understanding them that the healthy part of me got on my bike and rode down to the Beverly Hills Public Library. I furtively hunted the shelves for books on homosexuality. In each one, chapter after chapter hammered home to a frightened child that all such activity was a result of mental illness. It was a disease!

I remember with such devastating clarity getting back on my bike and riding home with this horrible knowledge. It was calamitous. I was now educated. I knew for certain what I was and what it meant.

That was when my magical thinking became more than just a coping mechanism; it became the only way I thought I could survive. I had to compartmentalize my sexual feelings to keep from being branded forever as abnormal. I could keep it all a secret from my parents, and they would never have to know about my "mental disease." *There can't be two of us. There can't be two of us.*

I would never allow myself to feel a rush of exuberance without instantly quashing it, for fear it would somehow reveal all I'd been hiding. I was in suspended animation, like being on a plane from here to there, but never landing.

Meanwhile, my brother was getting arrested for various schemes and scams to get money for his heroin habit. My parents were rarely spared a month without having some horrible incident to deal with. Thus my secret became much more important to conceal. These pressures had been building up inside me for so long without my being consciously aware of them that their final denouement would soon almost destroy me.

The defining mythology of the family sitcoms of the 1960s—*Father Knows Best, My Three Sons,* these perfect white families that had no complexity, no trauma or real troubles—was as damaging an influence on children as Instagram-perfect pictures are for today's teens. But in my own life there was one exception: my friend Terre Thomas's family was even more idyllic than the one in the top-ten sitcom that her father, Danny, starred in. I spent far more time with the Thomas family than I did with my own. They were so involved and intertwined with each other, so demonstrably

When I woke up, I quickly fell back into the same free-fall panic. It was a flash warning that this fantasy world of compartmentalization I'd been living in for the last years couldn't continue. The jig was up.

I went to our family doctor, and he asked what was wrong. I couldn't very well say that my leg was paralyzed, because it clearly wasn't, so I said, "I'm just petrified for no reason."

He gave me one shot, then two shots, and soon I was close to comatose. It was clear to him that I was having a nervous breakdown.

I was so discombobulated I could barely function. I was put on the maximum dose of Valium, which stabilized me and at least prevented me from being hospitalized, although I was living like a zombie.

I was still doing nothing other than all-night wanderings and all-day sleeping. My parents weren't pestering me—as usual they weren't anything-ing about me. My friends had dispersed. In that year after high school, still hibernating in my very comfortable bear cave, I did realize that I had to do something other than my night foraging; this couldn't go on forever. There just had to be something I could do. What paralyzed me was that I believed I didn't deserve a future. Just like my parents' life of impermanence, I was renting a life rather than making concrete plans for one.

There was only one area that authentically excited me, and that was the world of entertainment. Simply, it resonated, not just as nothing else did, but as something I was instinctively drawn to. At least half of my friends' parents were involved in front of or behind cameras, and to me they were a lot more interesting than the other half, who were involved in making light fixtures, egg farming, and other industrial pursuits. From the time I started to ride my bicycle from one famous Beverly Hills house to another, my eyes were starlit with every aspect of the entertainment industry.

When I was eleven, one of my best friends' father, James Saphier, who was Bob Hope's longtime agent, took us to a matinee of *Peter Pan*, the first musical I ever saw. I fell dumbstruck in love with Mary Martin, who played Peter Pan—a character I was well struck to love given he also didn't seem to have any parents. I was so dazzled I wrote a little-boy fan letter to her, and she wrote me back on pale blue paper that I kept as a sacred text of my earliest yearnings for a show business life.

Another friend's father was Eddie Dukoff, Danny Kaye's manager, and he took us to the Hollywood Bowl, where Kaye was doing a patriotic Fourth of July charity benefit. Danny Kaye at that time was a supersized movie star of the first order. Afterward, we went to his dressing room, where a few people were congratulating him on his performance. A knock on the door interrupted us. His manager opened it, and a guy stuck his head in and said, "Thank you, Mr. Kaye, you were so great, but really, you should've spent more time performing instead of just introducing the acts."

Danny Kaye, who was just a few feet away from me, hauled off and slugged the guy, who fell onto my feet. Dukoff grabbed the man's legs, dragged him out of the dressing room, and closed the door.

How much more exciting that was than visiting the endless rows of my father's tract houses. I was captivated by all of it—the performances, yes, for sure, and the performers and their eccentricities, too, but also every aspect from playing with the stage curtains at El Rodeo Elementary School when I was in the fourth grade to invading every off-limits nook and cranny of the Fox studio, which bordered Beverly Hills High School—all these nuggets of show business had me in their thrall.

One of my very best friends was Doris Day's son, Terry Melcher, who was a kind of pied piper to all of us: fun and munchkin cute and always up for any trouble. Of course, I knew that his mother was *the* biggest movie star at the time, but she didn't act very Doris Day–ish; she was just a bubbly, happy, sometimes-absent housewife. Since Terry called her Doris, that's what I called her, too. But her third husband, Marty Melcher, who had adopted Terry, scared the hell out of me. One night I broke his rigid rules about not entering the main house without prior consent. I walked through their dining room looking for Terry while Doris and Marty were having an intimate dinner with Hedda Hopper, the wickedest witch of Hollywood columnists. Marty tried to ban me from the house, but Doris saved me. It was only after he had a heart attack and died that Doris found out that Melcher and his lawyer had misappropriated and lost most of her money, which forced her to do a television series she hated.

Every Saturday night in the summers we'd go to Lew Wasserman's for his daughter Lynne's weekly pool party. I was once arrested for joy-riding in Mrs. Wasserman's Bentley. Actually, if you were stopped by the police in Beverly Hills and you lived there, you were never really arrested; they just drove you home from wherever you'd misbehaved—unless you stabbed your mother's lover to death with a kitchen knife and your mother was Lana Turner. I knew about this famous scandal before anyone be-cause I was going home late one night, up our Bedford Drive, and an ambulance with its lights flashing was going very slowly in front of me. I instantly worried that my father, who'd recently had a heart attack, had had another, but they passed my house and stopped on the next block right in front of the Turner house. One lone police car was there as well. I saw a big black Cadillac pull into the driveway and out came the short, squat Jerry Giesler, a famous attorney of the day. I turned around quickly and drove the one block home, thinking something dark and nefarious must have happened. The next morning they arrested my high school friend Cheryl for the murder of her mother's lover.

Undeterred by the movie star violence up the street, it was slowly be-coming clear to me that the only thing that aroused my curiosity was the entertainment industry. It was inexorably pulling me forward. But how could I fit in, where could I begin? At nineteen, I didn't even have a Social Security card. I qualified for nothing. There was no list of starting jobs in the entertainment industry. I had no training in anything, had barely grad-uated from high school, and my sole "work" experience until nineteen had been a summer job in one of my family's businesses.

For some forgotten reason we owned a precision-toolmaking com-pany that made pitot tubes, one-foot-long metal cylinders that measure speed and altitude, for airplanes. Early one morning, I was assigned to take a rack of them to be silver-plated. There were twenty, and each cost $5,000. I carefully put them in the back of the van and set off on the freeway for the fifteen-mile drive. But . . . I'd forgotten to secure the rear doors and when I turned and went over a bump at high speed, one of the doors flung open, and out onto the freeway went the pitot tubes. And my summer job.

In my voracious reading I had learned there were mail rooms in theatrical agencies that hired hopefuls in a haphazard kind of training program. That was my first practical glimmer, and the dots began to form. I had met Abe Lastfogel, the owner of the William Morris Agency, the largest at the time, whose best friend was Danny Thomas; he was called Uncle Abe by everyone in the Thomas family. Lastfogel didn't seem very child-friendly to me; I always thought he must have been born in a tight suit and a bow tie. He was hardly Uncle Abe to me, but he was often a presence in their house, and therefore familiar.

Hmmm, I thought, *Abe Lastfogel and Danny Thomas*. More dots. *Danny Thomas and me and Abe Lastfogel's mail room.* Aha! The dots connected.

Danny Thomas was in Las Vegas performing at the Sands Hotel. I called and asked the operator to put me through to him.

"Who's calling?" she asked.

"Barry Diller," I said.

Very long pause.

Finally Danny got on the line. "Barry? What's happened? Is everything all right?" he asked, thinking that the only reason I'd call him is if something had happened to his children.

Quickly I said, "Yes, we're all fine here, but . . . will you do me a favor?"

He said, in his Talmudic, solemn way, "Of course, my son, of course I will."

"I want to work in the mail room at William Morris."

Thomas, at that time the agency's biggest client, said, "That's easy. Can I go back to my massage now?"

The next day, I was called by the head of personnel at William Morris. He ever so politely asked me to come in whenever convenient. I said, "How about now?"

Thirty minutes and a few desultory questions later I was hired.

And just like that my life began.

CHAPTER 3

That next Monday I burst out of my house like a cannonball to get to William Morris, which was less than a mile from my home. I'd found a way forward, finally. A lifeline to a life.

I arrived with an enormous interest in everything entertainment, but no interest in ever doing the actual work that brought revenue to the company. I was probably the only kid to get a job in that mail room who emphatically did *not* want to be an agent. You need a certain assertiveness, and since I had no sense of self, it was inconceivable that I could ever ask anyone to trust me with their professional life.

William Morris resembled something like a Jewish Vatican: it was a place with great traditions and rituals and odd rules filled with a very nattily dressed collection of short Hebrew men with their often eccentric—and sometimes distasteful—private pursuits (one of their most senior executives, a wiry, overly tan fifty-five-year-old man with a constant twitch in his right eye, literally cruised high schools to pick up girls).

The agency was founded by its namesake in the late nineteenth century, and for forty years after his death had been owned by his protégé, the aforementioned Mr. Lastfogel. Everyone, including senior employees who'd been with him for thirty years, addressed him as "Mr. Lastfogel." At five feet tall, the three-foot-wide Mr. Lastfogel was dignity in motion, striding purposely as fast as his little legs could go with focused and commanding confidence and determination. It was an energetic but uneasy transition from my sleepwalking life to an office filled with ambitious guys wanting to make their bones. I was a very different fish from all those guys—and yes, all guys—who came from places far grittier than Beverly Hills. Even though the starting money was pathetic, most of them had to live on it. By comparison, my circumstances led to an early and embarrassing crisis. After about eight months, I was called into the office of the head of accounting, a grumpy man named Lou Goldberg, who watched every dollar going out with a frown.

He barked, "We have a problem! We've been paying you all these months, but none of the checks were cashed! It's screwing up our books."

You'd have thought this must be serious money to arouse him, but I was making $50 a week.

I mumbled some nonsensical answer about saving them up to cash or whatever, but the truth was that I didn't know how to deposit a check. I was funded strictly with cash from my family's office, so I'd never had a bank account. And it was so little money I just let everything accumulate. The longer the conversation went on, the dumber I sounded. That this dim rich kid couldn't even cash a check didn't sit well with the Depression-era accountant. He recommended I be fired. I tell this to illustrate how cocooned I was about so many things, particularly money. The lack of money or the accumulation of it has never been anything but distantly vague in my mind.

I didn't grow up with gobs of it showered on me, but I always had enough, and no one ever taught me how to earn it. When I needed money for anything, I'd ask for it, and there it was. No questions asked, except once when I was nineteen. I'd gone to Acapulco to stay with a Mexican playboy friend who had a *palacio* on a private beach called Puerto Marqués. I got in a coin-flipping gambling game with another guest, who I didn't know was a cardsharping professional. I thought, *Well, this can't go wrong. It's a fifty-fifty chance that heads will come up.* He suggested we start at $100 and then double it: $200, $400, $800, $1,600, $3,200, $6,400, $12,800, $25,600. Tails came up every time. I stopped there and owed this guy $25,600. I went home and told my father it was a point of honor, that I had to pay it off. He refused, saying there was no honor among the thieves I was with. My mother surreptitiously gave me the money and I paid the hustler. What an incredible fool I was, so over my head, playing such a stupid game with money I didn't have with a person I later found out was a coin-flipping con man. I've always been thoughtlessly careless about money—the amoral consequence of having early wealth without earning it.

I didn't leave our house and its support system until I was twenty-three. When I reached my early thirties, my income finally surpassed my spending and I didn't need the family office for any help. It didn't even register that I'd become financially independent. I'd had enough money from my family to spend on whatever I needed since kindergarten, so I never could conjure the lack of it. Which explains why I have never made a decision that was related to money. While I wanted to be paid for my work with the best of them, it had no dictatorial role for me. Money to me was only a by-product of the work I was doing, never a motivation. While my expenditures grew exponentially from buying a lollipop at the candy store, it all seemed a natural progression from where I so unnaturally started. I am sure, though, that my situation allowed me to take risks in business that would daunt others. My motivation to succeed was never counted in dollars. It was simply to count as a person in the eyes of others.

If it hadn't been for Danny Thomas's patronage, there's no question I would have been thrown out of William Morris on any given day. While the tasks in the mail room were hardly meaningful, they were my first steps away from the magic boxes that had ruled my teenage years. I discovered things about myself that gave me confidence. I learned I could sound smart by picking up cues from smarter people and repackaging them in my own way. Most important of all, I discovered that if I was trying to solve a complex problem, I seemed compelled, *literally compelled*, to drill down to its essence, because when I got there—at the base level of understanding—my instinctual abilities would give me a surprisingly accurate sixth sense, allowing me to tease out the very core of the matter. Once I had that, once my intense magnifier was put to the issue, I had absolute conviction what to do. The stakes were small then, but I was discovering there was more to me than just puppylike enthusiasm.

I wasn't really working, I was studying. I had the world's greatest entertainment "library" at hand—the William Morris file room. It was a huge place with hundreds of metal file cabinets that housed the entire history of the entertainment business. I found excuses to disappear into it and deeply read every file from *A* to *Z*.

At William Morris in the 1960s, the primary job of a mail-room boy was to get out of there as fast as you could. The next step was to become an assistant to an agent, listen in on his calls, and begin to learn what his job entailed. By osmosis, you would emerge as a junior agent.

As a mail boy, you didn't really sort the mail; your job was basically to run around and pick up and deliver things, more like a messenger service. One of my duties was to take the day's mail to the post office in huge bags. One day, early on, I lugged the huge bag of mail to the parking lot, put it in my trunk, got in the car, and promptly drove home and went up to my room. Two days later the bell rang in my head—*Oh my fucking god, I forgot the mail!* It was still in the trunk of my car. I raced to the post office, but they refused to take it because it was already postmarked.

The post office clerk said I had to take it back and have every item re-postmarked. I thought, *Well, this is surely curtains.*

Somehow I talked the post office clerk into accepting the mis-postmarked mail and lived to spend another day mail-rooming.

There were eight or ten of us there at any one time. The mail boys either got their jobs through connections or were such fervid hustlers that they couldn't be denied. There were no requirements for being in the mail room, no college degrees needed or tests to pass. But to be an agent did take a scrappy charm, and a streetwise gregariousness. What it didn't particularly take was brains, since the main part of an agent's job is simply to sign clients. Selling yourself to a performer—who by definition is likely insecure and vulnerable—isn't a monumentally difficult obstacle. You simply need that savvy and confidence. I had neither, so I knew from the outset that I'd never graduate to junior agent.

The other mail boys loved doing the mail runs to the studios; there were people to meet and impress and contacts to file away for future use. But I wasn't learning anything other than the best driving route to the Valley. Lord knows why, given my life's taste for the fastest cars, I drove a blue Buick convertible—the first car I bought on my own (well . . . on my parents' own).

Once, though, during my runs, I did have the pleasure of accidentally knocking down Louella Parsons's Christmas tree and setting it on fire. I entered her dour, gloomy house and tripped over the five hundred presents (read: bribes) that were scattered around her dark living room. Parsons was the enormously powerful Hollywood columnist whose influence had only recently receded, but she still received those holiday tributes. I was so lucky to see the last gasps of old Hollywood life—the moguls who started it all were passing from the scene and with them their outsized exuberance, egos, and excesses. I remember a poignant scene from the lobby of the Beverly Theater when I was in my late teens and went to a preview of a new movie. The heretofore immaculately-turned-out great old mogul Jack Warner was emerging from the bathroom and it saddened me to see he'd left a pee stain on his trousers.

Early on I knew I wasn't much like the other guys in the mail room. They were so aggressive about "making it," while I was just oh-so-tentatively putting my ambition training wheels on. Then, one Christmas holiday, into the mail room walked David Geffen, a scrawny nineteen-year-old who looked more like a malnourished twelve. He introduced himself, saying he worked in the New York office, but wanted to use the holiday to find out what the L.A. office was like. I thought, *Whoa, now that's ambition*. I could actually feel the hunger for success vibrating out of him. I'd never met, then or since, someone with more focus, more pure drive and ferocious intelligence than David. Unlike me, who loves process, David is the most efficient problem solver ever born. No artificial intelligence will ever exceed his ability to go faster from problem to solution, or from poverty to so many billions. Despite all the biological aggression and occasional occupational conflict that has bubbled between us at various times over sixty years of knowing each other, I treasure him now as my best friend.

On one of my missions as a messenger, I was assigned to go to the airport to pick up Barbra Streisand. Barbra was already on her first step to stardom, coming out to L.A. to appear at the Cocoanut Grove nightclub. We aimlessly chatted along the way, then I dropped her off at the hotel, saying I hoped I'd see her again, and she, politely dismissive, said the same. The next night at a party the Danny Thomases gave for her opening night, she was surprised to see yesterday's chauffeur introduced to her as one of the guests. Over these sixty years, Barbra and I have become good friends, although I have definitely tried her patience. One night some years ago she was receiving an award, and I was to introduce her to a Hollywood audience of five thousand. She called me the afternoon before the event, and, naturally, the controlling one asked me to read her my intro. I did so, and at the end I made the unforgivable mistake of pronouncing her last name as *STREISand* rather than Strei*SAND*. She shrieked at me, and I vowed to do it right when I made the introduction that night. Of course, I got scrambled and didn't, and her glare at me as she walked out would have fried a fish.

I was rescued from messengering around the city by a mandatory three-month rotation, during which all mail boys had to spend their time mimeographing hundreds of copies of the interoffice telegrams sent out daily to all the agents. Everyone hated that job. The room was in the basement, and not only was there no natural light, but the job gave the boys no exposure to their higher-ups, and thus no opportunities to impress them. I, however, loved every minute and managed to extend my three-month rotation to almost three years. It wasn't the mimeographing—that I finished in half an hour—but it meant I could spend the rest of the day in the file room, where I was transfixed by the history of every transaction going back to the turn of the century.

Everyone wondered what kind of strange person would want to do that, but for me, with no college education and an insatiable desire to know everything about the entertainment world, it was the dream job. It was as if I had gone to Oxford to read show biz. I'd go up to the file room, bring a big stack of files back down to my little lair in the mimeograph room, and read my way through the history of show business.

I learned about Elvis Presley from the very beginning of his career—deals, contracts, the movie business, the concert business, the record business, his life, and the intricacies of the bizarre history of his manager, Colonel Parker. I knew before almost anyone else that the reason Elvis essentially would not tour outside the United States was that the very southern-sounding good ol' boy Colonel Parker was actually a Dutchman named Andreas Cornelius van Kuijk, and he had entered the country illegally. Since he had no passport, he wouldn't be able to get back into the United States.

At that time, the only professional relationship an entertainer, actor, or vaudeville clown had was with his agent and agency, and William Morris had long-term relationships with most of its clients. There were files in those cabinets on people who had been represented for twenty, thirty, forty years. And because the agency was so involved in every strategic issue its clients faced, the files were basically biographies of their professional and often personal lives. The file room gave me an incredible foundation of knowledge about the structure and workings of an entire industry. And it was that bedrock of knowledge that later allowed my instincts to develop so sure-footedly.

But none of my file-chomping was doing William Morris any good. They really should have fired me. And I did give them many opportunities to do so; if, as I've said, Danny Thomas hadn't been my sponsor, there's no doubt I would have been toast. And still I came perilously close. At one point, a scandal sheet began printing vicious, horrible things about people working in front of and behind the camera throughout the industry, with seemingly no boundaries to what it revealed. It was run by a man of endless meanness named Jaik Rosenstein, and everyone was scared to death of what he'd say in the next issue. Over a period of months, things started to appear in that newsletter that included quotations from memos that could only have been obtained from someone inside William Morris. So they did lie detector tests on all the mail boys to try to find out who was responsible.

I was petrified of the lie detector, since I held so many nonbusiness secrets and hid out in so many compartments that an investigator might stumble upon. Even though the document leaks had nothing to do with me, I was so paranoid about the central lie of my sexual identity that I worried it would seep somehow into the inquisition.

The man who administered the test asked me, "Have you ever taken files from the file room?"

I had to answer, "Yes."

"What did you do with them?" he asked.

"Well," I said, "I read them."

"Did you ever take any files home?"

"Yes," I answered too eagerly, "but I didn't give them to anyone!"

Apparently, I was the only person tested who admitted to doing something that was not allowed, and on that fact alone the woman in human resources recommended that I be fired—not because I was suspected of being the leak, but simply because I had taken files home.

Funnily, I had never done a lick of homework in my life before, breezing through school skimming all the surfaces, and now I was about to be fired for studying zealously.

But word reached HR: "Sorry, you can't fire him; he's like Danny Thomas's son." So I was kept on. But I was soon to face the ire of the ultimate boss, Mr. Lastfogel.

One day his driver was busy with Mrs. Lastfogel, and Mr. Lastfogel needed to go see Sam Goldwyn. I got hauled out of my tomb in the basement to drive the boss over in his ginormous black Cadillac. We got in the car, and he asked me to turn the radio to the news. What the hell did I know about radio news? The only radio I knew was rock and roll.

I began frantically turning the dial and couldn't find what he wanted. Mr. Lastfogel finally told me, "Stop the noise and just turn the radio off!"

Silent and sullen, we pulled into the Goldwyn Studio, where the narrow lanes were small and compact, with sharp angles around the huge soundstages. I was driving a little too fast, and a man shot out from around the corner directly into my path. I stepped hard on the brakes, and, thank god, missed hitting him. But when I looked into the rearview mirror, there was no Mr. Lastfogel in the back seat. I turned around and there he was, all five feet of him, lying face up on the floor staring at me, his bow tie perfectly in place.

A few months later I irked him again. He always came in on Saturday mornings, and would sit at his secretary's white Formica desk outside his office and go through his own mail in the quiet of the weekend. I was the mail boy on duty at the time, and when I saw him come in, I asked if I could get him anything. He said he'd like some coffee with milk. I went up to the Beverly Wilshire coffee shop and brought the brown bag back to the office and laid it on the secretary's desk while Mr. L. had his eyes down reading some memo. He had slung his white suede jacket over the side of the desk, and as I took the coffee out of the bag, it began to drip onto the jacket—four or five big brown spots. I saw Mr. L.'s eyes look up from the memo, following the trajectory of the drops.

"I'm so sorry!" I said, then grabbed the jacket and ran off to the men's room with it, thinking, *I'll just clean this up and bring it back nice and new.*

What did I know about suede and water? As I began brushing it and turning the whole side of it to mud, the suede came off in big patches.

I slowly walked back and placed the jacket on the desk, saying, "Oh, Mr. Lastfogel, I'm sorry, I've ruined it."

The boss of all bosses gave me a long doleful stare and said, "Just leave me be."

After almost three years at William Morris, I was beginning to feel like the Phantom of the Basement, scurrying up to the peopled floors to get my reading material, and then holing up to immerse myself in it all day long. They finally decreed that I had to become an assistant to an agent; so off I went to typing and shorthand school, which is the most productive formal schooling I've ever had. I still retain those basic skills, but I have no idea what the capital of South Dakota is.

My first "desk," as they called the job, was for the least-talented but hardest-working agent in the place. He had no charm, was incapable of any flashy agent talk, and was twitchy and gaunt; his internal nervousness made everyone around him uncomfortable. Nevertheless, he was the epitome of Mr. Lastfogel's dictum: "If you write it down, you won't have to remember it."

He wrote hundreds of meaningless memos every day. I would frantically transcribe his endless Dictabelts until my fingers were sore. Rather than stuffing those red Dictabelts in his mouth, I started to edit them down to the essentials—until he found out and "requested" my transfer. One day, the head of William Morris's New York office, Nat Lefkowitz, a gnarled, narrow-faced, and William Morris–appropriate "little man," came out to L.A., and I was assigned to be his secretary. He called me in for dictation and went on at least a half-hour monologue on why pay television would never work (this was in 1964). When he finished, I looked up after my furious scribbling and said, "Uh, Mr. Lefkowitz, isn't pay television inevitable as soon as it becomes technically possible?" He looked at me for the first time, said, "Who asked you?" and sent me to the typewriter.

There was only one person I wanted to work for—Phil Weltman, the head of the television department. He was a truly fine man who had come out of the military to work at the agency. When I met him, he was probably fifty; he looked like a Jewish General Patton and was the embodiment of the drill sergeant with a heart of gold. I adored him. He was extremely authoritarian, a real man's man. I was very much in awe of older men who had natural confidence, given my absolute lack of any. That kind of easy self-assurance seems to come much more naturally to heterosexual men who are sexually successful at an early age. I admired their lack of confusion about who they were and doubted whether I would ever be that sure of myself. I flat-out worshipped Phil Weltman. Even more than Danny Thomas, he was the father I would never come within two million miles of having, and I deeply wanted him to approve of me.

The job of being an agent is corrupting over time because you essentially lie for a living: you lie to your clients, who are being rejected; you lie to producers and directors and buyers of movies and shows—it can't help but corrode. But Phil Weltman was immune to that. He was not a major agent in terms of who he represented, but his long-term clients were loyal to him. All the now-famous (or infamous) agents who left William Morris in 1975 to start CAA—Michael Ovitz, Ronnie Meyer, Bill Haber—had been deeply influenced and mentored by Phil Weltman. When they built their headquarters, the only thing in the monster atrium was an honorary bust of Mr. Weltman. He knew how to train people who worked for him, which most agents didn't, and he was the first person to take any kind of interest in me and my development. And it was an interest that demanded I respond. It made me glow and wake up to the possibilities that came with having someone care about my future. I had waited twenty-two years for someone to have expectations for me—I would kill myself rather than disappoint him.

For those who can now never think of me as anything other than a boss, I have to say I was a better-than-good assistant. I was always a presentable young man in the strict suits and ties we all wore. My hair had begun to go in my earliest twenties and so I looked older than I was. There was no task I wouldn't do, tiny or large, no length to which I wouldn't go in order to make Mr. Weltman's life better. I've always longed to have me as my own assistant, because no one had a keener eye for every detail than I did. I anticipated perfectly. I discovered that I had this aptitude to sublimate everything into being supportive. Because I had so little self, I knew I couldn't be a principal, but I also knew I sure could suss out how to make the principal's life better, just as I'd made my mother's life better when I was a child. Where other people might assert themselves, I served.

I continued to work for him until he said, "You're going to have to be a junior agent."

I said, "I don't want to be a junior agent. Don't make me go."

He said, "You're going."

So I tried. I would go out with a few of the television executives on their rounds to the studios, and I had one or two little television accounts at the then-cheesy Warner Brothers Television.

That lasted for three or four months. I was no good at it, and I knew it.

I just didn't want to be an agent. Agents sell. You can't sell if you're impervious to being sold. I'm sure the cleverest selling can get to me in some way, but if I know that someone is trying to sell me something, I immediately lose interest. Consequently, I am a lousy salesman, especially if the sale is a direct appeal, an assertion of self.

I was, however, one of the few people at William Morris who knew how to thread a 16-millimeter projector. One night I was given the assignment of screening *Alice Adams* for Warren Beatty and Natalie Wood. He was just entering movie stardom and she had been a huge star since she was a child. Apart from their romance, Warren thought Natalie should star in a remake of that wonderful Katharine Hepburn movie about a social-climbing beauty. I was twenty-two and Warren was twenty-six. He and Natalie came in; I introduced myself and went into the projection booth to start the movie. It was an aged copy, and the film stock soon broke up in the machine. I turned on the lights, ran out, explained the problem, and said I'd be able to re-splice it, but that it might take five minutes. When it turned into ten minutes, Warren came into the booth and saw me on the floor trying to gather together about a hundred feet of film that spaghetti-tied out of the reel. It and I were a mess of tangled celluloid. He took one look and laughed. It was clear that no one could have fixed it, not even the editor of the movie. Warren could have tried to get me fired, but instead he said, "Fuck it, let's just all go eat," and Warren and I became friends.

I also met Jack Nicholson around the same time. Warren was a star when I met him, but Jack couldn't get a job except around the fringes of Roger Corman B movies. I had a little closet of an office then, befitting a not-quite assistant/not-quite agent, on the third floor—William Morris's Siberia—and Jack was wandering through the halls, looking for anyone who'd pay attention to him. He'd sit down and we'd rip around for a bit, and then he would move on to try to talk to someone with clout.

I had gone from loving every day in the file room to hating every day in the field, going out with these aggressive, confident agents to service and sell their clients. I knew I couldn't ever do what they did. The culture of the agency was very macho, and while I might have qualified physically

I had no self-strutting abilities. Since I couldn't and wouldn't participate in frat talk as I went on the rounds with these feral agents, I felt more and more alone. I was scared that not only would they find I had zero skills at the job but that the secrets I was hiding would be exposed, the anvil would finally fall, and all the progress I'd been making would be shattered. I was living in tightly choreographed compartments and the stress on me was growing. While I had begun to have some adult friendships, they were few, and most of my after-work life, my nightlife, was looking around corners for guys to fool around with and then never see again.

One day, I was talking to Warren about how anxious I was; he told me about the psychiatrist he had been seeing who he thought was a genius.

Warren said, "You have to go see Grotjahn!"

So I did and it was horrible. When I told Dr. Grotjahn I thought I was gay, he threw some babble at me about a truck with red meat in the back of it, and how the meat was going to fall off the truck and land on me. I fled into the street with those images making me far more anxious than when I had walked in.

It wasn't until an older friend of mine, seeing my distress and remembering what he'd gone through himself, recommended I go see Dr. Theodore Rich, who, I've everlastingly believed, saved my life.

Dr. Rich's kindness and decency—and the trust I had in him—helped me slowly rewire all that my mixed-up and magically obsessed mind had tangled into so many destructive misconceptions.

By the time I was twenty-two, I was emerging from my daze and finally able to get off Valium, the maximum dose of which had been steadying me since my nervous breakdown three years before.

But I was still at William Morris, it was clear I was never going to be a made man in the agency, and I was running out of time. That was when another of my lifesaving Thomases, Danny's daughter Marlo, and her new boyfriend came to the rescue.

———

Marlo had recently started dating Leonard Goldberg, a young ABC executive. She was already launched on her acting career, with her own apartment far outside the Beverly Hills city limits (meaning the Hollywood Hills), while I was an adult manqué, still living at home with my parents in their hacienda-style house, with a saltwater pool put in by Greta Garbo near two guesthouses that rarely had guests. It was like living in a hotel with some pleasant strangers always behaving politely.

Marlo had just started shooting her series *That Girl*, which was to become an iconic show about a young woman making it on her own. She would have these small dinner parties, to which she would always invite me as a kind of tagalong cub to fill out the table. Goldberg had been head of daytime programming in New York for ABC, but had just been promoted to vice president of current programming, the group that supervised the shows once they'd been ordered. One night I went over to her place and she introduced me to her new boyfriend and also new boss. Over dinner, Leonard argued that the major talent agencies were filled with conflicts of interest, taking big-package commissions that inflated TV and film costs. I argued back, defending the agencies—simply out of loyalty, but so strongly that it made an impression on Leonard. He thought I showed some spunk and spark.

No one had ever thought I showed spark.

Over the next months we spent more time together at Marlo's, talking of course about the entertainment business. Because I was a font of the file room's knowledge, I was able to hold up my end, and he took a liking to this outwardly sophisticated, though inexperienced, little friend of Marlo's. One night Leonard said that because he was moving to Los Angeles for the new job, he'd need an assistant. Would I be interested?

No one had ever offered me a job, much less one perfectly timed to rescue me from my flop show at William Morris. Before I could be accepted into the company, he said, I would have to be interviewed by Edgar Scherick, the head of all programming at ABC, and one of the three most powerful men in television.

I was told to go to the Hotel Bel-Air at seven a.m. and call Mr. Scherick from the lobby, which I did. He answered on the first ring and abruptly told me to begin walking to his suite in thirty seconds.

I started to sweat; I was still a kid who didn't wear a watch. *How many seconds have gone by? Probably eight . . .*

I started counting one one thousand, two one thousand, three one thousand, thinking I had probably blown it already. Then all of a sudden I was in the presence of the frenetic Mr. Scherick. In between phone calls and his breakfast, he asked me a few questions, and I stumbled through a few answers. It was kind of pro forma, some ancient concept that the head of programming had to interview every person hired—still possible when the department was about thirty people in its entirety; now it's in the hundreds.

After less than ten minutes I was ushered out of what was the first and last official job interview I've ever had.

A few days later I quit William Morris. As a courtesy, I went to the senior-most person I could find that day, knocked on his door, and said, "I'm going to join ABC."

He looked up from his fruit salad and said, "We sure wasted a lot of money training you." And out the door I went.

And on that very special day, literally that very day, Edgar Scherick, the czar of ABC, was fired! Quite incredibly, they reached down in the organization and picked none other than the young and untried Leonard Goldberg to be the new head of programming. What a stupendously inexplicable stroke of luck.

Serendipity, my lifelong lodestar, had made its first appearance.

From being a complete nonentity, the lowest training-wheel employee of a talent agency, I was going to be the assistant to the programming head of one of the three national networks. Having never in my life been east of Las Vegas, having never had a real girl- or boyfriend, and having never been within a thousand miles of the epicenter of media life, I was off to the New York City of 1966.

CHAPTER 4

I almost got stopped before I'd even started at ABC. Leonard gave me an assignment before I left for New York. He wanted me to see all the new series he was inheriting for his first season.

This was a decade before videocassette recorders, so in order to view the two-inch tapes, I had to go to ABC's local television station. Every day for about a week I drove over in the morning and stayed late into the night, watching what I thought were some pretty awful shows. The truth is, I never really had much interest—then or now—in series television, particularly since in those years they were cookie-cutter formulaic and unchallenging.

On the third day I got a call from Leonard saying, "We have a bit of a problem. The general manager of the station, Elton Rule, is angry about your speeding on his lot. Not only does he want to ban you from driving, he's questioning why I would hire such an immature and reckless kid who drives like a maniac."

Elton Rule went on to be president of the network and then president of the entire corporation. For years he thought my driving signaled a snotty low character. I'm pretty sure I wasn't snotty, but I still had a teenager's immaturity and little tutelage in proper adult behavior. And fast was just a thrill. Was and always will be.

A year later, after he was appointed president of the network and while I was still very much a junior in the program department, I was asked to pick him up at the airport in L.A. As I drove him into the city—driving very carefully—he asked me, point-blank, "When do you think you'll be leaving us for a Hollywood producer job?"

Elton Rule was an absolute god to me, running the network with the kind of confidence and surety I so admired. I was deeply hurt that he just thought of me as some sluff using ABC to get a start and then jumping off to become a journeyman producer. I knew even then that my ambitions were far greater than that.

I answered as carefully as I was driving. "I don't ever want to leave ABC."

With a skeptical and jaundiced eye, he continued the rest of the way in silence.

Elton had every reason to think little of that kid thoughtlessly zooming around the ABC lot. It would be beyond imagining for him to think that just three years later that kid would invent a new form of television programming.

For someone who's never been to a big city, there's few experiences as thrilling as crossing over the Triborough Bridge, looking out at a wedding cake of lights glistening off the skyscrapers, and hearing in the distance the growl and hum of New York City life. I was like a rube crossing the border from the provinces, saucer-eyed excited by everything I saw. I was deposited at the old and slightly decrepit Warwick hotel, across the street from ABC's headquarters, carrying all my worldly possessions in a small box: a watch (which I went out and bought after that first interview with Edgar Scherick!) and some jewelry, along with the few adult clothes (jackets and ties) I had. That was it.

Those first months in the thumping city were so overstimulating and disorienting that I started to have severe stomach cramps every night. As soon as I got into bed after my day at ABC, they would start, and it would take hours for them to ebb enough for me to sleep. I went to the doctor, and he found nothing wrong. I knew, though, that my Beverly Hills kid internal compass was rebelling and needed rewiring.

I'd never had an office before, and now I had a big one, with large windows overlooking Sixth Avenue. That avenue, grandly known as Avenue of the Americas, though I never heard anyone refer to it other than Sixth, was the home of the three national broadcast networks. I'd never had what was then called a secretary before, either; hell, I had been a secretary myself only two weeks before. Now I had one of my own.

Leonard Goldberg's great and good generosity meant he treated me as an executive from that first day instead of the typist I was qualified to be.

I was taking in everything around me with a wonderment that almost overcame my insecurity. I felt that I still knew nothing (which was true), that I was only there because of some cosmic accident (which was also true). But, accident though it was, I was soon to learn that ABC was the best possible place for anyone to carve out a TV career in the mid-1960s.

In those days, the three networks commanded more than 90 percent of all television viewing—but as the youngest of the three, ABC was the also-ran network. We were scrappy and adventurous, with a kind of nothing-to-lose sensibility that allowed us to take program risks that CBS and NBC would never do. CBS had been number one for many years and was referred to as the Tiffany Network. NBC, which had been founded on Toscanini concerts during the radio era, considered itself the quality network. It had been created by RCA primarily to sell radio consoles and then televisions, both of which it manufactured. By the time I arrived at ABC, NBC had just spent millions to adapt its programming to color; as a result, it was about to sell even more television sets.

I experienced a perfect example of the difference in the three networks on my first morning at ABC. I walked into the building and into the elevator, where an ordinary-looking man of no physical or sartorial distinction stuck out his hand and said, "Hello, I'm Leonard Goldenson." He was the founder and chairman.

I shook his hand and shyly said, "I'm your newest employee."

He smiled and said "Welcome!" and up we went in the elevator. Together!

The elegant and suave William S. Paley, CBS's chairman, would never have introduced himself to a new employee in the public elevator, because Paley had his own private elevator. Also, he was a time-honored snob and would have looked at my unruly suit and bad shoes and wondered what the hell I was doing in his classic Eero Saarinen building. At NBC, I would never have been greeted by Robert Sarnoff, its leader at the time and son of the founder, David Sarnoff. I would have quivered in the ornate lobby of the grand RCA Building, wondering which of the fifteen elevators I was supposed to take.

A few months in, I found an apartment, the very first time I'd had a place that didn't belong to my family. It was the ground floor of an old brownstone on the Upper East Side. Since it was winter in New York, a blizzard year, the garden was covered by five feet of snow—not pretty snow, just old, brown, slushy snow. The place had no natural light and was fairly gloomy, and I had only the most spartan furniture, just a bed, a bureau, and a lamp. There I was on my first night, hungry and alone.

Industrious person that I was, I went down the street and bought a steak. I put it in a frying pan, and the steak and the pan immediately caught fire. I frantically doused it with water, which sent the flames higher, and proceeded to pretty much burn down my kitchen. My first night of independence was also my last night of cooking.

Most weeknights I'd have dinner with my boss and his newly hired executive, Martin Starger. Len, as I now was told to call him, hired Martin away from the advertising agency BBDO, and the two of them shared a dry, sophisticated wit. They were New York fast and clever, making references to the insides of the television business that took me a long time to understand. But I drank in every word. I loved those dinners, loved being the little cub accepted into this rarefied wise and wisecracking world. I was jumping several levels up from the University of William Morris, being around these quintessential men on the make, with high-flying careers in the center of the media universe. The rhythm of their pace and patter was so different from my somnambulant California patois that my accent changed through these years, so much so that people have since assumed I was raised in the East. The changes were showing all over. I was shedding my sun-washed ways for the city-slicked sophistication of New York.

One of the many wonderful things at ABC was that if you wanted responsibility, you could simply take it. There were few rules, little governance, and almost no bureaucracy. The strictness came via the ethnic hierarchy: although the top bosses were all Jewish, the actual operations and running of the networks had white Anglo-Saxon presidents. Lower down on one side were the sales departments, populated primarily by gentiles, who interacted with the ad agencies and sponsors, where almost no one was Jewish.

But on the other side were the program departments, and they, like most entertainment businesses, were mostly staffed with Jews. In 1966, ABC was generally younger at each tier, and definitely scrappier, though it did parallel the bigger networks in these strict ethnic rules. It was an extraordinary environment for anyone with ambition because television was becoming the dominant communications and entertainment force, and the three networks were protected from competition by Federal Communications Commission rules that made it almost impossible for anyone else to horn in.

The contrast between high-toned NBC, elegant CBS, and ragtag ABC was everywhere, as much in New York as in Hollywood, where CBS had its architecturally striking complex and NBC had its campus headquarters in the Valley.

And where was ABC's program department? In low-rent central Hollywood, on the second floor above Sy Devore's tailor shop. Really.

So it was left to ABC to try anything to get attention and ratings. We were always shooting from the hip, taking risks. And the latest risk was picking Leonard Goldberg, an untried mid-level young executive, to lead its programming. He was lickety-split smart, moderately handsome with an easy confidence. When he started at ABC, there was very little talent in the place, and we weren't close to having a competitive on-air schedule. We'd have an occasional hit, like *Batman,* but never a really strong full night. As Len and Martin Starger tried to scare up show ideas, it fell to me to become the administrative glue of their operations, taking care of the details and making many of the decisions that didn't involve choosing series programming. My great good luck was that Len hated detail and I loved it. He was a little lazy, if charmingly so, and I was a firecracker. In a

few months I was basically running the operations of the program department, borrowing Goldberg's great power as my own.

Len inherited his predecessor's two-office suite, but instead of putting
Starger, his next-highest-level executive, in the office adjacent to his, as
had long been the practice, he installed me there with an earpiece that
allowed me to listen to all his calls.

Slowly but steadily, I came to know everything that was going on,
since he also had me in almost every meeting he took.

The education I was getting hourly and the borrowed power I was
using were a shock to my system, not to mention how it was shocking
those around me. I exploded in every direction with ferocious energy. All
that pent-up ambition I never thought I possessed shot out of me like a
cork from a champagne bottle.

My total ambition at that point was to be the person who takes care of
the "Person," meaning the principal. In that role I was fearless, intuitively
knowing how to move all the levers of people and power in my sole pursuit of satisfying the Person's needs and goals.

Never during that time did I even once think I would be anything more
than that, certainly not the Person himself. I could please people and intuitively knew what their issues and problems were. And I had the ability
to figure out in minute detail how to execute whatever was needed to help
them. I could "stand in" better than anyone else, but when the lights were
turned on and the shot was to be taken, I never thought I'd be the One.

Like a character in a fable, only protected by another's cloak could I
act like a giant.

I was everyone's busy boy. In my first month, the then president of the
network, a moon-faced, red-splotched Deep Southerner named Thomas
Waldrop Moore, wanted me to go out to Colorado and sit on a mountain for two months with a film crew waiting for a bald eagle to hatch
its eggs. Moore was a myopic outdoor enthusiast and sportsman, and he
thought the birth of a bald eagle would make a great special. I did not
want to give up New York for a second now that I had found my place in

it, and I somehow shimmied my way out of that assignment. It turned out the bald eagle had a miscarriage anyway. My job careened from ordering Len Goldberg's argyle socks to telling the head of specials to hire the famous photographer Bert Stern to shoot a documentary on Twiggy (the "it" model of the 1960s), from buying the talcum powder that Goldberg doused all over his body to buying a movie package for millions of dollars.

Those first couple of months moved so fast, with Goldberg trying to get his arms around his new job and me getting my legs organizing the department to best serve him. We quickly weeded out the tried and tired summer-seersuckered group we'd inherited and replaced them with fresh blood. One of our first hires was a young man named Michael Eisner. He was gangly and goofy, but with an irrepressibly interesting mind and spirit and came in to meet me for the job interview, thinking I was Leonard Goldberg. After twenty minutes of frenetic talk I thought, *Fantastic!* We had mostly old fossils and bureaucrats, and here was this guy who was whip-smart and enthusiastic about anything in his sight. He had more energy than his limbs could carry and more ideas than his mouth could coherently get out. For the next sixty years we would move in and around each other's work lives. Even though in later years we had turmoil and tussles when he fiercely ran Disney and I was fiercely at Fox, he is one of my rare lifelong friends, and serves as a most perfect director in one of my principal companies.

When I first moved to New York, I thought that city was going to be my permanent home, but soon found I was never going to have geographical permanence. For the next thirty years I would be a nomad, my only constant the planes that connected New York and Los Angeles. While historically the command-and-control systems for networks were in New York, filmed and taped series were mostly produced in L.A. Equally important, Leonard was now seriously dating Marlo Thomas, and he wanted to be with her as much as possible.

Because he'd gotten more and more dependent on my ministrations, it made sense for me to travel with him. So the two of us developed a pattern that went on for the next few years: we'd leave New York on Friday on the five p.m. plane, stay in L.A. the following week, and arrive back in New York late Sunday night. I would alternate five days in New York with ten days in L.A.—meaning basically that I didn't live anywhere. We stayed at the Hotel Bel-Air, a series of connected low-slung villas on a quietly luxe residential street.

I didn't have many friends, and that schedule didn't help me make a lot of new ones. I was so obsessed with my job and engrossed in this new life that I didn't notice much going on in the world. Other than an occasional secret date night, once with a young sales executive at ABC that quickly ended when I threw up on him on a Coney Island roller coaster, I didn't have much time for anything else than the work.

It's appalling that during those early years at ABC, when the Vietnam War was in full force, the country enmeshed in rancor, and all the young full-out in rebellion, I was barely aware that anything of significance was happening beyond network television. I had found a new way to be co-cooned from normal life.

At ABC there wasn't really a budget or quarterly reviews or any process other than using the Nielsen ratings to determine what shows were going to be on or off the schedule. The fight for every single ratings point was fierce. All life was wired to those daily ratings and how those huge audiences were split between the three networks. It was not unusual for the combined prime-time audience for the three networks to reach more than 100 million on a regular basis, such a contrast to today, when there is so much fragmentation that billions of people are watching hundreds of networks, and a single celebrity can have an Insta audience of 30 million. That concentration provided national unity, or the myth of unity, as against today's flood of information, disinformation, and cultural chaos. While yearning for simpler times is an old person's foolishness, the fragmentation of media, and the polarization particularly in news, and the tectonic plates of Hollywood shifting from the old major studio system to the control of trillion-dollar technology companies is not an altogether good thing. It has pushed creative decision-making too far down in the corporate structure of these giant businesses, and has changed the basic nature of the entertainment business. Back then, the rewards were the size of the audiences; now, buying a toaster from Amazon is the Prime (*sic*) business model. And as for polarization, it has rendered obsolete the concept of a trusted source for information—probably our greatest loss to the body politic.

One of the most important staples in programming in the 1960s was showing motion pictures after they'd played in the theaters. There were only two ways for audiences to see movies: you either went to the theater when the films were released or waited months or even years for them to show up on the networks. Movies, of course, were the major entertainment and cultural form that everyone worldwide paid almost daily attention to—home video hadn't yet been invented, so movies shown on television were its most watched and valuable commodity for the studios that produced them and the networks that aired them.

My first actual task, other than being the best assistant in the world, was to improve ABC's library of movies. No one else in the company had concentrated on that, and there was an opening, so I claimed it. I hadn't yet turned twenty-four.

For the major movie studios, revenue from the sales of broadcast rights was growing every year and becoming more and more vital to their overall earnings and financial health. This revenue often made the difference between a good and a bad year because it could temper their bad luck at the crapshoot of moviemaking.

In the fall of 1967, ABC had two movie nights: Sunday and Wednesday at nine p.m. NBC aired theatrical movies Wednesday and Saturday and CBS aired them Thursday and Friday. Who got what movies from the major studios was truly a haphazard process: basically, one big movie mogul would call up the president of the network, or even Mr. Goldenson, the chairman, and say they had a package of movies to sell and this was the price. ABC, the lowest network on the totem pole, got the titles the big two rejected. That process was about to change forever when I met a seeming madman who would go on to become one of the most important people in my life.

It all began when Leonard Goldenson placed an urgent call to speak with Len Goldberg. Len wasn't in the office, and Goldenson needed someone from the program department in *his* office immediately, and there I was.

Goldenson said, "Please come up right away. I have Charles Bluhdorn in my office."

Charles Bluhdorn (pronounced *blue-dorn*) was one of the great industrialists of the twentieth century. In his late and most exuberant thirties, Bluhdorn had just bought Paramount Pictures, and he was in Goldenson's office more than ready to deal. Actually, he was desperate: Paramount had been declining for years, making one expensive dog of a movie after another, which opened the door for the always rapacious Bluhdorn to take it over.

An Austrian immigrant, he had rag-traded his way into building Gulf + Western Industries into a huge conglomerate, doing everything from making car bumpers and pistons for jet engines to growing sugar. It took him only eight years to buckle together this giant agglomeration of businesses. He was like a rug merchant who couldn't be in any room without the urge to trade something. He was truly brilliant, had momentous energy, was charming and funny with his full-on Austrian accent, and had a voracious desire to bend everything and everyone around him to his will. He never walked into any room passively, never met anyone without trying to seduce them, devour them, mold them this way and that.

When Charles Bluhdorn got voluble, a near guarantee in any interaction, he literally began to froth at the mouth.

In I walked, not only having never been in Mr. Goldenson's office, but never having spoken to him again after our meeting in the elevator on my first day at the company. Bluhdorn had the energy of an electric grid and could hardly keep his seat as Goldenson told me they'd agreed ABC would buy a group of Paramount movies. Goldenson handed me the list and instructed me simply, "Follow up."

I politely asked Mr. Bluhdorn whom in his organization I should contact.

"Everyone at this pathetic company I just bought is an idiot, so just call me," Bluhdorn said. I couldn't believe this giant industrialist wanted to handle this by himself. What I didn't know was that Paramount was a vanity buy for him, opposed by his board. Until now all the other bread-and-nickel businesses he'd acquired had always been bought below book value. The only way he could justify buying the studio was to sell the television rights to its library of movies at a price close to what he'd paid for the whole company, a conniver's connivance.

Leonard Goldenson famously hated noise and confrontation, and given the hour he had just spent with Charles Bluhdorn, he was practically shaking with relief as he led us to the elevator.

As we rode down from the forty-second floor, Bluhdorn said that Goldenson had agreed to buy more than one hundred movies, but that it would be all right if I wanted to exclude ten from that long list. I smelled only trouble from that seeming generosity. Out I stumbled from the elevator, leaving Bluhdorn to descend on his own, while I scurried to my office and with mounting horror read the titles—one flop after another. I couldn't believe how many duds Paramount had made in the last five years. It was those duds that had given Bluhdorn the opening to buy the place, and now he was shamelessly trying to get us to bail him out. We couldn't air most of them—they would be ratings disasters.

I called Mr. Goldenson and gently asked him, "Did we actually agree to buy all these movies?"

He said, "Bluhdorn talked so fast, and with his accent I couldn't do more than just smile and occasionally nod."

He was pretty uncomfortable in the telling, as if describing a tornado that had blown through his office. With my best attempt at faking a big-boy voice I said, "Let me try to handle it."

And then, faking an even bigger big-boy voice, I put in a call to Mr. Bluhdorn. He got on the phone immediately.

I said, "We have a problem with these films."

"What problem? Your chairman and I just closed the deal!" I could tell there was already foam coming out of his mouth.

I said, "Our chairman wasn't aware of the actual movies, and I'm sorry, but there is just no way we can put them on the air."

There was a long pause, and he said, "Stay where you are. I'm coming over right now to straighten this out." Charles Bluhdorn coming to my office. Couldn't be. But, half an hour later, he strode into my office, almost violently threw off his jacket, sat down, and began to tell me in ever-increasing volume how he had bought "that stinker company Paramount" with borrowed money and that it was secured by the contemplated sale of these films to television. So he had no room to change the deal by a nickel; or, he said with a devil's smile, not a nickel more than 10 percent.

Pinned down by his small, bright, piggish eyes and looking for a politic way to get out of the commitment he seemed to think he'd made with Goldenson, I said, "Well, a deal this large has to go to the board of ABC for approval"—where that surety of statement came from I'll never know—"and I, speaking for the program department that has to schedule these films, I will say: we can't air them."

I just made that up, too. What had come over me? Here I was, twenty-three years old and going snarl for snarl with a titan of industry.

Now, I've played that moment in my head many times over the years. It wasn't a flush of hidden courage that came over me; I was still someone who would change almost any of my opinions to please a powerful person. But fairness and honesty were the only solid principles my generally absent father gave me. This raging energy ball named Charles Bluhdorn had somehow bamboozled my venerable old chairman into accepting this ludicrous deal. It wasn't fair and it wasn't right and I was loudly and righteously angry that he might get away with it. I stood my ground.

He got up, screaming, and strode toward the door. "I'm going up to Goldenson's office, and we'll *see* if he's actually going to renege on the deal!" Calmly, I said, "I don't think you want to confront Mr. Goldenson, since you've taken such advantage of him. Maybe instead of yelling at me, you and I should just sit down and see if we can find some other way to solve this."

A glint of compromise in the air, Bluhdorn sat back down, said he was hungry, and demanded I order lunch from a nearby delicatessen, which, thank god, was something I could do with total confidence. Over the next couple of hours we hammered through the list of every Paramount movie that still had sprocket holes. Finally I tallied it up: "There are about ten movies that would play okay and another ten we could bury in the summer months."

Bluhdorn insisted: "You've got to take all of them." The kernel of an idea forming, I asked if he planned to make new movies at Paramount or if he was just going to strip-mine the assets. That got him all frothy again and he bellowed, "Do you think I'm some small-time player? I'm going to revive Paramount and make it the biggest studio in town!" (And, he did.) I pounced on this and said, "Great. We'll agree to contract all those films if we have the right to swap the new movies for the old turkeys. In other words, I'll guarantee the dollars, betting you'll make better movies we can successfully run, which will partially offset the costs of making them, since these old movies are basically worthless." While I didn't fully understand it at the time, this was exactly the concept Bluhdorn had used to build up Gulf + Western: trading the made-up paper value of his stock and using it to buy better assets than the crummy ones he'd been able to buy at the beginning.

We made the deal, and that's how ABC eventually got *The Godfather* and *Love Story*.

Somewhere in the middle of that animated discussion, Leonard Goldberg returned and peered into my office. He later told people proudly, "There was this big mogul and my little assistant yelling at each other while devouring pastrami sandwiches—who knew?"

Somehow, defending what I thought was right and fair for my company, I became fearless, while at the same time I was able to calibrate just how far I could go. I never came off as arrogant or disrespectful to Bluhdorn, but I was able to hold firm against his tidal wave of aggression.

In that negotiation, I found out something about myself that has surprised me ever since.

I actually love confrontation. Arguing principles forcefully, loudly, and passionately was becoming the definition of me. As long as I wasn't arguing "self," I was fearless.

CHAPTER 5

So that was how I came to be in charge of the movie nights on ABC. No one gave me the job—I just grabbed it when nobody was looking, and it wasn't until years later that I was officially awarded it.

The owners of the movie studios, now fading old men, deeply resented television for taking away their monopoly on mass entertainment. Until I upped the game, the process for networks buying the studios' movies wasn't competitive. If a network bought the last package from a studio, it would generally get the next one. It was a staid and clubby arrangement, based on incumbency, not competition.

My first strategy was to bang on the doors of these old moguls—who had invented the industry—until they'd allow me to bid. Then I would bid up the prices to dislodge the best product.

The other networks had never been very savvy about buying movies, so I didn't have much competition. NBC and CBS had been doing business this old-fashioned way for a long time, getting all the best movies automatically. I wanted to shake the market up and almost shook myself out of a job.

I succeeded in getting better movies for ABC, but it did raise prices. To counteract that, I thought, naively, that if I signaled to the other two networks that I was going to pay less going forward, we would all be able to pay less in the future. It seemed to make sense in my legally uneducated mind.

My strategy was to leak my plan to *The New York Times* and *The Wall Street Journal*. That got big coverage, and the next day every studio head in Hollywood was calling Leonard Goldenson, demanding I be fired—for price-fixing!

I pleaded ignorance of the law and kept my job, but my bumptious pursuit of the straightest line from problem to solution kept getting me into trouble: I'd see the older executives at ABC to-ing and fro-ing with caution and delicacy, respecting channels and protocols and worrying that every action had consequence and risk that would upset their careers and financial security. I, on the other hand, saw only linear logic and was able to proceed directly, without the distractions of normal family life (and, to be honest, financial worry) or any of its curbing responsibilities. I was bashing forward all the time because I didn't see the risks an average person would.

This meant I was also thoughtlessly intolerant of my older colleagues' fear and complacency. I was far more frightened than they were, but my terror was of exposure, and that absorbed most of my fear-making capacity, leaving me fairly courageous on temporal matters as long as I was protected by the cloak of my powerful boss. I couldn't believe that they would ignore or defer a problem, large or small, because they had other things, mature things, family things, office political things on their minds. And so I became the odd-job specialist at ABC; any task that was gnarly and wasn't nailed down was now mine. I don't think I was obnoxious about it—just more or less oblivious to the effect my willfulness had on others. I would have been strung up by my heels somewhere along the way if I ever acted with arrogance, and besides, I've always thought it repugnant. If there's a deadly sin that often results from someone's success in business, arrogance should lead the list. Success and outsized ego breed it, but I had scarcely any ego to speak of, so little sense of self, that it was never even possible for me to act with arrogance, no matter how successful I became. Was I tough and argumentative and stubborn? Oh yes. Going deeper into every issue so I could get to the fundamental truth was what gave me the voice to win most disputes. Thus armed, I could argue persuasively and get my way without swagger or strutting. All those negatives from my early life, all that dysfunction, forged my own unique tools to succeed in business.

I was able to turn all those weaknesses into strengths—an alchemy all my own.

The one person I never got my way with was the über-powerful chairman of MCA, the wildly feared then "king" of Hollywood, Lew Wasserman. I'd known him since I was eleven years old as the father of my schoolmate Lynne. He'd intimidated me then and forever since. The only time I ever tried to negotiate with him, he wouldn't give an inch, not even a fraction of an inch.

I first approached him in business when I was twenty-five and buying a package of films from his Universal studio. I went to his office and said, ever so tentatively, that given we were buying sixty-four units at $600,000 each, couldn't you just cut one unit from that sixty-four? Two beats. He stared. He said, "No." Nothing more. Just no. Silence. The stare. And I folded like the cheapest tent. But as I got up to go, dejectedly knowing the fool that I was, he walked me out and, in that very quiet voice of his, said, "Next time you try this, be fully prepared to call the whole deal off if you don't get what you asked for. Because, otherwise, you never will." Out I went as the door closed silently behind me. It was the best lesson in negotiating and has stayed with me ever after.

The first time I smoked marijuana was at a dingy apartment in New York on a balmy summer night. And how lucky was I that the first experience came while listening—also for the first time—to the just-released Beatles' *Sgt. Pepper* album. I left at five in the morning, walking down the middle of Second Avenue, belting out, "We're Sergeant Pepper's Lonely Hearts Club Band / We hope you will enjoy the show."

For the next few years, whenever I wasn't in my work suit, I was getting high. That ended when Bert Schneider, my new hippie-dippie friend, brought me back a pound of marijuana from India. Bert was dating my high school friend Candice Bergen, and he was a rising television executive whose father was the chairman of Columbia Pictures. After the first toke of this exotic weed, I went quickly berserk, ripping my clothes off and baying at the moon.

I later found out that the marijuana had been laced with methedrine and I came within a whisker of going into a permanent psychotic state.

That ended that.

While I was gathering some independence, I was still primarily Leonard Goldberg's assistant. Which meant I was still on the plane with him every week going from coast to coast. And I began to hate flying.

"Hate" is not the right word; as the earliest indicator of my issues with control, I couldn't bear being thousands of feet in the air in a machine controlled by pilots behind a sealed door. For the first time I was thoroughly liking my life, and the idea that some "force" could take it away from me was beyond abhorrent. As those doors closed, I dreaded those first few minutes in the air until the Valium took hold. It got so bad that on flight days I would look up and pray for snow, sleet, fog—anything that would ground us. My increasing craziness reached its zenith one day when I was flying alone back to New York. Several hours into the flight, I began to hear this odd sound, a slow ticking noise.

Tick . . . tick . . . tick.

Pretty soon, I was thinking the ticking was exactly the way a bomb timer would sound. In my mounting hysteria, I called the flight attendant over and whispered, "*There's a bomb on the plane.*"

The captain came to my seat and asked me, "Did you just tell the stewardess there was a bomb on the plane?"

"Listen," I said. "Don't you hear it? *Tick, tick, tick!*"

The captain pointed up to the film projector that attached to the ceiling (that was how you saw films on planes back then). A movie had recently finished, and the end of the film strip was banging away rhythmically.

Tick, tick, tick.

This craziness couldn't continue or my career would be fatally compromised. I somehow got the idea that if I learned to fly, at least I would know what might be happening in the air other than my fantasies of disaster.

So out I went to flight-training school at Santa Monica Airport. They immediately put me in a little Cessna 150 with an instructor and we took off. After leveling, he said, "Now you take the wheel." Instead of panic, I felt utter exhilaration.

They usually don't give you advance notice for your first solo flight because it can be too scary for the student. My knee was shaking badly enough that the plane was wobbling as I took off. But once I was up in the air, I loved it, and I went on to fly fifty hours with my student license. I now knew more about how the whole flying thing worked and felt more in control. Forever after, flying for me was a glorious state of suspended animation, a pause button in the frenetic life I was living.

But I soon discovered a second, potentially more debilitating phobia: public speaking. Even getting up to give a short talk in front of a small group of people had me quaking. Again, control was the issue—could I control the normal anxiety or would it spin out into total collapse?

The first time it happened, a year or so after I started at ABC, I was in a small conference room, and I stood up to explain to a senior group of five executives my strategy for getting the best movies at the lowest cost. I started in, my voice strong and confident, when suddenly a completely separate track in my brain took over, and I found myself wondering, *What would happen if I simply fainted into the fruit bowl in front of me?* And then the answer fired through my brain: *What would happen is that my career and my life would be over in a flash.*

That panic sent my spine into spasm. For two seconds I used every bit of strength I had to overcome the panic—those seconds seemed to last an eternity. I recovered without them seeing the torrent of sweat inside my suit.

Flying had been about *not* being in control, but this fear of speaking in public was about *losing* control.

The worst of it was yet to come.

Every year at ABC, there was an annual convention for all the affiliated stations at which we told them about the next season's programming. It was a formal event, at the Century Plaza Hotel in Los Angeles, a thousand-person, two-day extravaganza, and I was ordered to present the section on movies.

It was not long after dawn when I got to the intersection of Wilshire Boulevard and Whittier Drive, across from the Beverly Hilton on one side and Robinson's department store on the other. There was no traffic that early in the morning, and as I sat in my car, the stoplight went from red to green and from green to red and back to green.

Okay, floor it, I was thinking. *Right through the plate-glass front window of Robinson's. What will I break? My arm? That might be worth it, not to make this speech. My leg? No, I'm going skiing next Thursday. What if I kill myself? Not likely, it doesn't look like there's any wall to hit.* Red to green . . . Green to red . . . Some part of me knew I wasn't going to crash through Robinson's windows. I'd just have to go through with it.

I got up in front of the thousand attendees, sure I was going to pass out. I had convinced myself I was weak when, at nineteen, I couldn't handle the flooding anxiety that almost felled me. I was now to discover just how physically strong I really was, how I could call on that strength to save me in a crisis. As soon as I heard my voice booming into the audience, I found my calm. When I stepped off the stage, I felt a level of elation few drugs could ever equal.

Overcoming these early career-risking episodes gave me enough clear sail to begin learning from some of the legendary captains and stevedores of the movie business.

I knew nothing of financing or accounting until I met Arthur Krim, the owlish-headed head of United Artists. He was in his sixties and very old-school. He wore three-piece suits even in his overheated office on Broadway. Krim was a lawyer who had rescued the decrepit United Artists from bankruptcy, but it still had a threadbare balance sheet and limped from film to film. Over the years, its movies were far more adventuresome than those of the majors: *The African Queen, Some Like It Hot, The Miracle Worker, West Side Story*. It took far more creative risks than the majors and, pound for pound, made better movies. In our negotiations, Krim insisted I make a side promise—not in writing—that we wouldn't air a film for a certain amount of time, even though we had a contractual right to do so. That way he could declare the revenue without compromising the timing of his releases. This was one of his trickier forms of accounting, and today it's a crime. But this was how wily old Krim was able to book the revenue from the films before they actually had income.

From Darryl Zanuck, who in his dotage was still smoking foot-long cigars as I sat half choking on the stench, I discovered the way he got movies made starring his various mistresses, none of whom had any acting talent: he would try to convince me to buy them up front so he could tell the financiers he had them covered regardless of the outcome.

From Steve Ross, the dealmaker who built Time Warner, I learned how posturing for no reason other than his worry about maintaining his supreme self-image could hold up a deal: he once kept me in my office in the deep of winter, after they had turned off the heat, until I agreed to something he hadn't even yet offered—because it would only be offered officially if he could count on my saying yes to it. His ego couldn't stand the possible rejection.

They were all full-blooded characters with their eccentricities, giant self-esteem, and supreme self-importance. They were compelled to stand out from ordinary men, so unlike today's managers and their undramatic and cautious ways. They were as theatrical in their means and methods as were the films they put up on the screen. I was often the last bridge these moguls traveled in their twilight years before the movie industry became more boringly business-sized and bureaucratized.

I also got to know Otto Preminger, the famously tyrannical producer and director, who was known as the Prussian martinet of the movies from the 1940s to the 1960s. He had made a notorious movie, *The Moon Is Blue*, which had not been sold to television because of its supposed immorality. Preminger personally owned the movie, and I wanted it for ABC. I thought it was brave and only indecent because the Catholic League had declared it so. He and I collaborated on editing it for television, and he liked that I stood up to him, eventually calling me his "little dummkopf." But for the first few months I was Mr. Diller; I usually looked around for whoever this Mr. Diller was, since no one had ever put a "Mr." before my name. He was formal, fierce, and scathingly witty, a great personality who'd had secret affairs with Dorothy Dandridge, a Black actress, as well as a secret son with Gypsy Rose Lee. When he invited me to dinner at his elegant, modernist town house, it was my first exposure to the highest European style of living, so different from the bland fare in the Beverly Hills provinces. I was so lucky these fabulous rogues were still around, and that they needed me to buy their old movies. I was paying special attention to them as increasingly few others were, and in appreciation they were in turn polishing me up with their world-weary gravitas and sophistication.

As the 1960s drew to a close, television was evolving. It had been growing audiences since the 1950s on a fairly bland diet of showing old movies and making half-hour comedies and hour-long drama series where the characters were in stasis for decades. There were long-running hits on CBS and NBC that had come from their dominance in radio, and ABC, being late to networking, had a hard time competing. I was making a little headway with getting better old movies, but the momentum was hard against us in series programming. We'd do anything to get attention and put on some fresh, flashy shows like *The Flintstones, Bewitched,* and *The Fugitive,* and they were occasionally enough to get us out of third place, but not enough to give us a sustained advantage. For my first two years at ABC, we searched frantically for a transformational concept. At one of the endless program development meetings where we tossed around new ideas, I asked if we might think about producing new movies ourselves, making them like a series, as we did half hours and hours, but with a different story every week. Make them ninety minutes in length—longer than a drama or sitcom, but not as long as a theatrical movie. That was such a radical idea that it was quickly laughed out of the room as impractical; it was conventional television wisdom that you had to have either continuing characters or presold movie titles to grab an audience. This had neither and was dismissed as far too risky.

I hadn't a clue how to pull it off, but I was excited by the idea, though. I loved its ambition and complexity, and I thought its sheer bravado and riskiness could actually alter the network landscape. Also I more than liked that it was contrary to every rule of the television game. I was turning into a classically querulous contrarian, and challenging everything was becoming my nature. I've never been a particularly good shepherd of repeating or sustaining any norm. I always thought conventional wisdom was . . . well, conventional, and therefore uninteresting. Those two principles—*never done before* and *never done quite this way*—have always got me going. If ideas don't have qualities of either I'm just not very engaged. Without my ferocious curiosity and focus aroused, I'm just like the next dullard.

I couldn't get this idea out of my head, even though it gained no traction every time I raised it. I couldn't even get it on the Program Development Report, which listed all the projects being developed and the costs associated with them. You couldn't develop anything without there being a budget for a script or pilot. Doing a series of movies was a long-range idea that needed long-range logistical planning. This would be difficult to accomplish since, at the time, "long-range" at ABC meant mostly thirteen weeks and out—the time it took to air a series, evaluate its success or lack of it, and cancel it or pick it up.

The failure rate at ABC for series was so high that the industry joke at the time was "The way to end the Vietnam War? Put it on ABC—it'll be over in thirteen weeks."

A breakthrough came via the most unlikely part of the company, in the person of its chairman, Leonard Goldenson. We only had one thing in common: his history as president of Paramount's distribution arm before he started ABC and my experience at buying old movies. But it was enough to make us bedfellows, as I was the only one in the company who knew anything about movies. While he was now a television man, he never gave up his love for feature films, and as I got more successful buying them, and dealing with his old colleagues at the major studios, he got more interested in talking to me about all things movies.

Goldenson was a diminutive, taciturn, quietly crafty old gentleman. He had purchased the bare bones of ABC in 1953 from the owner of Life Savers candies. Over the years, he became a rather benign-seeming cheerleader of his ABC management team, until they failed; then he would simply replace them with the next crop. His hands were never directly soiled with programming, and he'd make sure he was never in the direct line of fire when a decision went wrong. A lawyer, he'd risen up through the minefields of Paramount's movie-exhibition operations during the 1940s, a tumultuous period when the government sued to separate the makers of movies from their exhibitors so that studios could no longer own theaters. Goldenson emerged from that as the head of the spun-off United Paramount Theaters, and though he was a movie man in training and heart, he saw television as the future, so he merged his theaters with a bedraggled group of television stations to form the American Broadcasting Company.

Goldenson's network was profitable, but never flush, and Little Leonard, as we called him with affection—out of earshot, of course—stood small next to the titans Paley and Sarnoff. Nevertheless, underneath his dignity and decorum was a scrappy, shrewd fighter with enough old-movie-business blood in his veins to get excited about the idea of making new ones. Even for the small screen.

Every few months there was a review for senior management of projects in various stages of development. It was always a formal group, including the heads of sales and all the key network departments. About twenty people in the biggest conference room at ABC in New York. I was usually allowed in the room only when necessary, to talk about any new movie acquisitions.

On this particular day in 1967, Mr. Goldenson dropped in to hear what was going on. After one same-old same-old, boring idea after another seemed to be putting the crowd to sleep, I was asked if there were any great movies we could schedule for the next fall season.

I said, "The pickings are pretty grim, those great old libraries are getting exhausted and the new movies being made aren't as broadly popular."

This interested the old-movie maven Goldenson, and he asked me what could be done about that.

If I could have scripted it there wasn't a better opening. This was my moment. "What about making original movies on our own and programming them in prime time?" There was a fairly long moment of silence before the room erupted into comments. All of them against it.

"It would be impossible to produce and promote."

"We don't have the resources."

"We should just make better comedy and drama series and not mess with this nonsense."

But my man Goldenson was clearly intrigued, and he patiently waited for all the noise to quiet down. After a moment of slow contemplation, he said softly, "Yes, I can see the risks, but it's at least a fresh idea. Maybe we should explore this and I could help by going out to California and see if we can get some of the major studios to finance and produce them and thereby lay off some of the risk." That was a shock to the prosaic system: the chairman was going to engage directly in programming—something he hadn't done since Walt Disney came to visit him in 1954 to discuss his idea for Disneyland (ABC took an early stake in the park and put Disney's first series on the air).

You probably can't imagine how insulated the big motion picture studios were from the wider entertainment business. They were still strong enough to look down on and even hate television. They saw us as killing their golden goose—the theatrical distribution of movies—while ignobly they had to sell us their movies after they came out of the theaters just to stay alive. There was also no social or business mix between movie and television executives. Each ruled a sovereign world, with the movie people thinking the television people were beneath them. They thought of us just as purveyors of Kleenex and soda pop.

I'd been presenting these big-package buys to the board of ABC for approval, and Goldenson had come to like my sparky efforts to compete with the big guys. In a great surprise to me and all the others, he ended the discussion by saying, "I'll just take Barry with me, since he's gotten to know some of these old fellas."

With his entrée, we met with all of them. Most were exceedingly polite, out of respect for Goldenson, but noncommittal. We could tell that they weren't really interested. To them this was just another desperate act on the part of ABC—and one that would lose everyone a lot of money.

We were mindful that we didn't want any one studio to control the project, and we had thought we could entice several of the studios to divide up the twenty-four movies we'd need to fill out the first season. But only the youngest of the moguls, Lew Wasserman, showed some genuine interest, though he said he doubted ABC would make a big-enough commitment to make it worthwhile.

Lew Wasserman had built MCA—the talent agency initially called Music Corporation of America—into something so big that it had taken over Universal Pictures and become the dominant producer of all television series. He was intrigued and more than a little curious about our plans. He'd already started to make a small inroad with occasional two-hour-special movies for NBC, and he certainly didn't want anyone else getting into that game. He was becoming the most powerful man in Hollywood, and he sure was going to keep it that way. At the end of our meeting, he was the only one to say he'd like to think some about the project and would let us know if there was anything further to discuss. Both Leonard and I thought that was just another polite rejection, and we dejectedly boarded the next plane back to New York; Leonard, on principle, riding in coach; me, on the non-principle of inheritance, riding up front, where I'd always sat with Goldberg. Embarrassing in the extreme. The trip was considered a bust, but we were soon to learn how wrong we were.

A week later Len Goldberg and I were surprised to be called to a non-scheduled meeting in Mr. Goldenson's office. Lew Wasserman and Sidney Sheinberg, Wasserman's president at MCA/Universal, were sitting in the ABC chairman's office together with Elton Rule, the ABC president. They had called from Wasserman's nearby apartment at the Sherry-Netherland and asked if they could come over for a talk. Some talk—my project was about to be kidnapped!

They made us an offer, simple and remarkable: they would supply *all* of the ninety-minute movies we needed for $600,000 each. They justified the price as appropriate by comparing it with the $800,000 they were getting for the two-hour movies they were making for NBC. Plus, they wanted it to be exclusive. They would be the only supplier for ABC's movies, and the deal was exclusive for ten years. In order to gear up, they wanted ABC to commit to guarantee them $18 million, a huge sum for any network.

Wasserman said no one else in Hollywood could make these movies in volume, and given their huge TV operation, they were the only ones who could produce them at a reasonable cost. My bosses were impressed with their power and confidence, and I think they were intimidated by Wasserman's dominance over television production. To my more than dismay, I had to silently watch Goldenson and Rule give approving murmurs to everything Wasserman and Sheinberg said.

I was only able to ask one question: "Would you agree to let anyone else produce even a few of the films?"

Wasserman said, "No, we'll do all or none, and the price isn't negotiable."

Elton Rule then said, "You've made a compelling proposal. We'll get back to you quickly."

I had hoped to have many suppliers make the movies and keep the operation inside ABC. Now my project and I were going to be sidelined, and we, principally me, would have no involvement or control. After they left, Goldenson said that if MCA was going to partner in such a big project, it gave ABC safety in making such a huge commitment. Finally, ending the meeting, Elton Rule said, "We really ought to consider this one-stop-shop offer. They'll be responsible for financing and delivering the product, something we have neither the experience nor the wherewithal to do on our own. If we're going to take such a big risk, it'll be great to have MCA behind it." Everyone in the room except for me nodded in agreement. They all were in favor, and it seemed there wasn't anything more to discuss. Hesitatingly, but enough to stop everyone from getting up to leave, I started to speak. "First of all, MCA makes cookie-cutter films on a vast assembly line with efficient-but-boring in-house producers. Second, they'd control it totally, and we'd never get out from under the Octopus"—that's how the all-powerful MCA/Universal was known—"and this is our one chance to be in control and not give everything over to the

Hollywood factory. The only way to be successful with such an unproven project is to treat each movie as a stand-alone project, based solely on the material, and be open to every talented person who has a good idea. That isn't the MCA way."

Elton, who abhorred open conflict and didn't appreciate underlings' opinions, especially mine, said, "I'd sure trust MCA far more than I would trust a very junior member of the program department."

Stung, I nevertheless wouldn't let it go: "And, as is usual for them, the price is way inflated. I know I could do it for far less. I could keep us independent of the MCA Octopus that's been able to take over most television production and keep the networks basically out of producing shows." That was a reference to Wasserman's political strength in having gotten the FCC to bar the networks from owning most of their own production.

This confident but somewhat bombastic claim was followed by a long silence, after which Elton Rule ended the meeting, saying simply, "This is too big a decision to be hasty—I want us to think about this." And we were dismissed.

Dispirited, Leonard Goldberg and I returned to his office. Our idea was being stolen, and there didn't seem to be anything we could do about it. I was certain they'd go with the power and strength of MCA and poof would go my big chance. Two minutes later, Elton Rule called Leonard and said, "I think Universal made a wonderful offer and we ought to do it with them." He said Universal asked for a quick answer or they'd take *our* idea and see if they could sell it to NBC.

Goldberg said it'd be a shame to give up total control to the Octopus. Rule asked how we could do it ourselves; we had zero expertise in direct production. How could we be sure we could pull this off without a big studio behind it? At this do-or-die moment, and far more politic and subtle than I would have been, Len asked Rule to give him a few days to see if there was any alternative to Universal's offer. Rule said, "You have a week, but I'm really skeptical." Len, with his usual generous delegating, said to me, "Game on, go figure it out."

I went into more than overdrive. I attacked on three fronts: the costs, the creative, and an argument for our maintaining control instead of giving it up to Universal. I was convinced that $600,000 for each movie was a made-up number, with no basis other than it was what they demanded.

Of course, I couldn't know, since I'd never produced more than a postage stamp in the mail room. I had to learn fast on bottom-up budgeting, figuring out just how many days it might take to shoot a ninety-minute movie.

How much ABC sales could get for the commercials.

What independent producers might be available, since I doubted we could count on the major studios to produce at our costs.

How to come up with a framework for actually making deals with those producers.

How much each film would cost.

I needed to figure out all these things in areas where I had no experience—I didn't even know the right doors to knock on to find the answers.

And I needed to know all this within a week, and all I had was my untutored brain and the energy of a speed bunny. I made up a production plan on pure instinct and common sense, though I couldn't figure out how to pay for it.

I pored over shooting schedules and production budgets and figured the lowest amount we could make them for was $450,000. The sales department said they'd be able to cover, tops, $375,000. After knocking my head against every available wall, I took a long shot and went to our own station group and asked if they'd agree to put up $75,000 in return for the right to air them after they ran on the network (and this is why you still see them running fifty-some years later in the early-morning hours on local ABC stations). Thus I was able to guarantee—yes, there I was, Little Me from the Mail Room, *guaranteeing!*—that we could beat Universal's price by $150,000.

My most potent argument for doing this in-house was that we should never give financial and creative control to anyone, much less give one producer exclusivity over an entire programming area. This just made practical sense to me, but this need for control was also very much primal. As time went on (and as will be underscored endlessly throughout this story), my desire to be, my need to be, in control has never wavered. I raged at not being in control of my very self, so being able to be in control of everything else was beyond mandatory.

With two days to go before Elton Rule's deadline, we trooped up to the top floor and entered his spare, elegant lair. I told him I had a counter-offer to make to Universal. We'd agree for them to make a chunk of the movies at our $450,000 price, but with no exclusivity, and we'd produce the majority of the rest ourselves. He was impressed with all the work I'd put in, and agreed it was a fair compromise. We made the offer. It didn't take a minute for them to respond—a flat "No! Our offer isn't negotiable." The arrogant underboss of Universal, Sid Sheinberg, said, "Either you do it with us or fail on your own." There it was, that supreme negotiation ploy, the ultimatum.

Thank god for that arrogance, because I think it was that—more than any of my wondrous arguments—that got ABC management to back our plan to produce the *Movie of the Week* all by ourselves. I'd won, miraculously selling through this huge project, but now what? No one had the courage to ask the ABC board for formal approval. We never made a pilot or did any intensive development. We just kept moving forward because no one stopped us and there weren't mechanisms in place at the ABC candy store to check and balance the costs we were incurring. And the truth is, there was no "we." It was just me, twenty-five, without a title, without a staff, and without a portfolio, in charge of the most ambitious program venture in television. I think the main reason I wasn't pushed aside by someone more senior—and almost everyone at ABC was my senior—was that they all thought this was an incredibly risky project that would most likely fail. The consensus was: *Stay as far away as possible from this high-wire act.* And yet I never—then or later—ever felt cowed by the risk of failing. My one primary fear had the by-product of eliminating almost every other fear a rational person would have. It wasn't that I had found courage—that was never going to happen—I just have never seen business projects as risky. My blindness for that is rooted in the stark fact that I've only ever been really deeply frightened by the consequences of homosexuality. Everything else is small beer. What a trick of the mind it was to allow me to act with such bravery.

Chapter 6

Until then I never imagined I could be a "creative" executive.

Except for my aggression in buying movies and making the concomitant deals, almost all my experiences had been administrative. I was strictly the person behind the person who had creative talent. I thought I was just the enabler for the people who could make creative decisions, and my one early experience at being creative cemented that inadequacy deep into me.

Quinn Martin, one of television's most successful producers, had twenty-one straight years with at least one top-ten series, including *The Untouchables* and *The Fugitive*. He was a complete autocrat in every aspect of making television. Condescending to all network executives, he had a reputation for chewing up and spitting out "suits," as executives were called. Martin had presented a script to us based on a book called *House on Greenapple Road*. He conceived it as a pilot in the form of a two-hour movie. Because I was the buyer of movies, the script development fell into my inexperienced lap.

During the first script meeting I was all alone with the mythic Mr. Quinn Martin (he was actually born Irwin Martin Cohn, a much less fearful moniker), to give him the network's notes. I remember sitting in a chair that was much, much bigger than I was, feeling very tiny in the great man's presence.

The truth was that I'd never really read a script before. I didn't know that scripts were more like blueprints, not meant to be read as prose. I didn't understand that words and scenes were laid out just so they could be visually interpreted. I started asking questions about illogical transitions and gaps in the storytelling. My points weren't completely stupid, but I couldn't articulate them to a pro, particularly to someone who wanted only blind approval from the network, and certainly not notes from an uneducated twerp in a stiff little suit.

He mercilessly laid me out from one end of the room to the other, ridiculing me in excruciating detail and telling me exactly how dumb I was about scripts. He said, predictably, that I was just another network "suit" and added I was far too young to even fit properly in it and wasn't entitled to have opinions on anything other than skateboarding. I walked out reaffirming my clerkdom and swore I'd never get near anything creative again. I would be the best assistant the world ever saw and never step out from under Leonard Goldberg's protective cloak. But now, with the *Movie of the Week* beginning production, I had to overcome my antipathy to creative affairs and dive right into making editorial decisions. It's always been true that my career was one long case of "fake it until you make it," and here was my earliest need for the biggest fake imaginable.

It took endless hours to figure out that scripts were visual guideposts in telling stories and many more hours, even years, to learn how to interpret and help shape them. And longer even to trust my instincts in creative decision-making. Beyond that we had no infrastructure. Nothing, no one. Not a single executive at the company had any experience in actually ground-producing anything. I was suddenly the sole executive in charge of what would become ABC's most costly program venture ever. And we had only eighteen months to get this all together before we had to air our first movie. One dumb step in front of the other, making mistakes, bouncing off the walls, course-correcting as we went along, head down. That was my process and . . . over time Process became my one true mantra.

Rules of order had to be established quickly. My first baseline law was that each movie had to be easily explainable in a sixty-second promotional spot and in one full-page *TV Guide* ad. No one had ever before used advertising to sell television shows. Series sold themselves through reviews and word of mouth. ABC's procedures were that all on-air and off-air advertising was handled by the robotic and conventional advertising department, which reported to the sales department. I argued that because we were doing a different show every week, we needed to do our own marketing, make our own spots, and design our own ads. Not knowing the monster they might be creating, they let me have all that, largely because it was going to entail a lot of extra work for a project that had little chance of success, and so why bother arguing about it? I also mandated we'd need our own business-affairs team making deals, because no one at ABC's legal department had any experience in this area.

I very stealthily put together my own vertically integrated operation at ABC, a mini production studio operating inside a television network. Since the founding of radio, where advertisers produced the programs, which carried on through television, this was the first time a network had ever produced anything internally other than news. I was left alone and unguarded, and I learned from scratch how to make movies. Every experience I've had since then has been informed by what I learned during this classic start-up—the step-by-step process of micromanaging every piece and part of an emerging enterprise. The very best way to learn to be a manager is to start something from zero, where each granular step in creating the next job teaches you every task. Managing top-down is exceptionally challenging if you haven't had the experience of managing from the bottom up.

I knew we had to grab the audience's attention each week—that the base idea for the movie was instantly promotable and instantly compelling. Years later, at Paramount, we were said to have invented the high-concept movie, which dominated the movie business for twenty years, until sequels and franchises and the Marvel Universe subsumed all, but that strategy, in fact, had its beginnings at ABC with the *Movie of the Week. Repeat forever . . . it's the idea, the concept, that either resonates strongly or doesn't. Execution is of course vital, but unless the execution is pure poetry, it won't help attract an audience.*

Any really solid story idea that could be explained in a declarative sentence qualified as a *MOW.* Judging a good idea from a bad idea is completely instinctual, and only effective if you can keep your instincts clean, not cluttered or corroded. The daily drip of cynicism that this business generates in carloads has to be constantly exorcised. It helps if you have broad avenues of mainstream, general interests. But those instincts have to be kept pure, not influenced by anything other than the idea—not by who the director is going to be, or by who the leading actor is going to be, or by relationships, or by anything other than the single qualification: *Is this a good idea?*

If you can answer that question purely on its own, without trying to appraise its commerciality, or any other distracting issue, that's really all you need to proceed.

Instinct is what I prize. Not research or data. Those who try to apply metrics to these basic decisions waste a huge amount of time and money. And experience doesn't necessarily give you an advantage. It may even be a hindrance, since experience can easily inculcate a cynical outlook. In the TV and film business, you have no choice but to fly by your instincts alone, and that's why it was mandatory for me to keep myself as naive and, yes, as undereducated as I could, so I could trust my instinctive ability to recognize a good idea. I force myself to remain naive in this way so many decades later.

With the hubris of someone untrained in the wiles and ways of the movie business, I offered one of our first films to Elvis Presley, a project called *The Ballad of Andy Crocker.* Elvis was then going through one of the worst patches of his career. He had worn out the rock and roll formula in films with a string of repetitive Paramount movies, so I thought that this really good script might be a cure-all for his career, giving him a role as an actor in a legitimate drama.

I called up his manager, Colonel Parker, and introduced myself. I said, "I have a really nice script, it's a drama, it's—"

Parker interrupted me. "He's not doing a drama!"

I said, "No, no, it's a wonderful acting part—"

Louder this time: "He's not doing an acting part!"

Quietly I said, "This could change the game for Elvis. He's never done television, but this is a movie—"

And Parker said, "Send me a check for a million dollars. If I cash it, he'll do the picture."

I said, "Don't you want to read the script?"

Parker said, "No! I don't think we'll do it, but send me the check."

I said, "Well, we can't pay you a million dollars—our movies don't even cost a million dollars—but we could break our top and pay a hundred thousand—"

With that, Colonel Parker hung up the phone.

We were good on titles in the early days.

Women in Chains was one of my favorites; it was a horrible movie, but what a promotable title.

Scream, Pretty Peggy wasn't bad, either.

Sometimes the staff would ask, "Is it commercial?" and I would brutalize them, because rather than using their instincts, they were trying to predict the public's appetite, which I said then and say now, over and over again, simply isn't possible. Neither is using research to help make decisions. No amount of research on ideas is worth the paper (or computer screen) it's printed on. Data can tell you what *has happened*, not what *can or will happen*. Data is often harmful to instinct, and I believe this to be true for making not only creative decisions but many business decisions. PowerPoint can be the enemy; structured information often narrows the sieve just when you need to broaden it out in the spaces between information and real understanding. Overtraining our brains on data alone doesn't confer an advantage, and it can be a deterrent if it's the only decision-making component. That's often the problem with MBA students, who come armed with all the business tools and case studies but little simple human instinct. I do not believe that using instinct rather than deep, hard numerical or fact-based data to help with decision-making is the lazier process. Too much information can overload, overcomplicate, and obscure what is at the essence of any proposal: Is it a good idea, and does it make any common sense?

You rarely get the perfect project or the perfect script. In all my experience I probably haven't read ten scripts out of a thousand that are so fully realized, so utterly and incontrovertibly great that you just scream, "Make it!" One of those, though, was the day in 1970 that Leonard Goldberg, who had recently moved on from ABC to run a large television production company, called up and said, "You must read this script right now." It was called *Brian's Song*, the story of the deep bond between a Black and a white pro football player, one who will die of cancer. I wept as I read it. I called him up and said, "We can only screw it up from here—it's perfect—let's go." Often referred to as one of the finest television films ever made—and one of the greatest sports films as well—it was nominated for nine Emmys and won five. Another of those few times, Dan Curtis, a leading ABC daytime producer, sent me a manuscript of an as-yet-unpublished novel called *The Kolchak Papers*. I read it in two or three hours—it was the contemporary tale of a vampire in Las Vegas—and I told Dan, "This is as good a story as I've ever read." And what a great idea: Las Vegas, a city most alive at night—the perfect place for a vampire to live.

Out of that novel we made *The Night Stalker*, which turned out to be so good that we held a screening for the senior ABC management, who all said, "That's a great movie. We should release it theatrically!" I fought against that, saying, "Yes, it's a great movie, but it's a *Movie of the Week*, and that's where it belongs." We aired the film in early January 1972, and it became ABC's highest-rated *Movie of the Week* at the time, drawing about 50 million people, a record. *The Night Stalker* spawned a sequel (*The Night Strangler*) and a television series (*Kolchak: The Night Stalker*), and it was followed by two more made-for-TV movies and a subsequent remake of the series. All that from one good idea! We ran fast and loose that first year—we had to in order to get a new movie made and aired every week. Some were good and some were bad, but all of them had the highly promotable concepts I'd insisted upon.

Finally, after more than a year of preparation, in 1969 we were ready to make our debut. Leonard Goldberg left ABC that same year. Without his gigantic generosity and belief that I had real ability, I would have never gotten anywhere close to being responsible for much of anything other than ordering the daily essentials of his life. Instead, he let me fill every vacuum at the ABC store. Now he and his vast cloak of power were gone, and I was all on my own. The stakes for me couldn't have been higher; I was like a cat on high alert.

We had scheduled the series in a key time slot—Tuesday at eight thirty—and if it failed, all of Tuesday night would go down the drain. I was worried that our first movie, *Seven in Darkness*, was so on the nose in hitting the high-concept nail with the biggest possible hammer that it might just be laughed out of people's houses. It was the preposterous story of seven blind people in a plane that crashes on a mountaintop and their descent at night down that mountain. It was melodrama at its most basic and starred a group of old-timers led by Milton Berle and old-school-not-really-movie-stars Dina Merrill, Barry Nelson, Arthur O'Connell, Alejandro Rey, and Lesley Ann Warren. I watched it with dread that night and didn't get much sleep as I waited for the ratings numbers that would come in at seven the next morning. And they came in a gusher—35 percent of the entire television audience had watched all the way through. About 30 million people. And every week after that for twenty-four weeks, we were the number one show. A new movie every time.

We were a smash.

It had been so improbable, so risky, so discounted, with everyone predicting failure, that I was the only one associated with it. A twenty-seven-year-old television star was born.

Because I also still had responsibility for buying the big feature movies at ABC, my area of programming was now the most successful on the network. As my reward, and when the title "vice president" still had currency, I was appointed one—the youngest VP in network-television history. As Leonard Goldberg had once said about me when he saw me holding my own with that industrial magnate Charlie Bluhdorn, "Who knew?"

Those five never-to-be-imagined years, from ages twenty-five to thirty, were built on the foundation of my reading program at William

Morris. I had absorbed the history of the entertainment business in my bones, and it gave me the building blocks for making decisions without having any practical experience. Out of my blunt nature came my most defining aspect of management: I encouraged and insisted upon extreme argument in every creative area. It was loud and it was something of a free-for-all, and every voice got attention if that voice had passion. I was like a bandleader conducting lots of dissonant instruments clanging together. But if you listened, really listened to this cacophony, out would come, after exhaustion and sometimes late into the night, the refinement of an idea into something actionable. I called it "creative conflict," and since then I've prized it as the best process for decision-making. It was sometimes tedious and often more than boisterous, and it was certainly not for everybody, nowhere near politically correct by today's often oversensitized standards. But I learned to use it to tease out the base truth of whatever was up for discussion, because at some mostly tortured point the truth rang out in my head and I knew what to do. Eventually, I adapted it to fit into almost all my business decisions, and it's this process that has since guided me more than anything else. I've never thought decision-making should be peaceful. Despite today's standards of enforced and usually dull civility, I still believe passionate, argumentative debate is the best way. While I'm comfortable with it, I also accept that some are not, and I don't want anyone to participate if it doesn't excite and stimulate them.

Our first season of *Movie of the Week* was such a success that the program department ordered up a second night, and when the second season exceeded the first, they ordered up a third night. We were now making the absurd number of seventy-five movies a year! By then I'd built up my own fiefdom inside ABC, a vertically integrated mini studio, one that, contrary to any studio operation in history, never had a loss on a single picture. Fake it until you make it, indeed.

CHAPTER 7

I had so much early success, you might have thought I'd have conquered what I saw as the biggest danger in my developing life. I'd conquered other phobias, but fear of exposure still had a tyrannical hold on me, so much so that it stunted any chance of my having a fulfilling personal life.

Until very late in life I never believed that I deserved one. Other people make plans, have goals and expectations. All I had growing up was magic boxes that warded off the danger I felt. Even when I was forced to give them up when I had my nervous breakdown at nineteen, I'd not replaced them with any kind of emotional maturity.

I wasn't dating women; I was still seeking out men in all the subterfuge-driven ways of those times. Enmeshed in my work, I never felt particularly lonely, until one weekend during that first summer in New York.

Los Angeles was always warm, but almost never hot-hot, and when it was, it was a dry, easy-to-breathe heat. But that Fourth of July weekend in New York, it was over a hundred degrees, and I dreaded being in all that steaming concrete.

I had met this guy and he invited me to spend the weekend with him on Fire Island. I'd never been there before. He worked for a talent manager, was four or five years older, and sophisticated in all ways I was not. So out I went with him to a place called the Pines, at the time a lower-key version of the all-gay Fire Island community of Cherry Grove.

Since I had never been in any kind of ghetto (other than a rich one), I wasn't prepared for a place that was all guys, all the time.

I was trying not to show how alien it all felt. He took me to a slew of parties and then to a dance club. All I thought about while I was avoiding the popper-soaked dancers surrounding me was that all too soon I would be going back to the house of a person I hardly knew and was growing to dislike as he pushed ever closer on the dance floor.

The wood-frame house had been baking all day. I was exhausted, and we fell into a creaky bed, where I quickly faked falling asleep. I lay there sweating until about four in the morning, and when I couldn't stand it any longer, I snuck out and walked down to the main pier.

No one was around, and it was silent except inside my buzzing, panicked head. I saw a sign saying *In an emergency pick up phone for help*, and help was what I needed at that moment.

A water taxi took me, all alone, across the bay, and I arrived on the other side around five in the morning. I went to the train station, but the first train back to the city wasn't coming until seven, so I wandered around the silent streets of Sayville with its huge ancient arching trees swaying over neat white-framed houses. It was like a postcard for small-town Americana family life. The opposite of the scene I'd just left.

I found a perfect Norman Rockwell house and sat on the whitewashed steps leading up to a broad veranda. I thought about the past few months. I felt like a kid from the sticks all alone in the big city, trying to hide how small and lonely I was.

And just now, I had even failed at gay life. I broke down and cried the tears of a loser.

Finally, the sun rose and I went off in the dawn to get on the train.

I never discussed my personal life, low-light as it was, with anyone. Outside of business it wasn't much of a life anyway, because it was so over-controlled. Even though as the years went on I began to be realistic and understood that "everyone knows," I never wanted to make any declarations. So many of us at that time were in this exiled state, so stunted in the way we lived. Consider if you can what such a daily drip of that kind of dysfunctional life does to one's sense of self.

I hated having to live a pretend life, one that was totally silent on all the topics normal people talked about with each other. Of course I could have declared my sexuality, come out as some others were doing, but I was among the many at that time who were too scared to do so. If I had to be silent, I couldn't stand the idea that I'd also have to pose as a perfectly functioning heterosexual. The hypocrisy of that would be soul killing. I've always admired Rebecca West's comment about Noël Coward's life: "The impeccable dignity of his sexual life—reticent but untainted by pretense." For me, it was okay that no one asked and I didn't tell. But I wanted—needed—to adopt my own personal bill of rights:

I would live with silence, but not with hypocrisy.

I would never pose or pretend.

I wouldn't do a single thing to make anyone believe I was living a heterosexual life.

I wouldn't tell, and I wouldn't allow myself to be asked.

I would live my life within these constraints, and I would never do a single thing to delude anyone.

I would never bring a man as a date to a heterosexual event—not that there were many guys I was serious enough about to bring—but I'd never bring a woman as a "beard," either.

I would never lie, never make a false claim by playing roles, never pretend to be "dating" just for show. It would be difficult to be vacant on personal matters, but the idea of pretending was abhorrent to me.

I would have secrets, but I would tell no lies.

It wasn't courage—it was simply the minimum conditions of my conduct, and I recognize it now as the opposite of courage.

While I adopted stringent standards I could live with, I lacked the guts to openly and freely declare and define my life to others.

That day, though, after my Fire Island sojourn, as we pulled into Penn Station the buzz of the big city lifted my spirits. It was impossible for an ambitious person to chug into New York, surrounded by that vibrancy, and feel lousy about himself. Especially if that self was starting to make such a professional mark.

In 1970, we agreed to work with the producer David Wolper on a project called *Visions of Eight*. The idea was to approach the upcoming 1972 Summer Olympics in Munich by having eight directors take their own personal interest in one specific contest and each make a short film, their artistic vision of sport. To get together this extraordinary bunch of directors was some feat. It was an ambitious, original idea, and I wanted to be there while it was shooting. I'd never been to an Olympics, and since they were carried by ABC, and the Olympic Committee loved this idea for a movie, I would have special access to everything.

I thought it'd be much more fun to stay in the Olympic Village rather than the old German hotels the tourists were staying in. The security to get into the Village was stringent, even for those more relaxed times, but once in, it was a wonderland of brotherhood and friendliness. Every country had a small wearable decorative pin, and as the days went by, the way to say hello was to exchange pins; over the first days in the Village there was a happily frenetic race to collect the most. Sounds silly now, but it created a joyous atmosphere. There was one main housing structure, about ten stories high, and around it were a terraced series of condos for the athletes. Being the producer of this prized film, as well as a VP of ABC, I had a suite on the top floor overlooking the entire Village.

It was a euphoric place to be. And the Germans were trying very hard not to act fiercely Germanic.

At six in the morning, on the tenth day of the Games, all that ended with a hard banging on my door. Ten policemen swarmed in because my room looked down onto the Israeli compound, where eleven athletes had just been taken hostage by terrorists.

Then the cameramen came in from ABC, which would cover the whole horrible thing as it unfolded. The Olympic Village became an armed camp for the rest of the day, and I was not allowed to leave my room until news arrived that a Palestinian terror group called Black September had killed two of the Israelis and still held nine of them hostage.

All that day, the Germans, Olympic security, American security, and others, including the U.S. State Department—and of course the Israelis—debated who had jurisdictional rights: Who would supervise the transportation of the terrorists from the Village to the airport, where they would return the hostages if given planes and safe passage?

At first we got news the athletes were on their way to the airport, then we were told they were at the airport, and then we heard that they had all been slaughtered. It was shattering.

For those of us in the Olympic Village, it was as awful a wake as you can imagine. We had all been on an emotionally devastating roller coaster. People hung around to commiserate, and then got drunk. Nothing like this had ever happened at an Olympics before, and this one had begun with such a particularly beautiful sense of international peace.

Later that day, discussions began over whether to continue the Games. They ended up postponing them for a day and then held a memorial service, after which everything resumed. The thinking was that canceling the Games would have given the terrorists a win, and they wanted the Olympic spirit to prevail.

I couldn't help but resent the conduct of the Germans; I had watched throughout the day how heavy-handed and rigid they were in attempting to get the hostages out. In contrast, I observed the Israelis trying to persuade them to handle the situation without provoking more murders. Correct or not, everyone around me felt that the Germans' mistakes had gotten the Israelis killed.

After the memorial service, I couldn't stay another minute in Munich or in any part of Germany. I went to the airport and looked at the snapping departure boards and picked Amsterdam because it would take me out of Germany faster than anywhere else. I wouldn't set foot in Germany for another thirty years.

I've mostly forgotten the actual content of the films we made, but it doesn't take much to bring back the image of those black-hooded monsters on the terrace below me.

I can't recall most of the films we made for *Movie of the Week*. We made so many, and some were just solid good work, and some won praise and awards, and there definitely were some turkeys. But there was one I'll never forget and am most proud of. It was called *That Certain Summer*. The writers, Richard Levinson and William Link, came to me with a story they were developing. It was about a divorced father forced to explain his homosexuality to his teenage son. In the history of broadcast television no one had gotten near homosexuality, other than in turgid and tragic documentaries. I knew it was controversial, of course, but I thought the story had great drama and better-than-great humanity. The story they wanted to tell was of a divorced man, living in San Francisco with his male partner of many years, who is about to get a visit from his teenage son. The boy discovers that his father is living with a man and runs away in shame and disgust. The father and the lover go out searching for him, and when the boy is found, the father explains to him, "Some people say what I have is a sickness, something that has to be cured, but what Gary and I have is a kind of marriage. We love each other."

This was 1972. The American Psychiatric Association still listed homosexuality as a disorder in the *Diagnostic and Statistical Manual of Mental Disorders*. There had never been anything positive about homosexuality shown on any of the three television networks. There were no portrayals in national media that didn't stigmatize or ridicule gay men. Levinson and Link were asking me to make and air on ABC something truly groundbreaking—a positive portrayal of a gay couple.

Levinson and Link were tall and short, respectively, and utterly straight. They were top-of-the-top writers and producers of mainstream fare, and this subject was an anomaly. We never discussed it, but of course they knew about me and of course that's why they brought it to me rather than NBC, the network where they worked almost exclusively.

After reading their outline, I told them emphatically I wanted to do it.

The only consideration for me to do a film was whether it was a good story to tell. This one, of course, did have an additional consideration. A consideration I felt deeply about, but I did worry there wouldn't be any way to get through this without linking the subject to me personally, and that scared me. While I knew in one compartment of my brain that everybody I worked with probably thought I was gay—and my rules precluded me from claiming otherwise—I had never come out.

While so much has changed over these last fifty years, what hasn't—at least I believe it hasn't—is the agonizing pressure on most young men and women at the first glimmerings of their sexuality. That sexual excitement is usually accompanied by—it certainly was for me—sheer terror. Nature and nurture make every adolescent young man want to identify as "one of the boys" in all their macho rituals. At the very least, they don't want to be separated from the pack just by being different, which often comes with ridicule, or physical abuse. To know in your bones at an early age that you're in such a minority, having no one else in your group to align with, is a very scary place to be. I've so envied those who had the courage to declare early and exuberantly. I've also thought it's kind of a counterintuitive blessing to be less than masculine in appearance and thus unable to get away with hiding: if you find a way to survive all the taunting, many emerge far stronger and less damaged than those who navigated that period with secrets and lies and subterfuge. But in either case it's an awful burden that society places on a young person.

For too long I justified my silence by believing that my "complex" sexuality would preclude me from being a poster boy for gay pride. In truth, I was just too chicken to tell anyone anything. I rationalized that this was an honorable position because I'd been adhering faithfully to my rules of behavior: never be hypocritical, never lie, never pose. Given all my own trauma I believed I didn't owe the world a defining statement. I was wrong. I should have been a role model, for whatever good that might have done for others. It's a guilt that will never leave me.

———————

While there was of course no law against portraying homosexuality on television, either dramatically or sympathetically, there was a very active broadcast standards department at ABC that vetted every line and every scene to see if it was fit to broadcast or not. At that time, the department of Broadcast Standards and Practices was the Supreme Court at all the networks. The rule of thumb for all ABC executives, from the most senior person on down, was: *Never air anything that will get the company in trouble with the Federal Communications Commission.* The FCC determined whether or not we were programming "in the public interest." That's an awfully broad definition, as was the fairness doctrine that stated that all positions on any controversial subject must be "fairly" covered. That fairness doctrine was eliminated years ago, and was a great mistake; it should still exist as a standard for all media. It made us aware we had a responsibility beyond ratings and sales. It might have kept us from doing some things we wanted to do, but it also meant that as broadcasters we had a greater duty because we held a public license. And there was honor and pride in that. Nothing in our current world of endless and overwhelming "communicating" would be hurt by having a fairness doctrine to adhere to. Having pride in upholding standards—it's still holding fast in some of our communicating institutions, but as we normalize behavior we wouldn't tolerate just five or ten years ago, it's increasingly difficult to feel positive about society's direction. I think the biggest crime of the Biden administration is that it came in with a pledge to restore a more civilized, selfless, and uplifting manner of governance and instead let us all down with its progressive elitism, personal ego, and cynical behavior. Such a shame.

With all that process and trepidation, *That Certain Summer* went on the air on November 1, 1972. It won the night and the week in ratings. Beyond that, it went on to win awards for the best television program of the year. Critics said it was "a giant step for television"—it put the subject of homosexuality in the mainstream for the first time, and while I've never done as much as I could have and should have, I'm very glad I was able to put this groundbreaking show on the air because it was a sympathetic and very human story that was viewed by a huge swath of the American public at a time when homosexuality was so stigmatized.

Over these decades, I've tried to do responsible work and make contributions furthering the cause of gay rights, but probably nothing comes close to what *That Certain Summer* did for a generation that had never before seen a positive gay story. Millions of heterosexuals also might have had their natural biases tempered and maybe altered by this love story of two decent men. And for gay men, it was likely the first time they had seen a portrait of two fine and decent men who also happened to be homosexual.

It was during this time that Katharine Hepburn first walked into my life. Walked, literally.

One day at ABC my phone rang and my secretary said, "I have Katharine Hepburn on the line."

Katharine Hepburn?

Why would Katharine Hepburn be calling me? I answered with the always appropriate but somewhat curt "Yes?"

And then I heard that unmistakable voice; it was either Hepburn herself or Martin Short doing his immaculate imitation. The voice said, "Mr. Diller, this is Katharine Hepburn. I just finished making *Glass Menagerie*, which I'm told is going on your network, and I don't think it should be interrupted with commercial breaks. The work is just too good to be interrupted."

I was a little taken aback by her directness, so I said carefully, "Well, Miss Hepburn, the thing is, this is a commercial medium, and the only way to pay for it is to have commercials."

She said, "Yes. I understand—I have ideas about that! Can I come over now to discuss them?"

I said, "Now? You mean *right* now—you mean here . . . ?"

She said "Yes!" and hung up.

An hour later, in strode Katharine Hepburn, no hello, no anything. She looked around my office, went right to the blinds, which I had drawn, pulled them all up, and said, "Light. You shouldn't shut out light."

Then she sat down and said, "Now, Mr. Diller, what are we going to do about this?" and waited for my response.

I said, "Well, I don't really know what we can do because you have to accept that commercials pay for the programming, and therefore they have to run."

She thought for a moment, then said, "Well, that's reasonable, but how many commercials?"

I said, "Well, a two-hour program would probably have about thirty minutes of commercials—"

"Thirty minutes! That's ridiculous!" she said. "You don't need all that money."

I said, "Well, I'm not going to argue the economics with you, Miss Hepburn"—we were Mr. and Miss for many meetings to come—"but aren't there act breaks in *The Glass Menagerie*?"

"Yes," she said, "go on."

"Well, what if we bundled our commercials into those act breaks?"

This intrigued her, but she said, "You can't break the acts with so many commercials."

I had a sudden inspiration. "Well, maybe we could sell it to one sponsor rather than lots of diverse sponsors. That might help."

A smile came over her face. "I like that idea!"

I had another idea. "Will you go with me to see if we could sell it to somebody?"

And she said, "Of course I will, Mr. Diller; I would be delighted to."

This no-nonsense kind of talk—and there could be no other kind with Hepburn—led us to trust each other and, over time, become friends.

I called our sales department, and they said the best candidate to be a single sponsor would be IBM, which was in Armonk, New York. So I called her the next day. "Would you go with me to IBM?" She immediately said, "Yes, when are you picking me up?"

I said, "I don't know . . . I'll have to ask for this meeting with these people and . . ."

And she said, "Pick me up this afternoon. I'm sure they'll see us."

I picked her up at her town house in Turtle Bay, we drove up to Armonk, and IBM saw us. Miss Hepburn and I sold them hard, and they ended up sponsoring the whole show—with only one commercial—and it was a tremendous success, nominated for six Emmys and winning four.

My friendship with Katharine Hepburn lasted for twenty captivating—and often irascible—years. It faded because of nothing more than benign mutual neglect.

Over those years, though, she'd come out to L.A. for this or that, and we'd go for long meandering drives to places that had potent memories for her as she told me the stories behind them. Sometimes we'd secretly go swim in the pools of houses she used to live in, sneaking stealthily around gates and shrubs, taking a quick dip, and then beating a hasty retreat. Two years after *The Glass Menagerie*, while I was still at ABC, she sent me a script she wanted to do with Laurence Olivier, directed by her great friend George Cukor. It was called *Love Among the Ruins* and was to be shot in London. I went over several times to supervise the production. Once, on the plane over, I had an attack of prostatitis. Unable to urinate, I was immediately put in Guy's Hospital upon landing. I woke up before dawn staring into Kate's face at the end of my bed. She'd stopped by on her way to the studio. "Get up," she said a moment after my eyes opened. I said, "Get out, I don't want to move." She said, "My father was an expert urological surgeon, and I know what I'm doing. You have to start peeing and the only way to get that to happen is to walk until it's forced out." I replied that she should leave me in peace until the doctors arrived.

"Nonsense!" She dragged me out of bed, walking me up and down the broad hallways of Guy's until I fled into the bathroom and out it flowed. She didn't even bother to say goodbye. *Love Among the Ruins* was a lovely television movie and went on to win the Peabody Award for best film of the year, as well as a sweep of six Emmys.

Madame Hepburn, several years later, had another effect on my life, this time leading me into my one and only somewhat significant relationship with a man during my early thirties.

She called me up and said, "I think you should meet my new friend, Michael Bennett. You two young people ought to know each other."

Young people! I was thirty-three years old, and Michael was thirty-two. Of course I knew who Michael Bennett was. His show *A Chorus Line* had just opened at the Public Theater in April. It was already a sensation, and the buzz was that it was the greatest musical *ever*. When Kate called me, the show was in transition, moving from Off Broadway to Broadway, and Michael was in the midst of tech rehearsals.

Why Katharine Hepburn thought Michael Bennett and I should meet—and what Michael thought of her suggesting it—will never be known, but I do know that putting people together without a personal motive wasn't Hepburn.

She simply said to both of us, "I think you'll like him."

Michael called me on a Friday, and I said, "Why don't you come over for coffee tomorrow?" So he came to my apartment at the Hampshire House Saturday morning. I'd just moved into this venerable, elegant building on Central Park South, not that it kept me from answering the door in shorts and a T-shirt. Michael was in an ill-fitting black suit that looked much too big on his small frame. His very white face was marred with black moles, but it was a face so alive with the juice of life and energy and magnetism that it made everything physically ugly about him beside the point.

Michael took one look at me in my Saturday shorts and said, "Uh, hello! I'll be right back," and he turned around and was gone down the hall.

Twenty minutes later he was back—in his own version of Saturday shorts—and we spent the next six hours transfixed with each other. We were two odd characters at highly auspicious moments in our lives: Michael was about to become *the* Broadway powerhouse, and I was just a month into an extraordinary new role. Maybe it was the mutual intoxication of the moment, but we were attracted to each other in every conceivable way. For a few months, it was a full-on romance. I went to his apartment and he cooked for me, he came to mine and I didn't cook for him, but he'd stay for a room service breakfast the next day. I'd have a long day at the office and then go meet him at the Shubert Theatre, where he was in previews before *A Chorus Line*'s opening. For a few months we squeezed each other in and out of our frenetic lives.

It ended because of a game of phone tag gone wrong over Thanksgiving weekend. We decided we were going to spend the holiday together in the Dominican Republic. Gulf + Western owned a resort there, and Charlie Bluhdorn had given me a huge house on the beach. To finalize the weekend details, I called Michael and we didn't connect, and then he called me back, and then either I dropped the call or he dropped the call, but however it happened, we never spoke.

The holiday came and went, with me sad and angry and alone in the Dominican Republic, and who knew where he went.

We both felt we had been ghosted, and each of us was too neurotic and probably too busy elsewhere in our lives to right whatever had gone wrong. A potentially lovely relationship went onto the rocks of our egos and insecurities.

As our careers careened in and around each other's, I didn't speak to him again for ten years.

By 1972 the *Movie of the Week* had matured into a steady manufacturing process, and I was getting bored by the very steadiness of it. I was looking for something new and risky. I had always wondered why novels that were rich in character and situation were telescoped down to two hours or less as films when there was so much story to tell. Sometimes a great director like David Lean would get to expand epics like *Doctor Zhivago* to more than three hours. But television had unlimited time, so why couldn't an expansive tale get told over as many hours as the story demanded?

It seemed so natural to me, and I couldn't understand why it hadn't been tried, other than it did break all the conventional rules. But at this point, I could get away with anything, and I just barged ahead with what I provisionally called the "novel for television." I needed a real-world test of the idea. Which meant buying a novel. I had enjoyed reading Leon Uris's *QB VII* a few years before. I thought it was a decent story, but the reason I bought it as our first project is that no one would sell me anything else. At that time, all successful books were sold to movie studios. No television network had ever bought a novel, and I wanted to find a known and successful title to experiment with.

I went to the famous book agent Irving Lazar and told him my idea. Swifty, as he was known to all but never called to his face, immediately saw that he could unload an unsellable book for this untried new television form.

Lazar would happily sell you a counterfeit picture on the wall, and luckily there hadn't been any takers for *QB VII*. Probably because its subject matter, dealing with Nazi castration, wasn't exactly appealing. But I thought it was a cracking good courtroom drama and . . . it was all I could get at the time. We bought and produced it with Anthony Hopkins in the lead, and in another television first it ran for six and a half hours over two nights. It was a monster success and was nominated for thirteen Emmys in 1974, winning six. The miniseries was born.

I went back to Lazar, who had now gotten some religion on television as a new market, and quickly scooped up *Rich Man, Poor Man,* a textured, expansive novel by Irwin Shaw. It was a perfect next project to establish the miniseries as more than just a onetime wonder. When the twelve hundred pages of script came in, piled high on my desk, everyone around ABC thought I'd lost my mind.

That book took twelve hours to show—definitely a television first— and it, too, was a huge success.

Soon, David Wolper, who had done the Olympics films for us, came into my office with an outline for a novel that Alex Haley was in the process of writing. It was called *Roots*.

I was fascinated and financed the writing of the novel and its development as a miniseries. In 1977 it made television history: that saga of an African slave and his descendants was television's highest-rated program for many years, won every award, and became that decade's cultural milestone. These miniseries were beginning to set the cultural agenda and would go on for the next five decades to be among the finest works that television, and later streaming, was capable of producing. Creating an enduring form for television is no small thing, and while I'm always hesitant to use the word, I am proud we created it.

In 1971, I was reading and loving *The Winds of War* by Herman Wouk, and I thought, *This is it! The big one!* A story spanning the lead-up to World War II, it was epic in scope. I called my pal Irving Lazar, who of course represented Wouk. In truth, it didn't matter whether Irving represented someone or not. If he didn't, he would simply call a writer who was represented by somebody else and say, "I've got a gig for you." He was famous for representing people he didn't represent; other agents would call him up, furious, and say, "I represent this person!" And Irving would simply say, "Tell that to your client."

Anyway, I called Irving and said, "I've just read *Winds of War*—"

And Irving said, "Forget it, kid." He always called me kid, no matter how old I got.

I said, "What do you mean, forget it?"

"First of all, Herman Wouk is a nightmare," he said. "Second, he will never sell anything to television. He *hates* television. Television has always butchered his movies with commercials. And third, his wife, Sarah, who acts as his agent, is worse than a nightmare."

Irving was so completely dismissive that I thought, *Now, here's a good challenge.* I badgered him to just let me meet the difficult Wouk. They lived in an unshowy, modest little house in Palm Springs, where the great author received me formally and quite coolly.

I explained what we were trying to do by adapting these epic novels with the time and care they deserved. The Wouks didn't watch television; they thought it was a wasteland of mediocrity. Additionally, he didn't like the adaptations of his wonderful novels *The Caine Mutiny* and *Marjorie Morningstar*, so he was not inclined to let any more of his work be filmed.

Somehow, even though we were the most unlikely of soulmates, we bonded. He came to trust me because I never prevaricated on the issues and never overpromised. Also, I never tried to be particularly friendly. His wife, Betty Sarah Brown, was constitutionally unfriendly and didn't trust anyone; I never tried to penetrate that facade. After six months of tortured negotiations, where we gave him the unheard-of right to approve not only the commercial interruptions but the commercials themselves, we were finally ready to produce.

Aired in 1983, *The Winds of War* ran for eighteen hours over seven nights and was followed up by *War and Remembrance*, which ran a landmark twenty-seven hours over twelve nights. Both starred Robert Mitchum, one of the first genuine movie stars to jump to TV. Its ambition was astounding—there's never been anything like it since—forty-five hours of epic storytelling, all devoted to Herman Wouk's World War II novels.

The development of the miniseries was the last major project I worked on at ABC. It did so much to elevate television from the drip and dry of half-hour and hour series, though it was that bromidic form that would soon come very close to derailing my high-flying career.

CHAPTER 8

I was thirty years old and had spent six years at ABC, going from taking drink orders for the executives to learning the craft of being an executive. At that relatively tender age, I was now seen to be a powerful force in media.

It was hard for me to go anywhere where someone wasn't shoving me a script or giving me an elevator pitch for what was usually some hackneyed idea. I was becoming too elevated for my own good, too isolated. I had hundreds of people working directly for me and thousands indirectly. I was no longer the underdog of dogs who everyone thought would fail. Instead, I was flying close to the sun. Shuttling back and forth from New York to L.A. every other week, a better-than-well-kept man living a mostly arid and work-cloistered existence. The interior of my life was fairly barren, but the externals couldn't have been plusher.

I had no actual home—I lived at the Hotel Bel-Air in L.A. and the Waldorf Towers in New York, two of the toniest addresses in the world, but the only personal possession I carried with me between them was my battered briefcase.

My single effort to plant something of permanence occurred just outside my bungalow at the Bel-Air. This was during my weed-smoking days, and whenever I left L.A. for New York I'd take my little grass snatch and bury it among the plants just outside my front door. My little marijuana patch bloomed for years before it was discovered and annihilated by the hotel gardeners.

Inside the corpus of ABC I was still a middle-management executive. I was getting lots of hot attention in the press, and I was paid lots of obeisance from people outside the network, but in the hushed gray-carpeted corporate halls of ABC, I was someone they assumed would never climb high up that corporate ladder. Instead, they expected me to do what every other top programming executive did, which was jump to the other side and become a Hollywood producer.

Elton Rule had by then become president of the network, and he had always looked at me a little askance. To him, I was just an overeager puppy dog who was getting more attention than deserved. Elton was a great leader, with magnetism and assured confidence. To me, he was a blond-haired Olympian god, and wherever he walked, gold dust and good luck followed. His successes were the people he led. Everything about him said that he was a winner, and if you were with him, you won, too. He always had a coterie of six or so executives around him, known as "Elton's men." They were the made men in ABC's cult of personality.

I had never been one of them, and didn't look, much less act, like one of them. They were all classic "suits," and I never got a suit to fit quite right, either sartorially or symbolically. In the summer of 1972, I was in London at the same time as Elton and Marty Starger, by then head of programming; they were being more than wined and dined by Lord Lew Grade, who dominated British television. He lavishly entertained U.S. media executives for the quid pro quo of getting his shows onto U.S. networks. On what must have been an off night, Marty invited me to have dinner with him and Elton. I had been at business lunches with him—but dinner? That was unexpected.

We dined at the Inn on the Park, a new modernist hotel that sat inelegantly near Hyde Park. Elton was not only a bravura leader; he was a bravura drinker, too. I was not, but I did my best to keep up. In the daze of the moment, I was almost shocked sober when Elton took hold of the conversation and said the words "I want to tell you that you're part of my team, and I value you greatly." It was said as a hallowed induction.

He was inviting me into his small made-men circle. After all those years being ABC's in-house exotic, I was unable to contain myself; tears streamed down my face, and I nearly slid under the table, Elton Rule's long-delayed acceptance filling me with undiluted joy.

That was truly my ABC high.

The next year would bring me low.

I was about to experience my first, and actually only, career failure, at least thus far.

I got promoted above my level of competence.

The network was continuing to do badly with its series television. So they asked me to become head of all prime-time programming—the true big leagues of broadcasting. I'd had my own internal operation making movies and miniseries where I didn't have to ask anyone for anything, so I really didn't want to give that up, but I couldn't say no to this huge promotion.

I'd never really liked series television, and had no facility for it. It was static and repetitive, and I was neither a strategist for how to schedule a network lineup nor an experienced developer of comedy or dramatic series.

The whole process—making a lot of shows, most of them failing, sitting in program-review meetings, and, above all, setting the schedule, the high task of the head of programming—was alien to me. None of it had ever triggered my curiosity; it all seemed like being on a perpetual rat wheel.

In the first few years I was at ABC, I got to sit in on the annual program scheduling meetings that included the head of sales, the president of the network, and five or six senior executives. I thought the whole process made no sense. They'd look at the pilots, they'd play with the big-three network program board, they'd move the magnetized pieces this way and that—Show X on Wednesday at nine? No, swap it with show Y at eight on Thursday!—they'd do endless, meaningless, complex research, which rarely projected anything correctly, and out would pop the next season's schedule.

During a lull I once asked, "Why do you pay attention to these re-search people? Why do you accept their prognostications as if they're sci-ence? It would be better if they came in wearing headdresses and bones around their necks because they're just witch doctors who give you false security over a process that is definitionally insecure."

They kicked me out of the room.

Now, having accepted the job, I was overwhelmed from the start by the relentless manufacturing regime, and I had no time, no ability, and no idea how to reform it. My heretofore solid instincts were doing me no good inside the tangled web of prime-time programming. I was lost and miserable knowing that under my watch sooner or later the whole sched-ule would collapse—and so would my big-time career.

Like something out of an old Western movie, over the horizon came the cavalry to rescue me in the always roaring body of Charles Bluhdorn, the chairman of Gulf + Western.

After our tumultuous first meeting at ABC, when Charlie tried to sell me all those bogus Paramount movies, we continued for years to haggle over those rights. He liked me because I was probably the only person in the entertainment business, probably in any business at this time in his ginormous career, who didn't tell him exactly what he wanted to hear. Charlie started to call me frequently, usually just to rant about some trans-gression by his executives, sometimes simply to ask my opinion about this or that nefarious project he was being pitched.

Charlie loved confrontation and argument, and from some devilish osmosis I learned never to give an inch when arguing with him.

Charlie started Gulf + Western as an auto-parts company, making the chrome bumpers on the front of cars. Before that, he'd been a coffee trader, and became a millionaire in his twenties. He could—and did—trade anything. He put the word "insatiable" into ambition, and he built his auto-parts business into one of the first conglomerates at a time when buying disparate businesses was popular, and before private equity took over the model. From auto parts to sugar to insurance in every corner of the world economy, he bought sound and cheap, using his stock to expand, each acquisition pushing the stock price higher and making the next acquisition easier. He was an industrial genius. An immigrant's immigrant, he was more of an American patriot than Americans born generations earlier.

Over the years, Charlie had attained an earned reputation for megalomania; along with that came a need to have a direct effect on any life he touched. The forces of his energy and power were almost impossible to resist. On meeting an actor for the first time, he was likely to say, out of the blue, "Why don't I make you a director?" He was constantly trying to rearrange everyone's life into something he could manipulate and control.

Charlie had often tried to recruit me to work at Paramount in various positions, but I always rebuffed him. I didn't want to leave my cocoon at ABC, and I certainly didn't want to work in the highly politicized regime at Paramount. Charlie was not used to rejection, so each time I said no, it only made him come after me more aggressively. I had no intention of ever going to work for him or any of the showboating executives he had at his movie studio.

Paramount had become extremely successful under Frank Yablans, the short, feisty, street-smart Jewish mafioso who was its president, and Robert Evans, the smooth prince of Hollywood, who was head of production. They jointly rode *Love Story* and *The Godfather* to studio stardom. But they made Paramount extremely dysfunctional, because the two of them had used their leverage to get extraordinarily good deals for themselves as well as a measure of independence that prevented Charlie from playing any real role at the studio. Charlie couldn't abide this, and kept trying to interfere in their decisions, while they did everything they could to hold him at bay. This made Charlie increasingly impotent and dangerously angry.

In early 1974, Andrew Tobias was assigned by *New York* magazine to write an article on Paramount's president called "The Apprenticeship of Frank Yablans." The magazine billed him as "The Toughest Tycoon in Hollywood."

I'd known Andy Tobias ever since I read his book *The Best Little Boy in the World* and had fallen right smack in love with him. The book was and is one of the best coming-out stories, and I can't imagine anyone reading it who wouldn't also fall in love with Andy. When I mentioned to the author Marie Brenner how great I thought the book was, she said, "He's a friend. You have to meet him!" So Andy and I went out on a few chaste dates. I think we both thought the better of romance and became friends instead.

One day, early in his reporting for the *New York* magazine piece, Andy called and asked what I could tell him about this strange character, Frank Yablans, and his even stranger relationship with Bluhdorn. Yablans had been saying nasty things to Andy about Charlie. Andy said I was his only friend in show business and he needed help as he tried to report on the Yablans-Bluhdorn relationship.

I had no ulterior motive in helping Andy and was not trying to manipulate him any which way, but I did winkingly and unwittingly participate in the fall of the Frank Yablans and Bob Evans regime at the studio, and with some irony, out of those ruins I became the chairman of Paramount.

ACT TWO

CHAPTER 9

The dominoes were about to fall into my lap. While Andy Tobias was reporting and writing the piece, Charlie Bluhdorn was constantly calling me to complain about the increasingly demeaning behavior Yablans and Evans were displaying toward him. All the while, I remained friendly with Frank and Bob; they knew perfectly well about my relationship with Charlie, and they thought I could be easily used as a pipeline to air their frustrations. Bob Evans would invite me to his glamorous house for dinners and movie screenings. These were state affairs, with the current cream of Hollywood, and I didn't qualify to be there, other than as Charlie's special friend. I was an exotic television executive with a lot of television power, but that was still greeted with disdain by all those sitting above the salt.

Bob and Frank had brilliantly positioned themselves as the "greatest film team in the history of movies." Losing them—or just risking their discontent—had the potential to topple the company. Their very public self-promotion was increasingly putting Charlie in something of a stranglehold.

Moreover, they were both represented by Sidney Korshak, the great mob lawyer, who had just extracted a breathtakingly audacious five-year contract that allowed them to both unilaterally order and produce movies in which they had a personal stake; a conflict of interest so enormous you could drive a convoy through it.

All through that summer of 1974, there was a Shakespearean plot developing around this triangle of outsized personalities. Neither Charlie nor Yablans/Evans ever knew that I was surreptitiously talking to Andy

Tobias. When I heard from Andy how vicious Yablans was in characteriz-
ing Bluhdorn, my motivation was to do as much as I could to make certain
Charlie wouldn't be unfairly or negatively portrayed. Hard going given
the delectable tidbits Yablans was throwing out. Andy told me Charlie
wouldn't agree to be interviewed, so it was up to me to be his defender. It
never once occurred to me that I was helping to open a door I would soon
be walking through. And, anyway, I was awfully busy just trying to save
my ABC schedule from disaster.

The *New York* magazine story came out on September 23, 1974, and it was
far more scathing and consequential than I could have imagined.

Charlie was described as "the Mad Austrian, sequestered on the 42nd
floor of the Gulf + Western Building, in the chairman's office—cradling
a tomcat in the crook of his elbow, with his back to the camera and his eye
on the stock market." The article went on to describe how Yablans was
responsible for Paramount's success and had essentially pushed Charlie
out of any control: "This man, Charlie Bluhdorn, ran Paramount single-
handed for a while after Gulf + Western bought it in 1968; Frank Yablans,
though he still talks with Charlie every day (and, we're told, does a sensa-
tional Bluhdorn imitation), has managed to beat the boss back to a largely
supervisory role."

This was the last straw. He was publicly humiliated, but had little
recourse, since he had just given Yablans and Evans a new five-year
agreement.

Soon after the story appeared, I got a call from Charlie asking me to
come see him as soon as I could.

As I walked up the street from ABC to the Gulf + Western Building, I
knew this wasn't just going to be another rant-and-rave meeting; Charlie
would once again be pounding on me to join Paramount. In the past, I
could change the subject or demur or outright spurn him. The last time he
had asked me to leave ABC and join Paramount had been at dinner at the
restaurant on the top floor of his building, when I scared the other diners
by practically yelling at him, "Charlie, see that waiter? I'd rather have that

job than work for Frank Yablans." Charlie was almost literally frothing at the mouth when he replied, "How can you say that? You're a little vice president of ABC!"

But this time, when I got to his office, he was quite calm and speaking slowly. It was Charlie at his most lethal.

He told me he wanted me to become chairman and CEO of Paramount, where Frank Yablans and everyone else would be reporting to me.

It was a stunning maneuver on his part. Paramount was at that moment the most successful studio in the world, and Evans and Yablans were the biggest executive stars in the show business firmament. He was going to curb their power and replace them with this TV guy. If it hadn't been Bluhdorn, I'd have laughed it all away. But it *was* Charlie, so it was real, no matter how foolish it all seemed.

After that shock, I quietly asked, "Charlie, would that mean I would have the right to fire Yablans on my own, without your approval?"

He said, "Well . . . yes." And then he qualified it: "Except you can't fire Yablans, because I'm not going to pay off that contract in the millions. But he'll report to you and you can tell him what to do, and I won't take his calls to hear him complain."

I told him I needed to think about it. He was momentarily dumbfounded by my reaction, having reasonably expected me to leap over the table to accept his offer. After a moment, he fairly shouted, "What is there to think about, you idiot? You're a lowly vice president of ABC, with no movie experience, and I'm making you chairman of Paramount Pictures!"

He did have a point.

Even though I was in a bad box at ABC and knew the end was nigh, this monumental shift in circumstances was too much, too overwhelming, and I said, "Still, I'm going to think about it. You can't ask me to give you an instant answer."

He sat back and said, "Yes I can. And you can give me the only answer a sane person would give—which is a grateful 'Thank you, and when do I start?'"

———

Standing up to Charlie Bluhdorn had become second nature to me; I knew that was my true and only power over him. I could feel his hot fumes following me as I got up and walked out of his baroque French-furniture-filled office. I said I'd call him the next day.

What was I doing? It was a stalling tactic. I needed to get my head around this ridiculous proposition for which I had zero qualifications. I was well aware that a big part of the offer was just Bluhdorn's thirst for revenge against Yablans and Evans. I didn't much desire being the trip wire in the mousetrap he wanted to set.

I walked down Park Avenue to my apartment at the Waldorf Towers. I realized that this was the first hard real-life decision I'd ever been forced to make. I'd risen so fast up the entertainment ladder without any friction inside the insulated corridors of one company that this frightened the hell out of me. Despite the shaky programming ground I was on at ABC, all I wanted was to crawl into a ball and forget what I'd just been offered.

When I got to the Waldorf, I called Marty Starger, the person to whom I reported, and told him I'd just been offered the chairmanship of Paramount. There was a long pause; he was astounded that his underling had been offered such a job—a Houdini-like escape from his poor performance running series television. I ended the silence by saying, "I don't think I'm going to accept it."

At that point, I still hadn't been able to think coherently. I just wanted it to go away. It was way too much, way too soon. Like Charlie, Starger thought my response was inane.

I had to tell Marty right away about the offer, because Charlie had said he was going to call Leonard Goldenson first thing the next morning to ask permission to make me a formal offer. I had told Charlie not to do so until I decided what I wanted, but I knew that Charlie Bluhdorn had a will not governed by what anyone else wanted.

The next morning I was summoned to Mr. Goldenson's office.

For Goldenson, the idea that I had been offered the chairmanship of Paramount was equally astounding. In his kindly old crocodile way, he told me gently, "You can't turn this down." He probably would have fired me as an acknowledged dolt if I had stayed.

Now, I know this is hard to believe, but rather than any wild exhilaration, what I felt was that I didn't have a choice, as if I were being pushed out onto a stage and into a big spotlight before I'd even put my long pants on. There I would be, for all the world to see, an impostor exposed.

I also believed that all this was the doing of a mad, willful, contrarian Austrian who was furious at the president of his company and wanted to use me to humiliate him. I was just an accessory to Charlie's vengeful whim. Nevertheless, of course I couldn't do anything but say yes, but with very little joy and not much enthusiasm. Here I was, thirty-two years old, being offered this opportunity, and yet all I saw was trouble and strife ahead.

The roller coaster I was on began to crawl along the track to the top; once it tipped, the ride down would be tumultuous. I hadn't anticipated it would all go so fast. My first conversation with Bluhdorn had been on Wednesday, and I was scheduled for my regular trip to L.A. on Friday. Charlie, eager for the sting to bite Yablans and Evans, asked me to postpone my flight by a day and come to his house in Connecticut on Saturday to finalize things. Thinking we'd just talk about it all without anything concrete happening, I was surprised when I arrived at his Ridgefield country house to be greeted at the door by Martin Davis, Charlie's henchman. Martin Davis was a dour Uriah Heep–type character who heckled from the shadows. On the surface, he was affable, with a quick, deeply cynical wit, but underneath he was an evil conniver. As head of public relations, he hid all the dark deeds taking place in the Gulf + Western Building. Barney Balaban had run Paramount in the years before G + W acquired it. Davis had been Balaban's assistant. Then, when Balaban was running the studio deep into the ground, behind Balaban's back, Davis helped finagle the sale to Gulf + Western, and Charlie made him his vice president of communications.

Martin told me he had already written the press release for my appointment, and while I was reading it in one room, Charlie was calling Lew Wasserman in another room to tell him the news. Charlie wanted the most powerful person in Hollywood to be the first to know that he'd bested the ungrateful and disloyal Yablans.

Charlie yelled at me to come into the room and put me on the phone with Lew, who was also rather startled at the news about the new statehood of his daughter's childhood friend. I was hardly someone he took seriously, but like everyone else in Hollywood, he didn't much like Yablans, so he congratulated me heartily. The ever-charming Wasserman told me he always knew I'd go places when, as a twelve-year-old, I'd beaten his wife at gin rummy at their Palm Springs house.

Meanwhile, Martin Davis was phoning out the story.

Charlie was eager for me to leave so he could go to his too-long-delayed weekly Bavarian lunch feast. The revenge on Yablans was just the appetizer.

Once out of his house and on the way to Kennedy Airport, I numbly looked out the window as the peak fall foliage flew by, finding it impossible to accept all that had happened in the last four days. As the plane moved westward, the news wafted its way to every nook and cranny of Hollywood, and its vicious tongues were wagging:

Who is this person—from television of all places!—and how did he usurp the two greatest success stories of the movie business?

Thirty-two years old and with no experience?

You've got to be kidding!

Television was still considered the underclass. To movie people I was an interloper from an inferior land. At that time, almost no actor who made movies would *ever* appear on a television screen. Film directors did not direct TV. Film producers did not produce TV. On studio lots, television stages were like Calcutta compared with the big soundstages reserved for moviemaking. I was clearly not cast right—or the right caste for this job.

By the time I got to the Hotel Bel-Air, the switchboard was filled with calls for me. I'd been living there for most of the eight years I was at ABC, and they took care of me as a kind of house pet, with the operator mothering me with concern at all this uproar on her phone lines.

Everyone I had ever known—and many I'd never met—wanted to offer congratulations. Just to get some actual air—as against most of the hot air on the calls—I went out to the pool and took the calls there, one after another, for hours. While I was outside, the hotel surreptitiously moved me from the studio suite I'd been in to the North Cottage, their most private and secluded accommodation.

That's the way Hollywood functioned in those days.

Next up was the required visit from the reigning éminence grise of Hollywood, the producer Ray Stark, who came to give me his "friendship" and to "guide" me in my new role.

Once I'd gotten all that over with, I never wanted a phone in my ear again, and was so exhausted from it all that I got into my new big bed and slept until Monday morning, when I went to see Bob Evans. He was full of goodwill, but said right away that he had no interest in staying on as head of production. He had just made *Chinatown,* and his new deal gave him the ability to personally produce movies. Being a company executive was no longer appealing. When I asked Bob who could replace him, he said, "No one."

Bob Evans made the *The Godfather,* and my high credit was a movie of the week about a vampire in Las Vegas—he had no intention of working for me. That rejection was nothing compared with what awaited me in New York when I returned later that week.

I was met at the airport by Mario, an angelic-looking (but soon to prove otherwise) chauffeur, who told me he'd been permanently assigned to take care of me.

In his big black Cadillac, we cruised into Manhattan, a very different ride from my ratty taxi trip over the Triborough Bridge eight years earlier when I saw the city for the first time.

Paramount's New York home office was in the mighty Gulf + Western Building, which had a perfect position at the southwest corner of Central Park. Years later, when Charlie was suffering from one of the many vicious attacks on his character in *The New York Times,* I wrote him a note saying, "The sun will never set on you or the Gulf + Western Building." Charlie burst into tears reading it. Years after, that building was reclad and gussied up into the Trump International Hotel—and I can't help but wish the sun had never risen on that.

At that time, all the movie companies had their home offices in New York. This had been tradition since the beginning of the movie business. Production was based on the West Coast, but all the major business decisions were made in the East. I would learn to like that separation of responsibilities: New York was the center of U.S. marketing and distribution activities, as well as the business and finance center. While Hollywood's importance was primary, the ultimate power was always in New York. The same had been true in television, so I was used to both the tension and the reality of how the two coasts played against each other. That effective balance of power is missing now; everything is L.A. based, much, I think, to the detriment of how movies are made and marketed. It's far better to have some distance, some check and balance, from the insularity and daily bullshit of Hollywood life.

I took a small office in the Siberia of Paramount's executive floor. Frank Yablans was encamped at the other end, with a majestic office, where he had his desk put on an ego-lifting six-inch platform, which was needed to add height to his Mussolini impression.

Yablans greeted me in his grand and garrulous way. He embraced me with congratulations, but it was hard for him to disguise the seething within at this diabolical insult from Bluhdorn. I was sure he thought it was just Charlie's way of taking him down a peg; I knew he was just adopting a smirkily smiling strategy until he could maneuver everything back to the status quo ante. Yablans had to believe that making him report to a movie nonentity was just an expression of Charlie's cruelty; he'd been a political warrior his entire life at Paramount and had gone through worse humiliations than this. If he could just keep cool, he'd find the right moment to demolish me. Then he'd be back as the rightful head of the company. Since I couldn't fire him and pay off his contract, my only strategy was to find a way for him to lose his cool and fire himself.

In the meantime, he planned for life to continue as before, and other than a gritting of his teeth here and there, all he did was substitute me for Charlie as an object to sidestep and ignore. And, of course, ridicule behind my back. In those first days, I ignored Yablans, knowing there was no point in being more than outwardly collegial. Besides, I desperately wanted to understand Paramount's operations from the bowels up—which was where Yablans was *not* to be found. Movies as a business and process were so different in pace and complexity from television that I had to hard-study how the place functioned. Even understanding what language was being used would not come easily. It's a lot harder to come in on top of an organization than at the bottom if you want to know how a company actually works. And I'm no good unless I understand everything down to the smallest molecule. No one really wants to tell the chairman anything other than good news and no one at Paramount was volunteering anything given how I was dropped onto the top of the Paramount mountain.

After a week of this discombobulation I flew back to L.A. for my first production meetings. We met in the Beverly Hills offices that Evans had established some years earlier.

I thought, *How odd is this? Here was this major studio, and we weren't on the storied studio lot, but in a fancy little boutique building in the heart of the tiny commercial district of Beverly Hills—a block away from the Bistro. This was the high-toned restaurant of the moment serving the movie business.* Sidney Korshak, the mob lawyer who was soon to figure so distressingly in my life, had a permanent table there, with a phone as its only decoration.

The reason they had this outpost for production was that when Evans took over in the late 1960s, Paramount was hemorrhaging money. Bob sold Gulf + Western on the idea that the problem with Hollywood was these old geezers wandering around the lot, thinking bigger was better and squandering money on old-time big-budget movies. He wanted a fresh take, separate from all that studio nonsense. This gave Charlie the bright idea of selling the fifty-acre studio lot and developing the real estate. In a typical move, Charlie sold half of it impulsively to Immobiliare, a Vatican-related and deeply corrupt Italian company that was expanding all over the world before it imploded in scandal and the suicide (or rumored murder) of its CEO. The idea was for it to be a joint venture between Paramount and Immobiliare, but the deal was impossibly complex and no one really understood the terms.

Evans said, "Don't bother with this ridiculous Bluhdorn real estate deal, because the studio lot means nothing to our business." Nevertheless, it all seemed so crazy to me, and I got the contract, determined to understand it. We'd sold the studio land seven years before in this faux joint venture with the Italians, but there hadn't been any real estate development on it—a curiosity that no one could explain. Yet Paramount had been paying for all the upkeep of the mostly dead lot for all these years. I had a meeting with the "observer" from Immobiliare that first week. At first I thought he had wandered in from the *Godfather* shoot. Immobiliare had recently been indicted for fraud and for being a giant mob-controlled business. The "observer" wore an impeccable suit, spoke awkward stiff English, and didn't have a clue about any real estate developments, but he thought the studio was being taken care of with efficiency, and he wanted me to tour it with him to see how clean it was.

All I knew at that point was that all the costs of operating the place were paid for by Paramount, not Immobiliare. It didn't make any sense. But so far, nothing about Paramount was making much sense.

One of the first people I saw when I got to L.A. was Francis Ford Coppola, who was just finishing the rough cut of *The Godfather Part II*. We had dinner and, waving his arms emphatically, he said, "Move back to the studio."

I hadn't thought of it until he said it, but I instantly realized, *Of course! I mean, we have a movie studio, we're in the movie business!*

I'd just become chairman of a movie company, and I didn't want to go to a little boutique in my old stomping ground of Beverly Hills. I wanted to go to my fifty-acre studio.

We put the Beverly Hills building up for sale and moved back where we belonged.

And, as for where I belonged, I didn't want to continue living only in hotels. In Manhattan I'd moved into a company-owned apartment in Hampshire House, and in L.A. from the Hotel Bel-Air to a house in the rising canyons above Beverly Hills. It was a somewhat bastardized Spanish terra-cotta'ed house with a three-hundred-year-old great oak tree in its courtyard that I wanted to own more than the house itself, though the place did come with a projection room, as its previous owner was the head of Columbia Pictures. "Projection room" is a term of Hollywood art from the 1920s that describes how movies were screened in private homes—at that time and up until digitization, the equipment necessary was massive: two huge arc light projectors manned by a projectionist changing the thousand-foot film reels every ten minutes.

That first day, in a conference room in Beverly Hills, we had my first production meeting. Frank Yablans had come out for it, and there was just Bob Evans, two of his assistants, Frank, and me.

I opened the meeting collegially, asking what our plans were, what movies we were making or considering. Yablans interrupted me, launching into a monologue about how the movie business wasn't like television and didn't follow the bureaucratic processes that I was probably used to.

His tirade was designed to show that I knew nothing, and he didn't try to hide his disdain.

When that didn't get a reaction from me, he crudely went for disparaging gay jokes, but I ignored him. I knew his tactics were to manipulate me into firing him, and that was the one condition Bluhdorn had imposed on me. I knew I could *not* breach the Yablans agreement. Paying off the huge multiyear deal would be beyond embarrassing for Charlie. Not to mention financially foolish.

So I just sat there, taking his subtle and not-so-subtle barbs. It wasn't nice; it made me feel queasy and small and even more out of my league amid these over-the-top personalities.

To conserve the little dignity I was trying to hold on to, I got up abruptly and said, "Sorry, I have another appointment."

What I did learn, however, and depressingly, was that there wasn't much in Paramount's larder. Yablans and Evans had spent most of the last year making their own bloated deal rather than developing new movies. The whole place was now wired to their egos, and there was no one underneath them to get anything done.

What I also knew by the end of that meeting was that there was no way Yablans was going to serve out that five-year contract.

Before I could really start, Frank Yablans had to go.

People magazine began publishing around the same time I started at Paramount, and it put me directly in its early sights. Over the ensuing decades, *People* has become a cheerleading celebrity book, but at the time of its launch it wanted to be snappy and snarky about people in entertainment. And they were homing in on me as a juicy target.

The gossip columnist Liz Smith, whom I didn't know at the time, was a junior editor there. She called me up cold and said, "I want you to know they're doing a story on you. And it's mean and homophobic."

At the time, executives were not really written about very much in general-interest publications. You might see stories in the trades, or in rags that wrote about gossip in the movie business, but those had little circulation.

People ended up publishing a story, but instead of what I feared, it was titled "Failing Upwards"—how this hapless "kid" from network TV with not a single hit show to his name became the head of Paramount for all the wrong reasons. As negative as it was, I was relieved: it was 1974, and it was better to be called a failure than a fairy.

By the way, I now own *People* magazine.

After I got back to New York, there was more of the same. Frank had told everyone that I was just Bluhdorn's toy, and since it was beyond absurd that I could run Paramount, Charlie would soon tire of the game and get rid of me. No one wanted to speak to me or look my way. I was invisible.

What was I to do? Everyone at the company reported up through Frank Yablans, and they knew any cozying up to me was curtains for them. Yablans just continued to ignore me.

Out of total frustration, I got a copy of the Yablans contract and read it word for word. Several times. Usually in employment contracts at senior levels, there's a detailed description of the duties. I discovered that there was no description of actual duties for the president: no definition of his authority, and no defined responsibilities.

I had found my way to kick Yablans out of his cool.

I composed a simple one-sentence memo to *all* the staff of Paramount worldwide. It said FROM THIS DAY FORWARD, ALL EXECUTIVES WHO PREVIOUSLY REPORTED TO MR. YABLANS NOW REPORT DIRECTLY TO ME.

And I signed my name.

Literally ten minutes after I'd had it hand-delivered to Yablans, my office door swung open so hard on the hinges that it actually cracked, and a fuming Yablans came roaring in.

"What the fuck do you think you're doing with that idiot memo?"

I responded calmly and quietly. "Frank, I have every legal right to do exactly that, and it's done. You have an employment agreement that I'm fully respecting. So go back to your office and figure out what you're going to do for the rest of the day, since I don't need anything from you right now," and swiveled my chair to the window.

Yablans thundered out of my office, presumably to read his contract.

I figured that aside from storming around, he wouldn't do anything to jeopardize his titanic salary. He had to know he'd never get another deal within a mile of this one.

Frank called Charlie right away. Charlie, true to his word, wouldn't take his call.

I'm fairly certain Charlie really thought that hiring me was a good comeuppance for Yablans's arrogance and insubordination, but that after a while somehow Yablans and I would find common ground. Charlie and everyone else in the business thought Yablans was a genius distributor, and after he suffered a little humiliation, this would go the way most Hollywood relationships cynically went: the money would talk and no one would walk.

But, deluded by his own self-image of grandeur, Yablans simply couldn't take this hit to his reputation . . . and he quit. Cold. Just like that.

I didn't hear it from him. His lawyer called.

Sidney Korshak.

In his deep, intimidating voice, Korshak said, "This isn't working. He's out, and we have to settle it."

I replied, "There isn't anything to settle. I'm perfectly happy for him to stay if he wants. If he quits, which is what you're telling me, then there's no settlement, he just goes home."

Korshak said, in that low and menacing voice, "You seem like a nice kid, but you're a little naive. I'll deal with your boss," and he hung up. Sidney went to Charlie, and fearless though Charlie usually was, he was a little scared of Korshak.

Charlie then called to tell me, "Sidney thinks you're being a hard-ass and we have to pay him something or things will deteriorate. *Unpredictably.*"

Charlie hadn't liked hearing that word, "unpredictably." He'd told Sidney that I would be reasonable and to go back and work it out. But he said to me, "Don't be *too* reasonable."

"A million will do it," Sidney said; that was real money in 1974.

I said, "It's far too much," and offered a third of that.

Sidney called Charlie back and said, "The kid's a total prick."

Charlie called me, almost whining, and asked, "Why are you causing so much trouble? It's not that much money for peace, and this is making my heart race."

I told him, "You wouldn't let me fire Frank because of the money, and now it's my job to save the money! Besides, Yablans is a thief; he's been getting bribes from Sumner Redstone for years." We had recently discovered that $100,000 worth of diamond jewelry was sent to a certain address every Christmas from a certain Boston jeweler. Boston was where the theater-owning Redstone lived; it wasn't hard to trace it.

Frank had been so nasty that I couldn't bear letting him take advantage of us, and I had the leverage. What could Charlie do, given that I'd just gotten the job? So I held firm both on principle and on what I thought was solid ground.

But Charlie Bluhdorn was paranoid on a good day. In the middle of all this negotiating, Frank Yablans's wife told someone who told Charlie's also-paranoid wife, "Frank wants to knock Charlie out on his fat ass, literally."

Underreaction was not in Charlie's tool kit. First, he locked down his personal floor in the Gulf + Western Building, then doubled security everywhere. Then he hid in his office.

Coming from the neat-and-tidy world of broadcasting, I couldn't believe I was in the midst of such a circus.

After several hours I was finally allowed up to Charlie's lair. I told him I really didn't think Frank was going to machine-gun his way into his office, but Charlie didn't want to hear any of that. He demanded that I settle immediately with Yablans, whatever the cost.

I called Korshak and was told he was at the dentist. I asked, "Could he be interrupted?"

The reply was "No, of course not."

I called repeatedly for an hour and a half, wondering what possibly could be taking this long. Finally they said, "Mr. Korshak has just left the dentist and has gone back to the Carlyle Hotel."

I found out the hotel was only five blocks from the dentist. I called the Carlyle and asked for him. No answer.

I called back in fifteen. Still no answer.

Another fifteen. The same.

Meanwhile, Charlie called me and said, "Maybe Frank has an accomplice . . ."

Caught up in this farce, I felt my own paranoia set in. I began to think something might have happened to Korshak. How long could it take to walk five blocks? Maybe he passed out or fell down or something!

So I called security at the Carlyle and insisted they send someone up to Korshak's apartment to see if he was there and okay. I was relieved when, just a few minutes later, my secretary buzzed to say that Korshak was on the line.

His deep, gravelly voice spoke very, very slowly: "Never. Ever. Send anyone. To find me."

I said, "Oh, Sidney, I'm just glad you're okay! I was worried something happened to you."

He repeated, with even more sinister softness, "Never. Ever. Send. *Anyone*. To find me," and hung up.

I wrote him an apology and sent it over, and after a few hours he called back. In quick order, we settled the contract, and that was the end of Frank Yablans at Paramount.

It took several more hours, however, to persuade Charlie to unlock the doors and return to what no one else on the planet would call "normal life" at the Gulf + Western Building.

CHAPTER 10

Every early rock I turned over had something foul underneath. It wasn't enough that we had no movies in development. I had to keep clearing the underbrush, one of the first involving my old friend, the legendary agent Irving Lazar. Swifty had a round, bald head and wore very thick horn-rimmed glasses, which seemed to make his eyes bulge out of their sockets. He was also known to wear his Sulka underwear only once before throwing it away—for reasons that thankfully remain unknown.

Paramount was paying Lazar as a consultant, which made no sense to me. But apparently, though Yablans was an unattractive, bombastic, Napoleonesque character, he was also socially ambitious, so he'd made a deal with Lazar for services that didn't exist on paper and couldn't really be pinned down. Irving was socially prominent in Hollywood as well as internationally. Yablans was using him as an entry into those worlds.

You couldn't be an agent *and* a producer; there was a law against that. Yablans had gotten around the law by defining Lazar as a "consultant" in his contract.

I thought this would be easy. I called Irving and said, "I've noticed the only thing that's happened in the two years that you've been doing this 'job' is that you sent the company forty-eight thousand dollars in restaurant and hotel bills." This was in addition to his salary! "Could you tell me what projects you've been running, as I can't find any record of that."

He said, "I established Frank Yablans in the community."

I told him, "Now he's gone and I don't want any establishing"—

especially at $100,000 a year. I said, "I love you, Irving, but we just can't justify this, so I have to end the agreement."

"Over my dead body will you break this agreement," he said.

"Well, then from this instant forward you are to have no drinks, dinners, or hotel rooms charged to Paramount. You are to not render any services."

He said, "Well, yes, I guess you can do that, but you're paying me every nickel you owe me!"

"Irving, you didn't *do* anything. I don't *want* you to do anything!"

His response was "Okay, you'll still pay me, but I'll let you pay me over ten years."

Corruption and crooked deals were rampant.

But that wasn't all.

Next I discovered that there was no one home.

There were fewer people working at Paramount than at any of the other major studios. Paramount had pretty much gotten out of the television business because its bosses had no interest in the "inferior" form. The biggest show they had, *Mission: Impossible*, had just ended, and the television division was basically shut down.

The success of *The Godfather* and *Love Story* provided Evans and Yablans with a nice shelter, and *The Godfather Part II* was coming soon—a movie, by the way, that both of them thought couldn't and shouldn't be made. Even Coppola didn't want to do it. It was Charlie Bluhdorn's majestic salesmanship that got that picture made.

Every day I was confronted with the realization that I'd come from clean-as-a-whistle government-regulated broadcasting into a business where ego and self-promotion corroded everything. It astonished me to see an entire company wired to the asses of its senior management. And the company's owner, in the person of Charlie, acted like an old-time emperor. Between frantically buying companies and trading every hour of the day in whatever markets were open, Charlie would occasionally call me with his perennial idea for what he said would be the blockbuster of all time: the tale of Sitting Bull and Hitler at war with each other.

Yes, true. Sitting Bull and Hitler.

Unlike broadcasting, which was fairly steady, and focused on the narrow ratings race, where all the networks had enough of an audience to draw in advertisers and deliver profits, the movie business was boom or bust. All you had were box office revenues. There were no subsidiary earnings at that time to count on. It was a hit-driven business, and you lived or died on the theatrical box office. Also unlike broadcasting, the business at Paramount was run on bluster and braggadocio. Broadcasting might have been a little bloodless, but I was finding the movie world filled with a lot of self-promoters and charlatans from all nations. I was totally untutored in how to separate the talented from the chaff.

Broadcasters had, at that time, a sense of responsibility for what they did, and were, to a degree, programming in the public interest. Guardrails of any kind didn't seem to exist in the movie business. For all Yablans's bluster he was a master at distribution and marketing. And Evans was far from a slouch at running the production side. He had great theatrical instincts, and he made pictures better because of his intense involvement. The problem was, their enormous successes were done and gone.

Another indication that I was out of my little league was meeting Kirk Kerkorian. He was an entrepreneur extraordinaire who had flown de Havilland Mosquitoes during World War II, after which he built an air-transport fleet and then proceeded to play on bigger and bigger stages with bigger and bigger businesses. He bought MGM when it was leaking money and floundering, after its long reign as the number one studio. At the same time, Kerkorian bought an airline that was also in trouble.

Kerkorian had very few words for anyone about anything, and what words he used were monosyllabic. He was always direct and clear, and could be counted on to live up to his word. While he was extremely charitable, his contributions were always anonymous. He was an economic adventurer, the true essence of a high-wire industrial gambler.

At that time, he had recently opened the biggest hotel in the history of Las Vegas, the MGM Grand, which had gone violently over budget. Everything was going wrong for him when he walked into Bob Evans's house to meet with Charlie Bluhdorn and Lew Wasserman and . . . um . . .

me. Kerkorian's hope of making a deal with Paramount and Universal was his last gasp at averting bankruptcy. MGM owned lots of assets outside the United States and had a first-rate worldwide distribution company, but like Paramount it didn't have enough pictures to support it. Some years earlier, Charlie had persuaded Wasserman to combine the separate international distribution operations of Paramount and Universal into one company serving both. The idea pitched to Kerkorian was to join the distribution venture and sell some of the theaters MGM owned to raise cash for his hotel.

Charlie loved using Bob Evans's house for his secret meetings. Not only was it isolated and private, but Bob's cook made Bavarian hot dogs that Charlie craved.

Kerkorian arrived and was the definition of taciturn, waiting for what he must have believed would be a humbling offer.

Sure enough, Charlie and Lew, thinking that Kerkorian was helpless without a large cash infusion, lowballed the price for the theaters. Kirk listened, saying only an occasional no, to which Bluhdorn kept browbeating him, saying he had no choice but to leave the house with the needed cash. Kerkorian, impassive, finally got up and walked toward the door, not saying a word until he got to the foyer. At that point, beyond insulted, he turned to Charlie and said, "There's no deal here."

Wasserman, who would never acquiesce in losing his leverage, got up and said, "Well, that's that," and also headed for the door.

But Charlie would have none of it. He chased Kerkorian out to the driveway, screaming, "Wait, wait, Kirk!" But Kerkorian got in his car, closed the door, and started to drive off.

Charlie, hardly an athlete, somehow ran alongside him for a hundred feet, banging on the window, managing to get in front of the car to stop it. Kerkorian would not open the window; he just sat behind the wheel with a stoic smile as the standoff continued.

I watched the absurdity of these titans frozen in their positions. Slowly Charlie inched his way around to Kerkorian's window, his hands up in surrender and apology. He shouted acceptance of Kerkorian's price. Kerkorian simply nodded and drove off. Meanwhile, Wasserman shrugged and got in his car. A distraught Charlie walked back into the house saying, "I'm starving, I'm starving—bring on the hot dogs."

Oh my god, I thought, *I am so over my head.*

At the time, there was no such thing as "media." Movie studios dominated entertainment, and the five majors (Paramount/Warners/Columbia/Fox/Universal) had worldwide importance. If you ran one of these film companies, you were a prominent figure wherever you went. In those early years, though, I wasn't swanning anywhere; I was just trying to figure out this weird and dysfunctional studio I was now in charge of. Because I'd offed Yablans in such a public and brutal way, everyone was now afraid of me. And I was petrified that they would find out just how unqualified I actually was. Only if I slowed everything down could I begin to understand all the parts and then try to rearrange them into something coherent. I tend to make things worse in the beginning as I fumble around trying to get to base truths. Instinct, which I prize almost above all else, doesn't work very well for me in abstruse matters. I have to get to the core DNA on any matter, its logical essence, before I can add anything of value. For me this takes a lot of time, often to the irritation of faster thinkers. But when it does crystallize, I can't be deterred.

I listen with an extra ear, highly tuned to hear a new truth among the cacophony of voices in the room. And when I catch that note, no matter what I might have thought before, I'll change course in a nanosecond. If I've ever had any kind of secret sauce, it's the ability to hear conflicting creative ideas bombarded around the room and extract something valuable. Recently in a meeting, someone complained that I wasn't being consistent. I replied that I'm never consistent; I'll turn on a dime if I hear a better truth.

From the beginning of my time at ABC, everything for me had been "What's it about?" or "What's the story?" or "What's the material?" not "Who's the hot person of the day?" or "What was the last hit?" My focus had always been the idea, the story, the concept. I strongly believed that at Paramount we had to concentrate on developing scripts from the beginning rather than going backward and being dazzled by all the promoters with stars and packages, which was the way movie studios were then run.

But before making any plans for new movies, I had to deal with the current releases, most of which were in disarray.

Even *The Godfather Part II* was in trouble, as hard as that is to comprehend today, when it's rightly thought to be one of the great movies of the ages. Soon after I started, I walked into the projection room, and there was Francis Ford Coppola and millions of miles of film he was trying to cobble into a coherent movie.

The rough cut was almost five hours, and as dramatic as the scenes were it was almost impossible to follow the story.

Francis had flashbacks throughout and multiple storylines. I was confused from the start and never caught up. The sequel to *The Godfather* was so anticipated and so hot that we had guaranteed a Christmas opening to the exhibitors and Francis had only a few months left for final editing. The lights came up after the screening, and I was wet with worry—somewhere in there was a truly great film, but I had just entered the big-time movie business and wasn't going to be much help in getting it to that greatness.

Not that Francis wanted any help. He'd made the film under some duress. Charlie had hounded him to make a sequel, and Francis resisted as long as he could, but finally Charlie's vociferous sledgehammer—and lots of money—made him acquiesce. Francis's stipulations were that he be left alone and not have to deal with Evans or Yablans, both of whom had driven him crazy on the first *Godfather* and then seemed to take credit they didn't deserve for its stupendous success.

Coppola was exhausted, but still seemed confident he could pull it together. I was skeptical, but told him the only thing I could do to help was to tell him where I was confused by all the flashbacks and flash-forwards. He did streamline them into a coherent whole, and in the end it was that shifting back and forth in time and place that was the triumph of *The Godfather Part II*.

That was the rightful high of my first season, so high that it almost obscured how low our upcoming prospects were. The 1975 roster of movies included *The Day of the Locust* (a beautifully made but depressing Hollywood tale that no one wanted to see), *Sheila Levine Is Dead and Living in New York* (about which I will say no more), Jacqueline Susann's *Once Is Not Enough* (which itself says it all), *Mandingo* (a Black sexploitation film), *Mahogany* (the troubled Diana Ross follow-up to *Lady Sings the Blues*), and Burt Reynolds's *Hustle*. Crowds rushed to see *Godfather* when it opened in December, but the descent from that triumph was swift. No one showed up to the opening of *The Day of the Locust*.

In my first full year, the company's output dropped from twenty-three movies to twelve, and Paramount went from first to last place among all the major studios. With Bob Evans gone, I had no head of production. I had no head of *anything*, and the place basically ground to a halt. There wasn't poor morale; there was *no* morale, because there was hardly anyone there. Those who stayed had no faith in me. I had to learn the differences between making *movies* and movies of the week; hundred-day shooting schedules instead of ten; real stars and totemic egos versus B and C stars and starlets. All my experience was upended going from the small to the big screen. Hollywood is not very tolerant of the learning process—maybe no businesses are.

Desperate to get something going, I was easily manipulated into agreeing to make an adaptation of Hemingway's *Islands in the Stream*. It was a prestigious but boring tale of catching a fish.

I took Bob Evans's suggestion and made Dick Sylbert head of production. A lovely man of great style and taste, he'd been an honored production designer who'd worked on some of the greatest films of that period. But an executive he would and could not be, which of course I found out about a minute after appointing him. It was a thoughtless move by a desperate novice. I then turned to David Picker. He came from a storied movie family: his father was in charge of movie theaters and his uncle was a high executive at United Artists. David had a very successful run in charge of production at United Artists and had become a producer. He had just finished the biopic of Lenny Bruce starring Dustin Hoffman and directed by Bob Fosse. I made him head of production, but for the life of me I couldn't figure out how he made decisions. David famously once said that if he turned down all the pictures he'd made and said yes to all those that he turned down it would probably come out the same way in the end. "Oh my god" to that. Once, when we were on a plane together, he went through ten scripts in the four-hour flight, while I got through two. I asked him if he could read that quickly and he replied, "No, I just decide in the first twenty pages whether to say yes or no." I knew then this wasn't going to last.

The differences between films and television were so stark that my first few years at Paramount were a train wreck. Other than *Godfather II*, the only hit we had that first year was *Three Days of the Condor*, an intricate political thriller about rot within the CIA, directed by Sydney Pollack and starring Robert Redford and Faye Dunaway. I thought the best way to sell such a complicated plot was to do a very sexy full-page ad of a shirtless Redford in the arms of Faye Dunaway. This elicited a call from Redford on the Sunday it appeared. He said that the ad had "disrobed him" in front of his kids. It was a push too far, he said, and we should take it down immediately. I thought it was a great way to sell the film, so I refused, and that was the last we saw of Robert Redford for five years, until he brought us *Ordinary People*, which would go on to win the Academy Award for Best Picture.

Television had airdates to meet, while movies meandered about until they solidified. Another difference was that television was a national business, while movies were mostly promoted city by city and predominantly in newspapers. I had begun questioning this method, because I knew how effective television advertising was—far more efficient than just putting a big ad in *The New York Times*. But given that movie people never watched television—or pretended not to—the only support they wanted was bigger and bigger *New York Times* ads.

The old rascal producer Joseph E. Levine was the only one who braved releasing a picture all over the United States at once. The major studios preferred to open their pictures in a few theaters in key cities and then roll them out slowly to the rest of the world after publicity and positive word of mouth spread. Levine upended that by opening in thousands of theaters, but only with exploitation movies like *Hercules*. The idea of a major studio doing that on an A-list release was odious to the old guard at Paramount. When I suggested it, that proved to them how unsuited I was to the big time.

I couldn't understand why opening a picture nationally, using television, wasn't a better idea than what they'd been doing. I had learned long ago that ad making was mostly about saying no to the ad makers. As in, "No, it's just not good enough," and "No, you can't go home until you make it better." The standard process at Paramount was to review three or four concepts that the ad department corralled from outside vendors, toss them around for a few minutes, and pick one.

I came to understand that denial—refusing to accept an ad that didn't jump off the page and resonate—was the only thing that mattered. I've always believed that if you push people past their endurance, good things come. Rarely does a great ad or a great TV spot appear on the first try, and when it does it's clear instantly and you don't have to talk around it. What I call "torturing the process" works. Saying "It's okay" or "It'll do" is repellent. Never compromise.

There wasn't an idea for a movie or an ad or television spot I didn't torture: we had the noisiest, rowdiest sessions that lasted into the night, trying to come up with ideas for movies, with the best advertisements, and it was usually after some exhaustion that original ideas emerged.

Some people truly hate that process; they don't like collaboration, don't really like creative conflict. It's messy and noisy, but I loved every minute of it. The longer it went on, the more stimulated I was, and the more exasperating it probably was to those I could never convert to this extremely demanding process. Those I did convert continue to tell me how much it contributed to their successful careers. Those I didn't called me the boss from hell.

During my lengthy teething time, Paramount became a distant fifth among the major studios. Not a good place to be, since, when I started,

Paramount had led the industry. Charlie couldn't stand that we were being beaten by all these other companies.

He was constantly saying to me, "Why don't we have *Kramer vs. Kramer*?" or "Why don't we have this or that hit?" Every time he saw a successful film he'd call and ask why it wasn't ours.

I kept saying, "I don't care what others have, or about their success; I only care what we do," and I didn't always say it calmly after the fifth harangue. But it was true. I've never cared much about competition. I'm not envious or upset by others' success, and I don't think their success diminishes me. No one has to lose for me to be successful.

I found I could hold my own in these everlasting arguments with Charlie, and I liked knowing that I could stand on my own two feet, that I wouldn't fall apart, that I would be able to advocate for whatever it was I was arguing for or defending, despite the volcanic eruption spewing from Mt. Bluhdorn.

While he was impossible at times, he never stopped me from doing what I wanted to do to organize the company or hire the staff. The combustible Charlie wasn't a collaborator. He criticized results, raged at what he thought were mistakes, but he let me build his company my way, even though I think he probably preferred the rollicking roller coaster of big highs and lows and Ruritanian drama that was Paramount under Yablans and Evans.

It was a difficult period for me because, above everything, I wanted to please him. I wanted to do well for him. He had taken such a huge risk on me.

In his own way, Charlie was unreservedly loyal to me, but he was increasingly eager for positive results and I wasn't providing them. The world thought I was driving Paramount into the ground. The ex-Paramounters were out there actively mocking me as a parvenu who was destroying their institution. I knew that all I could really do was stay the course—my course—and hope all the doubters were wrong.

CHAPTER 11

At the end of my first tumultuous year at Paramount, I met Diane von Fürstenberg. While there have been a good many men in my life since the age of sixteen, there has only ever been one woman, and she didn't come into my life until I was thirty-three years old.

There are many complex aspects of my relationship with Diane: romantic love and deep respect, companionship and world adventuring, then disappointment and separation, and finally marriage. We met in 1974, separated in 1981, reunited in 1991, married in 2001, and have spent fifty years intertwined with each other in a unique and complete love.

I have never questioned my sexuality's basic authority over my life (I was only afraid of the reaction of others). And when my romance with Diane began, I never questioned that its biological imperative was as strong in its heterosexuality as its opposite had been. When it happened, my initial and surprised response was yet another "Who knew?"

I'm well aware that this part of my life has caused confusion and lots of speculation. A relationship that began with indifference, then exploded into a romance as natural to us as breathing, surprised us and everyone else. It really is the miracle of my life.

Much has been written about us, whispered about us, wondered about us. So I'll just start at the beginning and let the story unfold.

It began at a party at Gil and Susan Shiva's, two über-socialite friends of mine who lived in the very elegant Dakota apartment building on the Upper West Side.

And I was pretty sure it would end there.

Shortly after I became chairman of Paramount, Gil and Susan gave a congratulatory dinner for me and invited their very high-toned friends, few of whom I knew personally, other than my awareness of their social superiority. This "informal dinner" meant that the men wore suits and ties and the dinner service ended with finger bowls; it was a social stratum to which I was unaccustomed and disinterested.

After being introduced around the room, I was standing alone next to the fireplace feeling I did not belong in this group, when Prince Egon von Fürstenberg walked up to me and said, "Your pants are too short."

They were.

I hadn't ever paid much attention to suit life or social life, and had little experience being around people who spoke at least three languages—simultaneously.

It wasn't much better when I was introduced to Egon's wife, the deliriously glamorous Princess Diane, who politely and dismissively said "Hello!" and quickly moved on to give a big embrace to someone more familiar and certainly more at ease than I was. She looked through me like cellophane, and I left that night thinking that neither her casual obliviousness nor Egon's put-down of my pants would ever induce me to see either of them again. The only positive outcome from that night was that I went to the tailor and had him lengthen my trousers.

Nine months later, I was returning from my first vacation from the agonies at Paramount. My work was so stifling and airless that despite the studio's perilous condition, I just had to get away from it for a little while. Sam Spiegel had lent me his grand boat, the *Malahne,* for a cruise in the South of France. He asked me if his friend the great Irene Mayer Selznick could join us. Katharine Hepburn had introduced us because Irene, the daughter of MGM's founder and titan Louis B. Mayer, knew everything about how big studios ran. Hepburn felt Irene might be a help to me. She was and we became friends. I'd brought along David Geffen, and at the first night's dinner it was quickly clear that Irene and David had an almost physical aversion to each other. Irene regally condescended to young David's biting Brooklyn brilliance, and it was all tight asses until David said, "You know, Irene, you're a cunt." To which Irene gushed out a big laugh, all tension ceased, and all was calm except for the boat itself, which broke down outside Saint-Tropez.

I arrived home to an invitation for a dinner Diane von Fürstenberg was giving for my close friend Sue Mengers, the funny and feisty big-time agent who handled lots of stars. Sue was then the prime leader of Hollywood social life.

I immediately declined. Diane von Fürstenberg's apartment was the last place I wanted to go.

Outraged, Sue Mengers called me and said, "How could you *not* come to a dinner being given for me?"

I said, "I'm not coming. I don't like that woman."

Sue said, "Of course you're coming. It's a dinner for *me* and it has nothing to do with how you feel about her." She added, "It would be too insulting if the top movie person in New York didn't show up at a dinner for the top agent in the world."

So I went. The dinner was called for eight, but I showed up around nine thirty, thinking, *I'll stay for a few minutes, do my duty to Sue, and exit.*

When I walked in, people were just finishing the buffet dinner and were lounging all over Diane's elegantly louche apartment. Without any reference to ever having met me, Diane greeted me with a dazzling smile, saying, "I'm so glad you came." I was instantly bathed in such attention and cozy warmth I couldn't believe it was the same woman I'd been dismissed by a year earlier.

We went around together saying hello to the people I knew and being introduced to her friends. There were seventy or so, every one of them some New York or international person of social or artistic note, or whatever kind of note gets noticed.

As we walked, we made little asides to each other, and then, like the gym scene from *West Side Story* when everyone else fades away and Tony and Maria are left alone, Diane and I found our way to a sofa, far away from the rest, and we stayed there for a long time. There was a glow around us that was setting off sparks, accurately described best by the French as a *coup de foudre*. Flushed and completely discombobulated, I said, "I've got to go," and she walked me to the door.

I was functioning without a brain, not a thought in my head, being willed on by pure primitive urges.

We stood at the door, and I said, "I want to call you," and she said, "I want you to."

As I walked to the elevator, I knew something heretofore unimaginable was about to happen.

All my life I'd been mostly un-seducible—by a man or woman—held back by shyness and, to a degree, fear, yet here I was with no restraint at all, knowing I was going to see her again and that nothing was gonna stop that.

I called the next day and said, "We'll go to Pearl's," an elegant modernist Chinese restaurant that was very popular. When I got to her apartment, she said, "Let's stay here and have dinner. I have better Chinese food than Pearl's."

And so, with the dinner served by her Chinese butler and cooked by his wife, we ate in her formal dining room. Afterward, on the same sofa as the night before, we wound around each other, making out like teenagers, something I hadn't done with a female since I was sixteen years old.

Now, this has always amazed me: there was no effort, no reasoning, no what's-going-on-here, no ambition, no anything. Other than sheer excitement. I thought, *Well, this is a surprise!* I certainly didn't feel, *Oh my god, what does this mean?* I was simply existing in the moment, a rare place for me.

The next week, we went to the opening night of the New York Film Festival, and a third of the way into the movie we left and, finally, went off to Pearl's. Then it was back to her place and we repeated what we had done the week before.

Diane left the next day for Paris, and I flew to L.A. She had recently separated from Egon, and had been dating an Italian journalist, with whom she was in the process of breaking up.

While she was in Paris, we spoke three times a day. After too much of this long-distancing I said, "Come to California."

She called her boyfriend in Italy and told him not to come to Paris because she was leaving the next day to see me.

She wrote this to me on the Air France flight to L.A.:

> *Barry Diller, Barry Diller . . . this name I kept hearing among people . . . You were a mystery to me, you are a mystery and you probably will keep being a mystery . . .*
>
> *I probably need you more than you need me and you probably are more of a man than I am a woman . . . I like your image, your mystique, you are someone people talk about, I like that . . . and then I like the rest: the real stuff . . . your heart! I love your heart, I know your heart . . . I know you have so much to give and I want to get it . . . D*

I picked her up at the airport, we came back to my house with the ancient oak tree, and that was the first time we spent the night together. The next morning, she came downstairs and said, "I've never been in a house that is so unlived in, so vacant. There's nothing in the drawers!" She was right: the furniture was all from Paramount. I hadn't had any time to buy things, so the prop department essentially furnished the house. You'd open a drawer and inside it would say PROPERTY OF PARAMOUNT PICTURES.

The next morning Diane went down to the kitchen, where my British butler, Derek, was standing. He said to her, "Madam, may I ask you? Did you sleep with Mr. Diller last night?"

She simply said, "Yes, I did." The next day was a Saturday, and we were at the pool with some friends. What happened then between us was an explosion of pent-up demand, and we ran to the guesthouse. David Geffen, who had been one of those at the pool, walked in on us.

I caught a glimpse of David's more-than-astonished face as he quickly closed the door.

The next days we were together in every happy way. Then she had to go to New York. When I drove back to my house from the airport, I found these little sweet notes she'd hidden everywhere, and every time I found one my smile expanded. She'd gotten to the airport early, so I got in my car, zoomed down the freeway, and caught her on the escalator for a final goodbye.

I was full-up ecstatic as I went to sleep that night.

The changing of my life's guard that day wasn't limited to Diane. In the middle of the night, my mother woke me up from my happily slumbering state to say that my brother, Donald, from whom I'd been estranged for many years, had been shot and killed in what the police called a "drug-related incident." He was thirty-six.

What stark bookends these events were: the beginning of my life with Diane and the end of the siege of pain my brother had inflicted on my parents. He had racked up a criminal record going back twenty years— burglary, drug sales, embezzlement, a short prison sentence. There were very few days in those decades that my parents weren't trying every which way to extricate him from his drug life. In the early hours of that morning so many years ago now, when my mother called to tell me of his death, I persuaded them not to pursue any further investigation into how and why the murder happened. I urged them to let this book close for them. And it did. They climbed out of their preoccupation with my brother's travails, and became a contentedly interdependent couple with no trauma and a lot of happiness for the rest of their lives.

I've never been able to let go of bitterness toward my brother. It's been almost fifty years since his death, and I have little sympathy for the life of trouble he had, and none for what he put my parents through. There is so much insecurity I carry from his cruel and contemptuous treatment of me that I can't find it in me to forgive him. I suppose it doesn't matter now, but I should have some compassion for him. I'll never know what drove him to drugs at such an early age, or how from our conformist neighborhood he became such a rare outlier. He didn't grow up in a culture of hopelessness, though he was contemptuous of life in Beverly Hills and of our family. Whatever its effect on anyone else, it must have been such a painfully calamitous journey for him.

I returned to New York the next week. Diane and her children—Alexander, five, and Tatiana, four—were on Park Avenue, and she moonlighted every night over to my place.

Within the space of one week, it was as if a giant tectonic plate in my life had shifted.

From that moment on, Diane and I were together.

I told no one about our relationship in its early months. I didn't want to shine any outside light on us because I wouldn't and couldn't put any definition on it and I'd never talked about my personal life and thought to do so now would be exploitative. I had kept my private life distinctly private, and though I had a growing public profile, that profile always had business guardrails around it.

Diane, on the other hand, had been a glamorous public figure ever since she and Egon first arrived in New York. They were the young and pretty prince and princess. Then she started her own business and, as has been true ever since, she *is* her brand, her brand is her, so there's no line between private and public. After a few months, as we began going out to various events, it was becoming clear to the world that we were some kind of together.

People started saying, "Huh? What is it with this person? We thought he liked only men."

Much of the speculation subsided when it was clear to all we couldn't keep our hands off each other. We weren't particularly conventional characters, and were so demonstrably in love both inside and outside the house. We were, though, still the subject of interest and gossip from people in the film and fashion worlds. But we were mostly oblivious to anything other than being together. Well, maybe we did prance a bit, enjoying the attention. Diane had recently bought a country house in Connecticut that she called Cloudwalk. It was originally a tobacco farm that had been bought by Evangeline Johnson, of the J&J Johnsons, with the most elegant pool designed by Frank Lloyd Wright. She didn't want only a city life for her children or for herself. I had no conception of country life, and I was a little nervous when I went up for the first time to meet Alexander and Tatiana. I found every excuse that Saturday morning to avoid meeting the children, and I knew I was in another universe when I walked into the great room and four-year-old Tatiana bluntly asked me, "Who are your friends?" Eight months later, Diane bought a grand apartment at 1060 Fifth Avenue, and I moved in there. I moved into her life more than she moved into mine. I'd never exactly been poor, and I was now making a helluva lot more than a living wage, but Diane was selling twenty-five thousand dresses a week and was on the cover of *Newsweek*. She and her husband, Egon, had been on the cover of *New York* magazine the year before as the "it couple." She was European royalty by marriage, and while I wasn't exactly chopped liver, the relative contrasts of our lives were pretty extreme.

I had never had a sustained relationship before this. I was thirty-three years old, a deer caught in the headlights of a full-on romance, with no training or experience to cope with my teenage emotions. I would get inexplicably hurt by something Diane said or didn't say. This was stuff that adolescents, though it drives them emotionally berserk in the moment, learn to navigate with relative equanimity. Having not had what anyone would call a normal adolescence, I had no resources to cope with these wild swings. And I couldn't even begin to articulate my feelings. I often just froze, unable to thaw. I had so totally bottled things up my whole life into safe compartments of denial that I knew no way to work the levers when emotions couldn't be contained. While I was, on the surface, a mature man, I was a teenager emotionally.

We went on our first trip to Santo Domingo, where Gulf + Western owned a huge sugar plantation and had developed a luxe golf resort on the southeast coast called Casa de Campo. We had our first fight there. Whatever hurt it was that stung me I no longer remember, but I had to get away. I fled on my motorbike up into the rocky hills of the Dominican mountains and slowly unfroze as I dodged potholes along the unpaved road. Why was I so emotionally unprepared for intimacy? When I was eight years old, I had given up believing my mother could protect me from my brother or from my emerging sexual confusion. I became a "walker in the city," all on my own, not dependent upon anyone. Now my emotions were all over the place because an actual person was becoming important to me. I didn't just *want* her, I *needed* her, and that banged hard into my built-up self-protections. But all that receded as I drove back to the house, and found Diane standing in the driveway, instantly stitching me back together with her huge earth-mother heart.

On Diane's twenty-ninth birthday, New Year's Eve 1975, I got her twenty-nine diamonds. I didn't know what to wrap them in, so I put them in a Band-Aid box and gave it to her as we were walking into the surprise party I was throwing for her. With Loulou de la Falaise as my cohost, it was a fusion of the worlds we all inhabited: New York and Euro society, movie and fashion stars. On my birthday, February 2, she sent me this note:

> My darling: Today is your birthday and it makes me terribly nervous to think how I could make it so nice for you as you made it for me on my birthday . . . I want you to be me and me you . . . forever! I have my own life, and it is nice, you have your own and it is nice . . . but ours is and will be better, because we have each other to fall on, to rely on, and to breed! You are strong enough for me to be weak, and I am strong enough for you to be weak . . . Happy birthday . . . Diane the little one in your shadow!!
>
> P.S. Do I make you stronger?

On March 22, 1976, she appeared on the cover of *Newsweek* in a story that described our relationship in some detail, including this passage:

> Her nights are spent either working or making the rounds of film screenings with Barry Diller, Chairman of the Board of Paramount Pictures. At thirty-four, Diller is as much a boy wonder as von Fürstenberg is a superwoman. And singularly underwhelmed by her title, he refers to her as "her Lowness."

I even took Diane to the preview of one of my earliest Paramount films—*Won Ton Ton: The Dog Who Saved Hollywood*—one of the worst movies we ever made. I was in my second year, and the studio was still a disaster. Diane had become a superstar, and I was still flailing.

Even her Chinese butler told her, "He's going to get fired any moment!"

I'm not so sure the word "settled" should have ever been used in a sentence with me and Diane, but during many of those Paramount years, it seemed to apply. We were living in Diane's apartment, where we and the children were becoming our version of a nuclear family. I hadn't actually lived with anyone since leaving my childhood home. Even the word "lived" is a little off, as I hadn't been doing much living. I was inhabiting hotels and had few possessions of my own. For the first time, I entered an abode where I wasn't the first person to turn on the lights. Where when I came back at the end of the workday there was someone and something to greet me other than room service. I wasn't lonely or pathetic before because I was mostly careering, but now the fireplaces were lit, there were children's noises and birthdays to celebrate, and holidays with presents and all the family activities I'd never experienced in my parents' house.

When not in New York, Diane was selling her dresses worldwide, and I was much of the time at the studio in Hollywood—or we were traipsing around the globe together, pulled to this or that country for work or just escapades. We were once in Hong Kong on a Friday, where the construction boom was so booming that we had a headache from the noise, but had to stay over the weekend for a meeting on Monday. I said, "Can't we just get out of this place—go somewhere?" Diane knew Imelda Marcos, the wife of the Filipino president, so she picked up the hotel phone and . . . just called her. She invited us over to the Philippines, just like you'd ask a neighbor to come on by for dinner, and asked us to stay with her in the presidential palace, so off we went. Off we always went, cruising on friends' boats in the Mediterranean, flying to a party in Paris, skiing in St. Moritz or Aspen. Oh, the glamorous life. But the children were always with us on holidays, and I was getting to know them as actual people, and sometimes becoming something of a parent. Once, in Aspen at Christmas, we were having Chinese takeout for dinner. Alexander, then around nine, wanted to meet some friends down the hill. I said no, it was too late. He said he was going. I said not. A small matter, but our voices got higher, with him rejecting my authority and me realizing I actually needed to have some. Higher it went until he threw an egg roll at me and I responded with a volley of shrimp. It ended with us each drenched in soy and ginger sauce and laughing over who was the greater child. But they were beginning to bring me up in ways that I, in my previous louche life, could never have imagined.

I've lived for decades reading about Diane and me: about us being referred to as best friends rather than lovers. We weren't just friends. We aren't just friends. Plain and simple, it was an explosion of passion that kept up for years. And, yes, I also liked guys, but that was not a conflict with my love for Diane. I can't explain it to myself or to the world. It simply happened to both of us without motive or manipulation. In some cosmic way we were destined for each other. At that time the Europeans had a wiser attitude about this than us provincials. And today, sexual identities are much more fluid and natural, without all those rigidly defined lanes of the last century. I've always thought that you never really know about anyone else's relationships. But I do know about ours. It is the bedrock of my life. What others think sometimes irritates but mostly amuses us. We know, our family knows, and our friends know. The rest is blather.

On April 26, 1977, Studio 54 opened, and with it came the seeds that would end the first chapter of our romance.

On its first night, Diane and I went to a birthday party there for Bianca Jagger. We'd never heard of Studio 54. We got to the entrance on Fifty-Fourth Street, and there were hundreds of people in front. It was a genius level of chaos organized by Ian Schrager and Steve Rubell, who owned the place and were brilliantly using the birthday party as a means to get their new club off blazing.

We had gone to a pre-party at Halston's, and there were six of us in my car as we arrived. A path was cleared for the face-famous of our group, but by the time I got to the entrance, the doorman put up his big plank of a hand in front of my unfamous face and wouldn't let me in.

I said, pointing to the trailing figure of Diane, "I'm with them," but the hand pushed me back farther into the crowd. So I went to sit in the car, thinking that of course someone would quickly come and rescue me. Minutes passed. I sat and sulked and was about to drive off when a much smaller hand, that of Steve Rubell, the co-owner of the club, whom I'd never met, started pounding on the window. I lowered it to his fast-talking apology; he was horrified because this was his first big, important night, and here he had already offended the chairman of Paramount.

I went in with him to the bass-grinding beat of the music, and Bianca Jagger was atop a huge white horse being photographed by what seemed like every paparazzo on the planet.

Even without social media, that picture went around the world in all the newspapers. Studio 54 became the hottest nightclub ever. Each night there were thousands trying to get in, with Steve out front standing on a box and letting in only the famous and the unfamous-but-beautiful men and women who were hoping to change their status to famous.

This citadel of 1970s excess, celebrity, and sexual freedom became the place where everyone wanted to be.

We started going there all the time. With a group of friends, we'd begin at eleven or twelve at night at one of our places, drink, smoke, and whatever ("whatever" included marijuana and cocaine). I didn't take either, but I usually developed a contact high.

Properly stoked, we'd all head down to Studio 54, troop through that long lobby and be met by Steve, who always had a quaalude in his hand to palm to each of us. I wasn't abstaining from those. The club lasted only two and a half years before he and Ian were arrested for income tax evasion. But in that brief time it was the first stop for every notable person who came to New York and the regular habitat of people who either had made it or were pretty enough to think they would.

Everyone inside felt protected. It was a remarkable moment in time, before AIDS changed everything. The mix was far more intoxicating than any of the drugs consumed there, a carnival of people from the theater, film, arts, highish society, and royals, sprinkled with the young and the hot.

A big part of this swirl was the sexual freedom, both of the time and the place. Drugs of course pushed this, but more than the drugs it was the aura of Studio 54, the safety everyone felt inside its walls. It was as if we were cocooned in suspended animation, floating in a warming bath, and everything happening there was somehow safe and protected from any repercussions.

Unbelievably, my friends and I were there three or four nights a week until four or five in the morning, and then we would get up at eight a.m. and go to work. It was a good thing it all ended so quickly, otherwise none of us would have survived.

The heady life that Studio 54 represented was to have its consequences for everyone caught up in it, including Diane and me. The personal expression and extreme hedonistic behavior that so dominated the late 1970s were extraordinary for those of us who participated, and the group we belonged to in and around Studio 54 participated in the extreme. Given our behavior, perhaps we somehow sensed the auguries of what was to come in the 1980s, the death and disease, and wanted to make all the hay possible while the sun still shone.

Diane and I had now been together for almost five years. She was in her thirties, and she wanted to have another child. Our intense romance had evolved into our version of an everyday, ordinary couple. But the idea of a child meant, to me, settling down into a boring homebound family life, and I thought I was too young for that. I was afraid my fun life would become my not-so-fun life if we had a child together. I was enjoying too much an adolescence I'd never had. I kept imagining me driving a wood-paneled station wagon and living in the San Fernando Valley. And I couldn't get that image out of my mind.

I was finally very grown-up in my business life. Paramount had by then become the number one studio, but if I had a child, I thought I would have to grow up in every other possible way, and I willfully and selfishly didn't want to. Once my immaturity became clear to Diane, she began to move away from me emotionally, not that I noticed it at first, as our lives were going so fast. I didn't like the idea of slowing all that down into what I imagined would be suburban somnambulance. I was such a child.

We began to flirt with others, which further destabilized us. It didn't immediately drive us away from each other, because it was a time when everyone was flirting with everyone. But it was the momentary affair she had with Richard Gere and my overreaction to it that lit the spark that would separate us. He was in the middle of making *American Gigolo*, and the idea this was happening while he was working for me at Paramount made me feel too much the fool. I got angry and moved out of 1060 Fifth. We were unraveling, but I didn't and couldn't accept it. During the months that followed I tried so hard to save us, but I had lost the plot of it developing naturally with our own child and had no clue that my actions had irretrievably doomed our relationship. I flew back to New York from L.A. two or three times to be with her, knowing but not knowing, accepting but not accepting. I couldn't face it being over and couldn't do anything to stitch us back the way we were.

Toward the end, we were on a boat we had chartered, the *Julie Mother*, and Diane was reading Alvin Toffler's *Future Shock*. She was underlining passages in it with a fountain pen, in turquoise ink, and for some reason that really irritated me. She likes puzzles, and so we had some elaborate jigsaw puzzle on the table in the salon. When the boat was sailing, rocking in the waves, all the work we'd done putting the pieces together would wind up scattered on the deck. It seemed like an obvious metaphor for what was happening between us.

The only good that came of that trip is that we had to seek shelter from the wind and pulled into tiny Harbour Island in the Bahamas, which at that time was a mostly unknown, tranquil island with tutti-frutti houses, sixteen hundred people, seventeen churches, and a few ten-room hotels. We were its first serious intruders and over time brought others to discover it. In her last years, Diane's mother built a house and lived there, while the island became a glamorous and trendy getaway for the rich and celebrated.

Right after that trip, Diane flew to Switzerland to be with her mother, and when she came back, she asked me to have lunch at the Pool Room at the Four Seasons restaurant. I knew what was coming and dreaded it. She looked at me, very sensitively and lovingly, and said, "This is . . . This is over."

She wasn't going; she was gone.

My tears didn't dry up for six months.

Diane took the children and ran away to Bali, leaving New York, leaving her successful business, leaving Richard Gere. There she met a Brazilian man name Paulo, with whom she lived an alternative life on the beach—an elegant and well-furnished beach for sure—and she stayed there for several years.

It felt as if a part of me had been cleaved off. Each day, I thought I might be on the path to recovering if I could just make it to the bathroom in the morning without having the hurt and loss come rushing back.

At the lowest period, I drove through the streets of L.A.'s Venice, finally stopping when I reached the ocean. I pulled to the side and sat there staring at the boats passing out to sea from Marina del Rey. I was so deeply saddened by everything I'd pushed away. Fearful of becoming a father, and leading an adventure-less conformist life, I had ruined so much in pursuit of the adolescence I never had.

I looked out at all those boats gliding by. They looked like salvation to me, a lifeline out of my desolation. My historically protective biology took over, and a positive idea emerged: *Go get a boat.*

And the next week I did, my first adult one, a fifty-three-foot trawler. As I traveled back and forth to Catalina Island dozens of times, mostly alone, I began to put the few remaining pieces of my life together.

CHAPTER 12

My Paramount story took place over exactly ten years—September 1974 to September 1984. And from age thirty-two to forty-two. Those first two years were pathetic. I don't see things clearly until I've mucked around with all the moving parts and found a way for the gears to mesh. And, just like in a movie, at the lowest moment of my career, when it seemed the promise of my youthful success would be dashed in the ruins of Paramount—an incredible series of hits would come to rescue me. But it was much more likely that I'd be thrown out before they arrived.

There was no such thing as process at Paramount or anywhere else I could see in movieland. For the life of me I couldn't figure what rigor was employed to choose making this or that picture. It was all about what worked before, who was hot, and what the package was (meaning agents would put together all the elements and then put that "package" up for auction). It didn't make any sense to me. Everyone was hustling to get their picture made with whatever movie studio would say yes. It all seemed catch-as-catch-can: agents pitching, producers pitching, all of them selling against whatever you were doing in order to replace it with their own project.

The hits and misses of each studio had no theme, no center of gravity, nothing resembling a plan. It was all about staying under the maximum failure rate while waiting for that one movie to bat it out of the park. Every movie was a one-off, putting up your tent each time, taking it out to the public with all the puff you could puff out, then striking that tent until it was time to put the next one up. In so many ways it reminded me of a circus, and Paramount was the saddest clown there.

In television you were part of an economic cycle that needed product to sell to advertisers. If you didn't have a program at eight o'clock on Sundays, the screen would go dark. In the movie business, other than the distribution department banging on the production door to give it more product, there were no timetables or guideposts. The number of movies released by any studio varied from about fifteen to thirty a year, for no strategic reason other than internal rhythm.

I knew I'd fail if I tried to emulate the way things had always been done. I wasn't any kind of promoter and wasn't particularly good at the schmoozing that seemed necessary to grease everything along. If I couldn't come up with a system I believed in, an actual process that made sense to me, I'd sink.

At ABC I'd had a relatively small staff of very tried and tested people that I could touch and teach directly, while at Paramount I had two thousand under me and very few I trusted—most were just nattering away at me to get what they wanted, which wasn't at all what I needed.

The movies that came out during this period were just darts thrown at the board. I had to pitch and roll with whatever came my way. That made me a mark for every promoter and rascal in the film industry.

We made *Lipstick,* with Margaux Hemingway: a Dino De Laurentiis movie that was the essence of putting lipstick on a pig.

We made *The Tenant,* directed by and starring Roman Polanski: an odd, small film that had an even smaller audience.

We made *The Big Bus,* a parody of disaster movies that ended up just being a disaster.

We bought *Survive!,* about the survivors of a plane crash in the Andes, with Allan Carr producing. Allan was a blowhard version of a showman. I met him in the 1960s when he was Marlo Thomas's manager. After he had blustered his way into being a producer, he found this exploitative Mexican-made tale of cannibalism at high altitudes, and I thought it was a good concept. It was, and it made some money, but it was also embarrassing for the studio that had just made the *Godfather* films to release such a trashy movie.

In and around those we had a few successes, but they weren't without their own troubles. One was *Marathon Man*—the first and last time I had to be evacuated from a preview screening.

It was in San Francisco, and we ran a long cut, almost three hours. About half an hour or forty minutes in, the now-iconic and still horrific "Is it safe?" scene began—the scene in which the Nazi villain, played by Laurence Olivier, tortures Dustin Hoffman's character with dental instruments. It was about three times as long as it was in the final movie, and the audience wasn't prepared for such invasive violence to sweet Dustin's teeth. Dental work is particularly relatable, and with every question from Olivier—*Is it safe?*—followed by an ever-deeper plunge of his instruments into Dustin's mouth, the audience got more and more uncomfortable. It went on for what seemed like forever—*Is it safe? . . . Is it safe?*—and finally we lost the audience totally. They shouted and booed at what we were doing to them, and many charged up the aisles, enraged, as I fled to safety.

We ended 1976 with *King Kong*, the first remake of the 1933 original. During the year before it began filming, there were actually two versions of the movie in competing development. I spent months being harangued by Sid Sheinberg, the president of Universal, who owned the original film: he screamed repeatedly at me that we had no right to infringe on its property. The inimitable Dino De Laurentiis had brought it to us, saying he'd acquired the remake rights, but of course, being Dino, he really hadn't. Dino was the essence of the Italian impresario: great fun to be around, he would cook you spaghetti for breakfast at the start of most meetings, and he lived, as some small people are wont to do, an especially outsized life. Everything was large, even his furniture, and he loved red, so everything in his office was enormous *and* red. Although Dino spoke English, he had no nuance in his vocabulary. Many of his movies suffer from a basic misunderstanding of the rhythm, the tonality, the nuance of English. Nevertheless, he believed in the rightness of everything he said, and he controlled everything on his films.

One day Dino called and said, "I've found the actress to play Fay Wray. She's right now a model with no acting experience, but I'm sure she'll be a star."

I said, "A model who's never acted?"

He said, "Yes!"

I said, "Well, we should test her, right?"

He said, "Yes, but first I want to have her breasts augmented."

That was Jessica Lange. You'd never have imagined at that point that she'd go on to be such a superb actress, but Dino wanted her and that was that.

The movie wasn't particularly good, but it was big and it was brassily promoted.

Nothing much had changed in the fifty years of movie distribution: there were still thirty film-exchange centers that each studio maintained across the United States, and the distribution of film prints was a complicated jigsaw puzzle. I wanted to change this Pony Express method of distribution. I whittled our exchanges down to fewer than ten. FedEx had just been founded, and while the technology was still primitive, I knew lots of these analog processes were going to change. But innovation in Hollywood was mostly an accidental afterthought.

Here's one example: A young executive in the television syndication part of the company came into my office with a concern. Part of his job was to sell film and filmstrips to schools and for small-time syndication. Though profitable, it was a minuscule part of the operation—one that I barely paid any attention to. But this fellow came into my office and said, "I have seen the future and it's not film." And this was a guy who sold filmstrips!

I perked up and said, "What do you mean?"

He held up a bulky two-inch videotape cassette and said, "Eventually this thing that I'm holding is going to be a lot less cumbersome, and it's going to be the basis for a consumer business. It's going to be in every school, and it's going to annihilate our filmstrip business."

While I couldn't have cared less about his small-time filmstrip business, it occurred to me that if he was right—and if videocassette technology evolved and the cumbersome tapes then in use were to reduce in size to a more consumer-friendly cassette—movie distribution would also ultimately migrate to the home. If the consumer could be more in charge of what they saw and when they saw it, what a tectonic change that would be. But that first chance that technology might radicalize media was almost highjacked from the start.

It will probably amaze you to know that the actual recording and re-play of television programs became the subject of a Supreme Court deci-sion. In its arrogant and aggressive way, MCA tried to bludgeon through a theory that the very recording of its copyrighted television programs was illegal and that the new VCR devices that Sony introduced to do so should be outlawed. I thought it was an absurd position and told MCA we not only wouldn't support it, we would begin to sell video copies of our movies to consumers. MCA eventually lost when the Supreme Court ruled against it.

The home video recorder was the first of the technological advances that would take over the industry during the next forty years and even-tually end Hollywood's worldwide hegemony over entertainment. For the first hundred years of filmed entertainment, the five majors had never lost their primacy. They absorbed television, cassette recorders, compact discs, all forms of distribution; whatever disruption came their way, they bought or corralled it. It wasn't until the Netflix disruption, followed by Amazon and Apple, that their long period of total dominance ended. As did "movies" as we had known them. I've for sure got nothing against Big Tech and have made my (later) way by using screens as more than narra-tive forms, but I miss (and I think the culture misses) what was sometimes produced by those wonderful old ways when the major studios operated with such flair and flamboyance. Old folk always yearn for the "old days," but I don't know anyone today who's having any fun or earning much long-term profit in this new technologically dominated "movie" business. Algorithmic life can't be enjoyably led by anyone other than pure techno-crats, and it and its disciples are driving the lone creator with just *a good, pure, and instinctive idea to extinction.*

Around this same time, the cable industry was transforming itself: in-stead of simply delivering better video than local antennas, it was starting its own networks with original programming. Ted Turner owned a local television station in Atlanta called TBS and wanted to turn it into a cable

Me, costumed with horse

My mother and father in Yosemite

My brother, mother, and me in Lake Tahoe

The "walker in the city"

Unlikely Scouts, unlikely mother

The Danny Thomas family, plus Hedda Hopper, at the Coconut Grove

With Marlo Thomas

Photo by Ron Galella/Ron Galella Collection via Getty Images

In the stands of the Olympic Games in Munich, 1972

With Calvin Klein and Doug Cloutier in Malibu

With Diane von Fürstenberg in the Dominican Republic

On location for a hurricane in Tahiti, 1977

With Danny Thomas

Katharine Hepburn and Laurence Olivier
on the set of *Love Among the Ruins*, 1973

Studio 54 nights

Tatiana and Alexander von Fürstenberg, 1976

Premiere of *Grease* at the Loew's State Theatre

With Warren Beatty

Photo by Guy DeLort/WWD/Penske Media via Getty Images

With Adolph Zukor, the founder of Paramount (age 102), and Bob Evans

Attempting to shut down Diana Ross's Central Park
concert amid thunderstorms, 1983

With Martin Davis

Photo by Ron Galella/Ron Galella Collection via Getty Images

At my desk at Fox

Photo by Lynn Johnson

Outside a soundstage at Fox

Photo by Lynn Johnson

Sound mixing *SpaceCamp*, 1986
Photo by Lynn Johnson

At home in Beverly Hills, 1989

Photo by Annie Leibovitz

At the Waldorf Towers

Photo by Annie Leibovitz

With Rupert Murdoch

Photo by Ron Galella, Ltd./Ron Galella Collection via Getty Images

My father, 1991

David Geffen and Diane

Alexander, Diane,
and Tatiana

Diane and me racing each other while driving back to
New York from our Connecticut farm, 1977

Me, happy

With Edgar Bronfman and Herbert Allen

With Sumner Redstone

The Big Laugh

Sailing with Diane

Marriage at city hall, 2001

The IAC Frank Gehry building

The dog, Diane, and me in Jordan

With John Malone

Little Island under construction, 2016

Photo by Michael Grimm

Little Island

Photo by Michael Grimm

The Clones

Briefcase Diane gave me in 1976 (. . . still in use)

network. Turner had started to buy product for TBS, and he was frustrated because the studios wouldn't sell him anything but old reruns. The studios were rightly worried that the big-three networks would boycott them if they cooperated with competing networks like Turner's. Ted came out to L.A. and asked for a meeting. We had breakfast at my house, and before we even got to the food, he began pacing around my living room and ranting a shockingly anti-Semitic rap about what "the Jews in Hollywood" were doing to him. "They won't give me the product!" he yelled.

I'd never heard such talk and couldn't shout him down until he ran out of gas and slumped into a chair. At that point all I said was "Get out of my house."

I don't think Ted was or is anti-Semitic at his core. He was a stranger in a strange land, with instinctive southern prejudices. He was also a loudmouth who would say anything to make his point. Deep down he was really a humanist, and over the years I gained great respect for Ted as one of the media world's great characters and visionaries. He was funny, sizzle smart, and somewhat crazy, and with his solid journalistic values he built CNN into the first international twenty-four-hour news service. If only his good, humanist, and bombastic self were running it today.

As we were adapting to these seismic changes, I met many larger-than-life characters, most of whom were at the tail ends of their long careers.

Sam Spiegel was one of the greats of the movie business; he had won best-picture Oscars for *On the Waterfront, The Bridge on the River Kwai,* and *Lawrence of Arabia.* He was the consummate producer, taking enormous risks and controlling every minute aspect of his productions. He was also a connoisseur of everything—art, boats, wine—and particularly young women. He lived a luxurious life on a grand scale, and came to me with the idea of making a movie of F. Scott Fitzgerald's unfinished novel, *The Last Tycoon.* I liked the idea and I also loved getting to know the irrepressible Sam.

He was the essence of the rotund, cigar-chomping producer, but at the same time he was genuinely charming. That kind of bully and misogynist had to be charming, or he couldn't get away with his behavior. He was also a true satyr. He often said—and it was hard to know if he was joking—he only liked to have sex with virgins and, if he could find them, lesbian virgins.

Sam had an elegant boat, beautiful apartments in all the world capitals, and a fine art collection. He paid for all of that by often tacking their costs onto his movie budgets. He bought the *Malahne* inside the budget of *The African Queen* with the justification that it was shot on the water in Africa and he needed suitable accommodations for the shoot.

There's a great story about Sam Spiegel and Otto Preminger. At a train station, trying to get out of Germany before World War II, Otto said to Sam, "I have fifty thousand dollars and I'm terrified they might find it." Sam said, "Give it to me and if I get it across, we'll split it." After they crossed the border Otto asked Sam where the money was. Sam replied, "It's in your back pocket."

At one point in his career he worried that anti-Semitism was going to be a problem for him, so he officially changed his name from Sam Spiegel to S. P. Eagle. When that great mogul Darryl Zanuck heard that this was Spiegel's new name he wrote him a letter and signed it Z. A. Nuck.

In *The Last Tycoon,* we cast Robert De Niro, who was coming off *The Godfather Part II*. It also starred Tony Curtis, Robert Mitchum, Jack Nicholson, Donald Pleasence, and Jeanne Moreau and was directed by Elia Kazan with a script by Harold Pinter. What could go wrong?

Everything. I knew it wasn't going to work when I saw the first assemblage.

The rough cut? Various cuts? The finished film? It never found the right tone.

The Last Tycoon opened at the end of 1976, another commercial and financial failure. *Marathon Man* wasn't a huge success, either (although the line "Is it safe?" still scares the bejesus out of me).

King Kong made money, but given the hype, was a disappointment. And while I was trying to lay logical bricks to a sustainable business, I had to deal with the craziness of the industry itself, which entrusted millions of dollars to some of the most talented but nuttiest people on earth.

Elaine May had been making a film called *Mikey and Nicky*, with John Cassavetes and Peter Falk as a two-bit Philly mobster on the run and the friend who tries to save him. Frank Yablans had committed to it years before, but only because Elaine told him she would cast him in a starring part, and Yablans thought that would be a lark. But when Charlie heard that his president of Paramount was about to star in a movie, he refused to let him do it.

By the time I got to Paramount, the movie was long past shooting and had been in postproduction forever. I called Elaine and asked how she was coming along and when we could expect to see a cut.

Elaine said, "Well, I have problems with the sound, and I'm just going to need a little more time to get that right."

And I said, "Okay, fine."

A month or two later, I called her and said, "Hi, Elaine, are you ready to show me the movie?"

Again she said, "No, I can't because I can't sync the sound with the picture."

I'd never heard that one before.

Talking to Elaine was truly like going down the rabbit hole in *Alice in Wonderland*. Three, four, five months went by.

In exasperation I said, "Elaine, we're going to see this movie, so stop all these excuses."

Again she prevaricated, but this time I said, "I can't do this any longer. This film's been in the works for years, and you have to let us see where you are."

She said, "Well, now I can't show you the film, because we've taken it apart and the sound is on reels that still won't sync, so it won't make any sense."

I said, "Sense or no sense, we're going to see it."

Another few weeks passed and still no screening. In great frustration I called Elaine and said, "It's come to an end. Show us the film or we'll take over the production."

Bert Fields, the famous and fierce Beverly Hills litigator, got involved. Letters went back and forth, and finally we instructed the lab to seize the film. But when we went to get it, there was no film. It was simply not there. Fields and Elaine's agent, Sam Cohn, had devised a cleverly devious and circuitous route for transporting the film cans from one location to the other until the trail ran dry. No one could tell us where the film actually was.

We formally sued to get back what was legally our property. Notices went out demanding the film be returned.

After a few months of this insanity, an intermediary got Elaine and me on the phone directly. I said, "Elaine, can we stop this? You know in the end we'll prevail—the film can't stay missing forever."

"I honestly don't know where it is," she said, "but . . . I've been told that if you send a messenger to Eighty-First and Lexington, the film will be on the sidewalk."

We went to Eighty-First and Lexington, and lo and behold, there it was. To this day, I have no idea how or who got it there.

But she was right: the sound was not synced, and the movie absolutely made no sense.

People now think of *Mikey and Nicky* as one of the overlooked films of the seventies, something of a classic, but for me what made it classic was what I had to go through to get it finished.

I was learning that the movie business was only occasionally businesslike.

Sorcerer, a movie we coproduced and cofinanced with Universal, was another early nightmare, demonstrating the sheer perversity of some Hollywood luminaries. Based on the classic French thriller *The Wages of Fear,* our version was directed by Billy Friedkin, the very hot director of *The Exorcist* and *The French Connection.* It was a fairly simple concept: transporting nitroglycerin in a truck over mountainous roads without having it blow up. I never much liked the idea, but for all the wrong reasons went forward with it, largely because Friedkin agreed to shoot the whole movie in the Dominican Republic, where Gulf + Western had huge sugar operations. We could use trapped funds to help defray the cost. But because of Friedkin's (over)shooting schedule, it ended up costing double what we'd agreed. Finally it wrapped and I drove over to Universal to see the first cut. I thought it was endless and endlessly boring. Sid Sheinberg and I had arranged to meet Friedkin after the screening, and of course we were pretty depressed and unhappy that this very expensive film wasn't any good. Things only got worse when Friedkin walked in, dropped a tape recorder in the middle of the table, pushed the record button, and fairly snarled, "What would you like to tell me?" I nearly lost it. Instead, I said, "I have literally nothing to tell you," and got up and left.

Sid, however, stayed. Among many things he discussed with Friedkin was an interior scene in a hut—a bamboo thing like a tepee—with only two people. Sheinberg said, "I don't understand what they're saying. I actually can't hear it. Could you rerecord it?"

Friedkin said, "Absolutely, of course I can fix it. But we'll have to go to the Dominican Republic and reconstruct the set."

Sid said, "Excuse me, it's an interior scene; you can shoot it here on Stage Fifteen."

And Friedkin said, "Oh, no, no, no, we'll have to go back to the Dominican Republic, reconstruct the set, and it'll cost about a million dollars." With that snide response I didn't think there was any point in further discussion. We let him finish editing the film, we opened it, and it was a disaster.

The following year, we were going to show the film outside the United States. In a show of consummate prickdom, Friedkin went to the annual big distribution convention in London—one of those conclaves where distributors come from all over the world to see the upcoming films. He made a speech before the screening, saying, "Look, I failed, the movie's not a success, I want to do anything I can to help you. Anything you want to do with the movie—cut it, change it, call it something else—whatever you want, I'm here for you, because I feel a terrible responsibility for its failure in the United States."

In the audience was Danny Goldman, the head of our French distri-

bution company, who took Friedkin at his word and cut this walrus of a
movie down by a few minutes. Friedkin turned right around and sued
Paramount for violating his artist's rights in France.

I was beginning to think, *This can't go on much longer. This place is a train
wreck, and I'm the conductor.*

It was just about our lowest point. The finance people at Gulf + Western had even made a presentation saying that we should get out of the
movie business entirely. The return on capital was just too low for their
liking and the risks were too high. They thought we'd never master a
consistently profitable slate of movies.

I was besieged from every corner. From the media, from the community . . .

From Charlie.

If I hadn't been able to compartmentalize, I wouldn't have survived.
When all the dots are against you, the only way out is to *not* connect them.

I'd learned many times before that I tend to fail first before I succeed. I
need to make mistakes and then course-correct as fast as possible, one dumb
step to the next less dumb step.

After going through two senior production executives who were part
of the industry brigade, I abhorred the idea of trying again with someone
I hadn't worked with already. I didn't want to learn what someone had
done before, someone I'd interview for the job for a few brief hours and
then try to extrapolate from that to how we'd work together. It's a horrible process with a huge failure rate. Conversely, I had known and worked
for eight years beside Michael Eisner and just had to get him to join me at
Paramount.

Michael was now a senior executive at ABC, a big part of making it the
top network. But he was still a mid-level vice president and didn't have
much of a chance to get promoted. I asked him to become the president of
Paramount; that got his attention and he agreed to join me. He was just so
smart—ideas simply bounced out of him. He was capable of saying things
that were so ridiculous, and then, in the same breath, out would come

something absolutely brilliant. Individually, we were complete opposites; together we were an indomitable combination. He was brash and somewhat reckless with his ideas and enthusiasm. I was measured and endlessly logical and always wanted to be sure any risk was covered. And yet, while he would reference relatively obscure literary properties to emphasize the distinction between an educated, cultured person (him) and an uneducated barbarian (me), he actually was much more basely commercial than I was. He was also funny and we could laugh together, which is almost mandatory for me in any working relationship—even in the most dire discussions or ones of the highest frenzy, something much worse is wrong if you can't find a laugh somewhere.

I had become so fed up with the way Paramount operated that I began to pick people from the lower ranks who hadn't yet gotten inculcated into the egoistical methods of Yablans and Evans. I built up a group of young executives who understood my mantra: "What's the idea?" After that, they began to grasp how necessary it was to tear that idea up and down and yank it every way imaginable to find its essence, to see if it could survive such a tough Socratic process. If it could, we'd take the next step, and if not we'd abandon it.

That process applied to every aspect of what we began to do. How we conceived projects, how we developed the material, how we controlled it was how we differentiated ourselves from everyone else. We weren't interested in packages, already formed elements presented to us, with actors, director, and writers pre-identified. We wanted to control the idea itself and go from there. When the script that emerged was worthy, we would attach elements we deemed appropriate. Nothing and nobody was forced on us. This was essentially backward from the way movies were coming out of studios. We regularly held "encounter sessions" with our development executives, where we would go past exhaustion trying to eke out new ideas that we could then assign to writers. We shook down every step of the development process and controlled every element throughout production and release. We rarely gave final cut to anyone. Our way was different from the laissez-faire everyone else was doing, and it was much tougher for us to get major artists to work with us, so we were mostly left alone by the A-list community. But we were pure of heart and deeply committed to our way of developing material internally without distractions. It seemed so obvious to us, but was not in evidence elsewhere; *everything* was the idea, the story, the manuscript.

We also needed to change the relationship between those making the films and those responsible for marketing and distributing them. Historically, the distribution and marketing people complained that the movies were awful, while the production people complained that the movies were great, but the distribution people were screwing up their releases. The squabbling was exacerbated by the physical separation between production in L.A. and everything else in New York. I was often the beleaguered traffic cop arbitrating the daily disputes between them. I had to free both organizations from their sclerotic political past. I made it clear we wouldn't tolerate warfare between the coasts or any blame-gaming. I had always thought it was ruinous to allow politics to fester in an organization and I stamped it out whenever it appeared. All this grand tinkering was taking time we didn't have as the poor results of our early films cascaded around us.

In the early summer of 1977, I went upstairs and told Charlie Bluhdorn he really needed to think about replacing me.

I felt I had an obligation to give him an easy way out of this mess by resigning. As maddening as he was, as fiendishly difficult to deal with, I had grown so much in constant battles with such a supreme warrior. I admired him so much and so didn't want to disappoint him.

All through those early years at Paramount, while he endlessly criticized our lack of success, he never prevented me from changing almost everything in the company.

Sitting behind his delicate Louis XIV desk, in his gilded chair, so unlike the very indelicate person he was, Charlie let me go on about the abysmal current situation and why he ought to consider someone else. Usually I'd have to use every bit of my energy to keep up with his constant interruptions, but this time he just listened.

Then, when I finished, silence.

I had come to know that when Charlie was dead serious about something, his whole demeanor would change from unimaginable boisterousness to being still and pensive, speaking slowly and softly. Finally he quietly said, "I'm not replacing you, so stop this nonsense and go back downstairs and get back to work." Charlie wasn't ready to give up on me.

He couldn't accept his instincts about me were wrong. While he bellowed constantly, he'd never lost faith in me.

As that very desultory long summer wore on, I plowed through the last of the 1977 releases that were keeping us chained to the bottom.

And although I told Charlie he really ought to let me go, that I'd taken far too long to try to get it right, the working part of me knew in my bones that we now were properly organized, that the gears of our process were finally beginning to mesh. I was rock certain the movies we'd put in the works were of a whole different cloth from before. So I persevered.

I persevered because I knew that if we could get these movies to market, they'd succeed and show everyone that there was another way to run a successful studio.

And I persevered for Charlie.

CHAPTER 13

That fall season of 1977 was our Waterloo. We'd either break out or be broken.

One of the first projects we bought back in early 1975 was a novel called *Looking for Mr. Goodbar,* about a dedicated schoolteacher who spent her nights cruising bars and looking for sex. It wasn't exactly conventional material, but I never much liked conventional anything, and with the great director Richard Brooks attached, I wanted to make it. He had made wonderful films like *Cat on a Hot Tin Roof, Elmer Gantry,* and *In Cold Blood.*

When the final script came in, the unbelievably controlling Brooks made me come to his office to read it while he sat staring at me from six feet away. He then refused to deal with anyone at the company other than me. As a result I learned so much from him about the craft of big-time moviemaking. He was also the cheapest producer/director I've ever known, tough as the old shoe leather his face resembled.

I was so closely involved with this movie that I was the one who went to the review board to make sure we could get an R rating. The film was so sexual and violent we worried we'd get an X, which would have made it unreleasable. This was a crucial time for me. While I had growing confidence in what we'd been making over the last year, none of the films, including *Goodbar,* was thought to be commercial. They had no stars and no buzz. Our distribution department told me for months that exhibitors had no faith in us anymore and could no longer guarantee the best theaters. *Goodbar*'s controversial material made that even more difficult. But it was critically well received and a surprise success and gave us a few more whiffs of the fumes we'd been running on.

Then, two months later, we opened *Saturday Night Fever*. All of us inside the company loved the little movie we'd made, and with hubris we decided to preview it for the industry at the grand Chinese Theatre on Hollywood Boulevard thinking that if we were standing this tall behind it everyone would take notice. At five of eight, the place was practically empty. Our old-time head of publicity came over to where I was sitting and whispered in my ear, "Travolta's the problem; he's a television person. You don't put a television person in a movie. The kid just doesn't put asses in seats." Well, not old Hollywood asses. But two weeks later we opened the movie, and there were vast lines around the block at every theater across America. Television execs and a television star had broken into the movies. We were on our way. The next year, 1978, we went from last place to first among all the major studios. And we would stay number one for the next seven years. Miracle of miracles.

The most emotional moment for me, the most personal from those beleaguered Paramount beginnings, came after *Variety* headlined in big black type blazoned across its front page, SATURDAY NIGHT FEVER #1 IN 17TH WEEK.

A package arrived for me from the forty-second floor. Charlie Bluhdorn had the article encased in a silver frame. On it, he had handwritten the message "No one but no one deserves this more than you."

I still keep it close.

It was a shock surprise to the industry, this solid hit from nowhere, but it was emblematic of how we were changing how movies got made. Kevin McCormick, a young producer working for Robert Stigwood, saw Nik Cohn's *New York* magazine article "Tribal Rites of the New Saturday Night" and bought it. That article became the loose basis for *Saturday Night Fever*. We heard about it, thought it was simply a great and original concept, and started to develop it—no stars, no pedigree, no package, no nothing—just a *good idea*.

Dealing with Stigwood was a movie in itself. He was a British music impresario who'd worked with the Beatles and then the Bee Gees. He'd never made a movie, but had great instincts and was beyond a world-class promoter. In his early forties then, he was so pickled in alcohol he looked more like a lobster claw than any human being I've ever seen. He had that skinny, long, bright-red English face, and he lived a kind of grand life at a time when people were not really living grand lives. It wasn't good enough to rent a car in Los Angeles. He had his Rolls-Royce flown over.

I never thought Stigwood had any real sense of how to ground-produce anything, but he had the shrewdest instincts about talent and promotion. He was prickly and one of those people you wanted to talk to as early in the morning as possible. As the day wore on, particularly as the evening wore on, he was subject to late-night rages. He would drunkenly call me at ten p.m., eleven, midnight, and then two in the morning. We'd have these deranged conversations, and the more he went on, the more his anger and paranoia deepened. I finally banned him from calling me at night. But thank the gods he came to us, and thank the gods we took him in with all his excesses. Before he inserted himself into *Saturday Night Fever* it had nothing to do with the Bee Gees. As the film developed, its internal rhythm called out for a great music score, and right there was the intersection of the Bee Gees and John Travolta, and out came that historic disco dance scene, just like the uptown and upmarket ones I was separately experiencing at the just-opened Studio 54.

In their manufacturing, movies are such weird creatures. Each movie is its own separate industry, and they go through the alphabet of process from A to Z and then spin around again before winding up in a place that rarely is predictable. *Fever* was a particularly quirky movie: a good concept that became a better-than-good script without any central creative force animating it. There was no one person saying, "This is what this movie should be." It was a lot of kitchen helpers futzing around as it progressed from script to film.

I'm not sure where the original idea to cast John Travolta came from, but Michael Eisner and I knew him from his television series, *Welcome Back, Kotter*. All the distribution and marketing people threw up their hands and said, "John Travolta? From television? Hopeless."

Added to that, first we hired the director of *Rocky*, John Avildsen, and then fired him, replacing him with a mostly untried TV director, John Badham. All these Frankenstein-like parts came together while all those around us thought we were amateurs. It was heady stuff, and quite a shock to the naysayers.

Travolta became a superstar within a week of the release. When Princess Margaret came to visit L.A., I was seated next to her at a dinner. With nothing much else to say, I asked her whom she'd like to meet.

She said, "I want to meet John Travolta. Ask him to tea."

So I called up Travolta. He didn't know who Princess Margaret was. I explained she was the sister of the queen of England, and John said, "Sure, have her come over."

I said, "No, no, no, she's at the Beverly Wilshire hotel, and you have to go *to* her and have tea."

He said, "I'm not going to her. I don't do tea!"

Finally I said, "John, just go."

So Travolta went to the Beverly Wilshire, and when he came back, he said, "She hit on me!"

Robert Stigwood had signed Travolta to a three-picture deal, and we had shot *Grease* in the late summer of 1977, before *Saturday Night Fever* came out. It was a pretty shoddy production all the way through. Everything looked crummy, including the grass, which was supposed to be bright and green and was mostly patchy brown. Many of the shots didn't match. The pace was uneven. Travolta's instant fame created a dilemma for us, because after seeing the first rough cut, shortly after *Fever* had become a smash, we thought *Grease* was going to be a disaster. *Fever* was of the moment and *Grease* was a throwback bit of goofball nostalgia. We'd been geniuses in creating a superstar, and now we were about to be the dopes who killed his career in the very same year.

We screened the first rough cut at my house. Eisner was there, and I'd invited Bob Evans to join us because he was such a genius at postproduction. It was like watching a train wreck. The music and sound, on the prerecorded tracks, without full orchestrations, sounded cheap and tinny. After the lights came up, Evans said, "You have to junk it. This picture is un-releasable."

Everything was wrong. Evans was almost twirling around my screening room, saying, "You are going to ruin everything you built with him in *Saturday Night Fever*. Burn it!"

Bob was married to the former Miss America Phyllis George at the time, and for some reason she sat in their car in my driveway while all this was going on. Maybe she had come to pick up Bob, but she ended up sitting in that car for two hours. I remember going out and apologizing to her as we kept talking about what to do. Bob couldn't have cared less.

They divorced later that year.

John Travolta was getting to be a bigger star every week because of *Fever*; he had just received an Oscar nomination for the movie.

I knew *Grease* was bad, but also knew we couldn't abandon it. Our distribution and marketing people were now so stoked on Travolta that they'd set it up as next summer's big release. We were very, very worried, and had big fights with Stigwood because we insisted on reshooting some of the worst stuff. None of the other people involved seemed to have an inkling that the movie was so bad.

We reshot and recut what we could, but were so nervous that we secretly went to Hawaii to preview it. We were petrified that advance word would get out.

"Summer Nights" is the first number—Travolta on the bleachers next to the high school football field with his friends. He gets up and duckwalks down the steps, the beginning of a music cue, and the entire audience started to laugh.

We all groaned, "Oh no," because that was the best number in the movie.

But as "Summer Nights" went on, the laughter started to fade. After about three-quarters of that first song, which seemed to last an hour, you could actually feel the audience move into the groove, laughing with it rather than at it, and it built from there.

The energy changed totally, the audience was charmed and that carried exuberantly through the whole movie. Moments that made me cringe in screenings got huge laughs. And by the end, it was clear they loved it! It wasn't a screening-room film; it needed a big, noisy audience to enjoy it for what it was: a campy, silly, entertaining movie musical.

Grease opened, and everyone loved it. Period. It was a smash.

Everyone started telling me how great it was, and I'm sure I always had a look of bemusement on my face. I still thought it was embarrassingly sloppy moviemaking, but the younger the people, the greater they thought it was. What a summer that year of '78 was—we premiered *Grease* at the State Theatre on Broadway and had a joyous party at Studio 54, which was at the height of being the best nightclub in the world.

I was excited when, one day at the end of that summer, Robert Stigwood called and said, "I have our next Travolta project."

I quickly sobered after reading the script for *Moment by Moment*. I knew Stigwood had no sense of humor; otherwise I would have thought, *Well, he's just ragging me.* It was truly one of the worst scripts I'd ever read.

I called him and said, "Robert, you can't do this. You cannot have John in a hot tub with Lily Tomlin. It's just . . . You *cannot* do this. You think this is good? It's impossibly bad."

Michael Eisner and some other people at Paramount read it, and we spent days banging it around: "What are we going to do? We can't *not* make this. How can we turn down Travolta coming off *Grease*?"

But in the end, we did just that. We just couldn't underwrite this terrible idea.

I called Stigwood and said, "I know you're not going to believe this— we pass."

He was thrilled. He took it right to Universal and they said yes in ten minutes. I thought, *If I'm wrong on this one, they're going to crucify me.* But by then, we were in the euphoria of our remarkable turnaround. In addition to *Goodbar*, *Fever*, and *Grease*, we had two blockbusters: *Foul*

Play with Goldie Hawn and *Heaven Can Wait* with the masterful Warren Beatty. It turned out a year later that *Moment by Moment* didn't improve from the script stage. A bunch of very talented people made a really bad movie. It happens.

Even when things started to turn around, Paramount wasn't the easiest place for filmmakers to work; the conditions elsewhere were much less controlling than they were with us. My training stipulated that we had to be involved in every detail. At best, this management style created a productive tension between the studio executives and the talent that made the movie. I abhor the popular concept that filmmakers should be left alone to do their work. There are very few who do not benefit from a more objective opinion; whether they appreciate or acknowledge it is beside the point. This has nothing to do with my respect for the artists. When people get up onstage during awards season and thank executives for "leaving them alone to make their art," I gag. Movies are the greatest example of collaboration. And creative tension is productive; Kate Hepburn said, "Show me a quiet, happy set and I'll show you a boring movie." Yes, there are a few, very few, artists who can unilaterally keep the whole equation in their head and need no external vetting. And yes, there are a lot of dopes in the executive ranks. But good and talented executives should not abrogate their responsibilities because artists denigrate them as obstreperous and talentless "suits." Movies have become a directors' medium, while television has always been a producers' and writers' medium. Because of that, I really do think the quality of television is on average far better than the quality of movies.

There were a few cases, though, where the auteur concept held for us: we believed movies to be this odd compilation of dozens of tasks; depending upon our assessment for each individual movie, it was our role to supervise putting all those tasks into a workable stream. When we had a unique talent like Steven Spielberg, we could leave him alone to make and deliver us a film. But with many others we would engage and approve the key elements and wouldn't be afraid to step in at any time if things weren't going well. Most other studios had more of an absentee approach. Many of the talented filmmakers who had their first big successes at Paramount chose to make their next movie, or the one after that, at another studio. Our process was just much tougher and more demanding than elsewhere.

Turning down *Moment by Moment* was an obvious example; we were dubbed insane for not making it. But our narrow approach—that the material was all—gave us a blueprint for how Paramount should function.

I never wanted us to be rough, I always loathed arrogance, and I worked hard to be sure that our success didn't let that creep into our culture. But we were tough-minded about creative decision-making. I was proud we had a point of view and articulated it: sometimes it was smart, sometimes it wasn't, but in moviemaking, since "nobody knows anything," a balance of power is the best way to manage the messy process.

I also recognized that sometimes we went over the line and overreached. Other times, like letting the director keep his yellow grass on *Grease,* we didn't push hard enough. But on balance we were probably the only studio at the time that functioned on the belief we had ultimate editorial responsibility for our product.

We wouldn't put out a movie like Oliver Stone's *JFK*—which essentially said that Lyndon Johnson killed JFK—and then just shrug off that kind of recklessness by saying, "Oh, well, we let the filmmakers do what they want; we're not responsible."

Soon after we turned down *Moment by Moment,* we thought we'd found the perfect film for Travolta: *American Gigolo.* John thought so, too, and agreed to star. But about a month before the cameras rolled, John went to Michael Eisner and told him he was grief-stricken over the death of his mother as well as Diana Hyland, his girlfriend, who had recently died of cancer at age forty-one.

He slumped down in a chair in Michael's office, started to cry, and said, "I can't do *American Gigolo.* I'm too sad. I'm still in mourning. It's the wrong thing for me to do. You have to let me out of it."

Michael came down to my office and said, "John's just left, and we have to let him out of the movie because he just can't do it."

I said, "He's faking it and using you. It's too late to recast and he's perfect for it."

Michael said to me, "You have no empathy."

I replied, "You're just being conned."

Now, John Travolta's a good actor, and I was certain he had acted his way through his meeting with Michael. I believed he no longer wanted to do *Gigolo*. He was afraid of playing that character because of its somewhat gay subtext. For days, I said, "I'm not even going to hear of letting him out of the movie, full stop, period."

Then John came to my house one afternoon. I began by saying, "Right now, you are the biggest star in the world, and you worry you're going to screw it up. You're listening to this twerpy, inexperienced manager of yours, and it's leading you to the wrong decisions. This is a critical time for you, and when you've got a great script and a great part, you don't let anything put you off it." I went on with various examples of how his management had been mishandling things since his spurt to superstardom.

I don't think we even specifically discussed *Gigolo*, because my position was unchanged: he was going to do the movie or not be able to work elsewhere.

I felt very proprietary about him. After those two movies for us, how could I not? And I sincerely believed he should be the gigolo.

He left with a pained and hurt look. A day or two later it became clear that he was not going to show up for the first day of shooting and would take whatever consequences ensued. I had made the situation worse because he'd told his manager about my criticism of him, so they both hated me.

It was too late for further arguments, and I'd handled it badly, so I folded and we floundered around until we found Richard Gere, coming off his breakout debut in our film *Looking for Mr. Goodbar*.

Gigolo made him a star, and for extra good measure he would go on to break up my relationship with Diane.

Warren Beatty was by now a superstar, and my friend, but we hadn't ever worked together.

I knew he was making *Heaven Can Wait,* a remake of *Here Comes Mr. Jordan,* with Warner Brothers. I also knew he was having trouble with Frank Wells, the president of the studio, because the costs of the movie kept escalating. Wells was driving Warren crazy with the expenses he was charging to the production. He even told Warren he would have to pay personally for the water in the watercooler. As they got into preproduction, Warren hated the atmosphere so much he wanted to move to another studio, and Wells had grown to feel pretty much the same way. Warren called me and said, "What if I could get you my movie?" I said, "Great, send me the script," which, with Warren, was always the beginning of a topsy-turvy ride. He has an extraordinarily interesting mind; his point of view on almost anything will surprise you. He's a wondrously wonderful talent and a total control freak; he said I could read it if he was in the room with me. Warren never ever wanted to be rejected, something that's hard to pull off in a business where you are constantly being judged. He would do absolutely anything to put you in a position where you wanted something more than he needed you to want it.

In this case, Warren had been trying to get Frank Wells to believe the best course of action would be to just leave him alone and let him make his movie. But Wells was a rigid lawyer, and Warren's normal manipulations didn't work. He did, however, succeed in getting Wells so fed up that Frank basically said to him, "You know what? If you don't like it here, take it somewhere else." The timing had gotten a little too tight for Warren to play his usual games with me, which is the only reason I got to read the script before having to commit to the film.

I read it in an hour, and of course I loved it beyond love. I said, "We'll do it!" He and I made the deal on the phone in five minutes, but I thought, *It's never going to happen; he'll go back to Warners because it isn't officially in "turnaround,"* meaning the studio hadn't legally let it go. I was fairly certain Warren would never accept a formal, signed piece of paper that said he and his film were being rejected.

But a week later he said, "I'm free. I'm out." He turned the watercooler expense into a grand *bouffe* and insulted Frank Wells in such a manner that Frank just wanted him to go away.

A project with Warren Beatty, with hits like *Bonnie and Clyde* and *Shampoo,* was like striking it rich for a company that wasn't prized for taking on big stars and big movies.

Originally, the film was going to star Muhammad Ali, and the main character was going to be a boxer rather than a football player. Warren had also hoped to bring Cary Grant out of retirement to play the part that had been played by Claude Rains in the original. By the time it came to us, it was Warren starring with his current girlfriend, Julie Christie.

The shoot was a dream.

Meanwhile, our marketing department had come up with a classic poster: a picture of Warren in heaven, wearing a sweat suit with gorgeous flowing wings on his back. It was the perfect image and communicated instantly what the movie was about. There was a struggle over whether it would have a single or a shared director credit. Warren wanted the credit shared with Buck Henry, even though Warren actually directed the entire movie. For whatever reason, probably insecurity, he didn't want to be judged strictly on his own for this film.

Warren and company had made a perfect movie and we were as euphoric as audiences would soon be when it opened.

Foul Play, starring Chevy Chase and Goldie Hawn, had Michael Eisner's smarts all over it. I thought the movie was ordinary comedy fodder, not unlike a lot of current television series, and was really surprised when audiences ate it up like perfectly buttered popcorn.

We thought Chevy, who had just left *Saturday Night Live,* could be a movie star. Given our own television backgrounds, we were much more savvy than other studios about taking people from TV and putting them in films. No one but us would have made the Cheech and Chong doper movie.

Then we'd switch to more artistic pursuits. What a beautiful thing *Days of Heaven* was, a lyrically told and photographically dazzling movie by the complete auteur Terrence Malick. After its success, he told me he'd like to start right away on his next one. Four minutes later, he was still talking, and I had no idea what he was talking about. He could have talked for an hour, and I still would have had no idea. I mean, he was speaking English, but it was gibberish to my ear.

He said, "I need a lot of time to shoot and just experiment with things."

I said, "Okay. How much money will you need, do you think?"

He said, "I think about five hundred thousand dollars."

I was hugely supportive and said, "Okay." Every four or five months, we'd talk on the phone, and I'd ask him how it was going, and he'd just say, "I'm making progress."

Terry would occasionally call and say, "I've got this idea to follow a paraplegic in New Mexico in a footrace."

And I stayed encouraging. "Oh, good, good, good." For years. Literally five years! Finally I said to him, "You know, it's embarrassing when we have our meeting and the production staff goes through all our active projects, and then they come to 'Untitled Terrence Malick' and they look at me and say, 'What's it about?' And I say, 'I can't tell you, not because I don't want to or it's a secret—because I don't have any idea.'"

Every time I asked if there was a script, some footage to see, *something*, he'd say, "Not yet, not yet."

Finally, I told him, "I've got to bring this to some conclusion. You have to give us material to look at or at least tell us you know where you are."

The calls became less and less frequent. Finally, I gave him an end date and said if we didn't have any clear next step, any progress, we'd have to stop. The date passed. And our project stopped without any further conversation. It would be twenty years before he directed another movie.

But, by god, *Days of Heaven* was a gorgeous thing.

Everyone who had previously discounted us now thought we were geniuses. We were definitely on a roll, but we'd also get rolled every so often.

Our first big movie of 1979 was Walter Hill's *The Warriors*, a violent film that got big audiences in its first weeks, but actually sparked outbreaks of violence in a few theaters. The media covered it, and then there were copycat incidents from gangs spurred on by the gang mayhem in the movie. Against the producers' wishes, we pulled the release and abandoned the film. Everyone yelled at us, but the violence around the theaters was growing, and we didn't want to be responsible for its escalation.

I then had the displeasure of going into a jail cell, for the first and last time (one hopes). We were shooting Clint Eastwood's *Escape from Alcatraz*, one of the rare times Eastwood strayed from his home studio, Warner Brothers. My friend David Geffen was briefly head of production, and when he'd seen Eastwood's latest rough cut, he thought, *Well, I'm a movie executive and we're supposed to give notes*. So he very reasonably called Clint up and said, "I have some notes."

And Clint said to him, "Notes? Fine—you can give them to me while I'm packing."

That's how we got Clint's next film.

I went on location to Alcatraz Island to watch a day's filming. Eastwood told me I should experience a few minutes inside a solitary-confinement cell. That was one of the longest conversations we had. The total number of words exchanged between us from the start of production to the release of the movie was probably between thirty-six and fifty-two. It was a perfectly proper but distant and cold experience.

I called Clint after the movie was successfully released and said, "That was just great. What can we do next?"

There was a long pause. I guess I had deluded myself into thinking that we had built a relationship.

Clint said, "I'll let you know."

He returned to Warner. I never heard from him, and that was that for the next forty years.

I was now thirty-seven years old, never had a checkbook, never went to college, never used an ATM, never experienced many other aspects of normal life. Yet my instincts for choosing material and making creative decisions seemed to counterbalance my inability to actually relate to humans. As the 1970s turned into the 1980s, our little band of brothers and sisters—yes, we were earlier than most in bringing women into the senior ranks—kept chugging along, with more successful movies all across the cultural spectrum.

We picked up (meaning we didn't produce it; someone else had financed it, in this case Canada, and brought it to us to distribute) an irreverent comedy called *Meatballs*. It was Bill Murray's first starring role, as a deadpan camp counselor, and it was another smash.

Our successes were becoming ridiculously expected. There was a sense we could do no wrong. But when we first thought of making a movie out of the *Star Trek* series, which had ended ten years previously and had a relatively small audience, no one in Hollywood could believe that such great geniuses would try to take a middling, long-ago-canceled TV series and turn it into an actual movie.

Our self-described "shiny-ass accountant," Art Barron, Paramount's chief financial officer, was obsessed with resurrecting *Star Trek*. Ever since I arrived at Paramount, every once in a while, shyly, given his purely financial position, Art would say to us, "We ought to do something with *Star Trek*."

And every time he brought it up, we ignored him. We thought it'd be ridiculous to make a movie of that clunky old show.

Around that time, I began to think about starting a fourth television network. While Paramount had become very successful making TV series and had five of the top ten shows on the air, I had come to believe the three national networks had lost their individual personalities and were just dull.

Over time, the distinct images of the three networks had blended together. Initially, CBS had been Tiffany, NBC was live "specials" and color, and ABC was the shoot-from-the-hip network that would try anything. ABC had become number one, and as the other two tried to compete, the programming for all three networks had grown very similar. I'd always been a contrarian counterprogrammer and believed this opened the opportunity to start a brand-new independent network and began to scope out how to get it launched.

Our intrepid chief accountant turned show barker again suggested we ought to revive *Star Trek* as our first series. We found out that there actually were lots of die-hard fans of the show and that would at least give us a known quantity to promote.

We were going to call it the Paramount Television Service, and thought it would cost us $30 or $40 million to get it up. We developed the financial plans, and were ready to present the idea to Gulf + Western for approval, but with a recession on, many of its businesses had begun to falter, and the finance people put a freeze on making any new investments.

Paramount was so successful that I'm sure I could have pressed it with Charlie, but he was under such vicious scrutiny from the SEC for all sorts of supposed corporate infractions and I didn't want to burden him further. We shelved the idea, thinking we'd revive it when the economy and Gulf + Western's conditions improved.

But the idea of doing something with *Star Trek* gained momentum. If not a television series then maybe a new movie. The moment we announced it, there was a huge positive public reaction.

We had done no blockbuster moviemaking with presold titles, but I knew this was going to be an expensive project, so we went out and got huge guarantees from exhibitors for a Christmas 1979 opening.

Now all we had to do was make it.

Robert Wise, the director of *The Sound of Music* and *West Side Story*, joined on and we hired Doug Trumbull, the biggest special-effects person of the era. This was all before digital effects had matured, and before we shot a single scene we went through $7 million in abandoned effects. It all looked cheesy and so did our second and third iterations.

We didn't have a finished script when we began principal photography. But we had to start because we had to deliver for Christmas or lose our guarantees. I now had no faith that the movie would be any good. I just wanted it to open and break even and get out with our lives. I had gotten so concerned that I thought we needed to assign one person from our staff to do nothing but make sure the movie was delivered on time. We absolutely could not default on getting these huge guarantees.

Jeffrey Katzenberg, a very junior member of the production staff, was chosen for the task: he was wildly energetic, and I knew he would go through walls to get the movie finished. Jeff had no other job for about a year and had to endure our constant hectoring about the poor footage we were seeing—the visual effects that were in no way visually effective— and about the budget, which kept growing like a stinking weed. I told Jeff, "I don't care what you have to do; I don't care what it looks like; just deliver it."

Jeffrey was like a hummingbird. Compact and wiry with the work intensity of a beaver on speed, he started as my assistant, hired because I thought he was sparky and enthusiastic. He was the super-assistant of all time—he furnished our house in the Dominican Republic in three days, he got me diamonds for Diane's birthday, he ran New Year's Eve parties for me—whatever he did, he did with gale-force intensity. He was also irritating in his zealotry to run interference for someone who liked interfering—me. I had to get him out of my office just to keep peace with all the executives who resented his ambition, so I put him in the marketing department, hoping it would round off his roughest edges. Soon we moved him out to the studio in L.A. to get some production experience, which he sure did, eventually running Disney's movie operation, founding DreamWorks, and becoming the most ferocious political fundraiser of the age.

With prints still wet from the lab, *Star Trek* opened on Christmas Day. By noon there were lines around the block at every theater it was playing in across the country. Jeff had recently bought a small house on Carmelita Avenue in Beverly Hills. The next day I had a truck pull up to the driveway and dump $25,000 in pennies on his front lawn as our thanks for saving us.

He called me up and said, "You destroyed my lawn!" But he was very proud of those pennies.

CHAPTER 14

We'd been the number one studio now for several years and keeping us there was a constant slog. Thankfully, every once in a while we got a jolt of failure to keep us bouncing. We made a big movie of the dancer Vaslav Nijinsky's life, which unfortunately had no life.

On the opposite side of the ledger was *Friday the 13th*. As soon as I heard the title and concept, I said, "I don't need to know any more, just make it!" It was a huge hit, but I've always had an aversion to horror movies, so never actually saw it. I once got scared out of my suit seeing *The Exorcist* at the home of Motown's founder, Berry Gordy. He had about twenty people over, and while everyone else loved it, there was such shrieking and screaming that I ran into the other room. Richard Pryor followed me in and said, "Hey, pussy, can't you take it?" I couldn't.

On the silly side of things, we made *Airplane!*, one of those rare instances when the dailies proved prophetic. No one deserved to have as good a time as we did watching those dailies. Howls were heard from the projection room every day for the month it was shooting.

We ended 1980 in hot competition for the Best Picture Academy Award. Two of the five nominations were ours: *Ordinary People* and *The Elephant Man*. Robert Redford had brought *Ordinary People* to us when it was in script development. Redford wasn't going to be in it, and it was a pretty dour story of a troubled family, but he wanted it to be the first film he directed. He had been so upset with me over our advertising for *Three Days of the Condor* that I'm pretty sure we weren't the first place he'd taken it to. But I adored the script and had confidence he could pull it off.

We had a policy of paying first-time directors the minimum Directors Guild fee, which was about $60,000. When the film was finished, I was so knocked out by it that, before it opened, I wrote a note to Redford saying that he wasn't a first-time novice but an A-list director and enclosed a check for $750,000, which was what A-list directors were paid at the time. Redford never replied, and did go on to win his very deserved Academy Award for directing.

For a truly out-of-body experience, there was *Popeye*.

Robert Evans was deep into his cocaine period, and you can see when you watch the movie today that every single person was glassy-eyed stoned. There's so much false energy that you'd have thought we shot it at 33⅓ rpm and released it at 78 rpm. Jane and Michael Eisner and I were in Europe for a meeting with our international distribution company, and since the production was nearby in Malta, we thought we ought to go visit.

They'd built an elaborate Popeye's village there, and when we walked down into the harbor, it dawned on us that everyone in our made-up village—and I mean everyone!—was completely coked out.

Keep in mind we were making *Popeye* in a coproduction deal with Disney—whose only concept of *coke* was the drink sold at Disneyland.

Card Walker was the very reserved and taciturn CEO of Disney. He was the steward of Walt Disney's legacy, and all they were doing was copying what had been done by their founder. They were known to run from anything controversial.

I had become friendly with Card when I helped bring Disney back into the powerful trade group the Motion Picture Association of America. The studio had shunned the MPAA for decades, after Mr. Disney lost trust in his fellow moguls. He had insulated his completely independent operation from the rest of Hollywood, but after he died the studio lost its creativity.

Paramount had been so successful that one day Card called and asked me to lunch. He wanted to find out how we had organized things so successfully. I suggested that a good way to learn was to coproduce a few movies with us. He heartily agreed, and off we went to find suitable material.

Popeye seemed perfect—on paper that is. Superstar Robin Williams in his first leading film role, the great Robert Altman as director, and Evans producing. But a more addled set and movie couldn't be found.

I was embarrassed by how awful this movie turned out and what a box office flop it was. *Dragonslayer,* another coproduction, while not a fiasco, wasn't much better. I felt so bad because Disney had faith in us to help them out of the creative rut they'd been in. Instead, we just made it worse.

I called Card Walker and said apologetically, "Twice and out. We just can't take your money anymore."

By the late 1970s, cocaine had become the recreational drug of choice of many in Hollywood and New York. I'd never taken it given my general fear of hard drugs. Quaaludes, yes, like candy. But I hadn't even smoked weed in fifteen years, since the bad experience I had when I was twenty-two.

I still had a driver in New York named Mario. Sweet Mario was kind and gracious; everyone loved him for good reason—and, it turned out, for other reasons, too. While driving me from the front seat of the car, he had his own business going on in the trunk. It was only after I left Paramount and gave him up as my driver that a friend told me what had been going on behind my dim back. Apparently, Mario had been one of the prime cocaine dealers in New York, particularly to all my friends. I always wondered why they insisted that Mario drop me off first after our nights out. Once I left, Mario would open his trunk and deal out the drugs.

I was furious with all those New York high-society folk who never told me: they had put me in serious danger without a second thought. They all thought it was funny that I was so clueless, but if Mario was caught, who would have ever believed I knew nothing about it?

Michael Eisner and I fought about whether to make *Raiders of the Lost Ark* for more than a month. We weren't George Lucas's first or second choice for the project, but after several other studios passed—I presume due to the potential costs and the extravagant asks of Lucas's representatives after his epoch-making success with *Star Wars* a few years before—we were given the script to read. After the first twenty or so pages, where Indiana Jones gets chased down the mountain by a giant rock, I thought the opening segment alone would cost more than any movie we'd ever made. I told Eisner that this was going to cost dangerously high money and that, together with the toughest terms ever asked for by the creators of a movie, it was much too risky for us. But he persisted. I did like the script—it was perfect from the first word—and I had confidence that Steven Spielberg would shoot it brilliantly, despite (or maybe because of) the fact that his last film, *1941*, was such a disaster.

Michael and I negotiated with each other tortuously on every detail before we engaged with Lucas's representatives. Michael was right to win the risk argument and take on the movie, but I did make certain that if it was successful, we wouldn't be in the position of Fox, which had only a one-picture license from *Star Wars*. I insisted we had the right to make sequels on the same terms as the original, given that the terms on the original were so much higher than anyone else had ever received. I wanted to retch once, and then not have to regurgitate in a new negotiation if the film was a success. And I wanted it in the clearest, most unambiguous language that all the parties agreed to and understood; there would be no new negotiating if George Lucas wanted to do a sequel. After the squabbling, all was settled and off they went to make the movie, and miracle of miracles, they made it on budget and on schedule.

Some months later, we were invited to a screening at the old Sam Goldwyn studio. We had agreed that they could make the film without our involvement, so our first viewing wasn't the early rough cuts we were used to, but the fully finished film. Michael and I and a few other Paramount executives sat in a lonely row of seats in a four-hundred-seat theater. After the rollicking prologue, it was cheers and thrills to the end. It was, and deserved to be, as joyous a first screening as ever could be. And the film, of course, was a great smash.

Two years later, they were ready to make the sequel. And, despite all my contractual reassurances and guarantees, I was told that George wanted to change the terms. He wanted more. I was enraged. We had made such a big deal out of *never* having to be put in this position, and yet that was exactly what was happening. I couldn't believe it, and thought, *Well, maybe this is just the lawyers out on their own for more money.* I called George and said, "Can this be happening?"

He responded with cold clarity: "It just isn't really worth it for me to spend time on this for the current deal."

"This deal, the most generous in history, isn't worth it?" I asked.

He repeated, "No, not really."

I said, "But you made a legal and moral commitment to honor these sequel terms. Here you are, someone who doesn't live in Hollywood because you loudly decry the amoral atmosphere of the company town, and then you blithely renege on an agreement made in good faith."

He replied, "Yeah, well, it's just not worth it for me unless I get more money."

I wrote him a very long letter laying out all the arguments and ending with a plea for him to honor his agreement, but I never received a reply. And of course we renegotiated and made the sequel.

The only scene in *Raiders* I never watched—I closed my eyes tight—was the snake scene. I have a deep aversion to snakes and cannot watch one, much less hundreds. But that experience with George tested my aversion to cynicism. I hadn't expected to find that the Hollywood-bashing, take-the-high-ground George Lucas was actually a sanctimonious, though supremely talented . . . hypocrite.

There were no two movies further apart on the artistic spectrum than *Mommie Dearest* and *Reds.* I didn't pay much attention to the Joan Crawford film while it was in the works, thinking it was just an easily promotable idea: a famous movie star who treats her child abominably. I never read the script or watched dailies, but I was told it was a very unhappy set. So, when I finally saw the first cut, I was unprepared for such a truly awful yet wonderfully fun-to-watch movie. You really can't make one of those laugh-at movies with intent. Everyone involved thought they were making an intense drama, without irony or humor. The movie opened to awful reviews, but it developed something of a cult following; audiences screamed in laughter at Faye Dunaway as Joan Crawford madly destroying the despised wire hangers in her daughter's closet and chewing up the screen. Our marketing department had great fun with it, taking out full-page ads bannered with NO WIRE HANGERS—EVER! AND THE BIGGEST MOTHER OF THEM ALL.

We were the only company that really had fun with our marketing.

Reds was one of the rare times I got Charlie Bluhdorn directly involved with a Paramount film.

Warren Beatty had been working on *Reds* for a long time, as was typical for Warren—endless talk and talk and talk and rewrites upon rewrites. At one point, I was invited to read the script, which for Warren was tantamount to agreeing to appear naked in Times Square. It was a dense and complex love story against the background of the Russian Revolution; the lead character, John Reed, was the only American to have ever been buried in the Kremlin wall. It had great historical sweep and great ambition and I very much wanted to support it, but explained to Warren, "This is a sympathetic film about a communist, and while you may think it's amusing for a capitalist company to do this, I work for a protocapitalist, Charles Bluhdorn. I don't talk to Charlie about decisions to make a movie or not make a movie, but for this one I have to. I can't put Gulf + Western in a position of being taken by surprise by the controversy this film will cause." We were still very much in the Cold War with the Soviet Union (it would be ten more years before it would collapse). When the idea was put to Bluhdorn, he surprised us by saying that of course Gulf + Western would support the movie. He said the greatest thing about America is its tolerance, even encouragement, of open discussion on any subject.

We started to get into preproduction, and the budget was high, even at the beginning. We didn't expect high costs in cast and talent. But then Warren said, "I have to have Jack Nicholson play Eugene O'Neill, and Jack has to have a million dollars."

I said, "I'm not paying Jack Nicholson a million dollars to do four scenes." But, not for the last time on *Reds*, I got so worn down by Warren that I folded, and of course Nicholson was worth it.

The shoot was endless. Diane Keaton paid the biggest emotional price for that. By then, her romantic relationship with Warren was over in her mind, but not in his. That couldn't have been easy. And the way Warren works is exhausting. He is not a confident or consistent decision-maker; he's subject to constant self-revision.

And just as Diane and Warren had a different understanding of their relationship, we thought we had a mostly completed script to begin shooting, but in Warren's mind we didn't.

When you start like that, you don't need much more to go off the rails.

It was all incredibly slow and incredibly draining on the cast and crew.

But that was Warren's way, just as it had been on *Heaven Can Wait*. The difference was that *Heaven* had a locked script, which they faithfully shot. With *Reds*, Warren was constantly rewriting, even as we started shooting. By the end of the first week, we were already a month behind schedule.

To make it worse for me, nobody else at Paramount really liked *Reds* or thought we should be financing such an expensive movie on such a controversial subject.

It all got completely out of hand. Not only was the picture way over budget, but there was no end in sight. We didn't even know what location was next up. Running out of pages to shoot, it would shut down for a month or so, then move somewhere else in the world. An average shooting schedule at that time was around sixty days. *Reds* went on for almost a year. There were something like 160 shoot days. In today's terms, the picture would probably have cost more than $300 million.

Eventually, I had no choice: I had to tell Warren that this production had to come under some kind of discipline and control. We had awful fights about it over the phone at what would be the end of his day and the beginning of mine. He wanted to do what he wanted to do, and I kept saying, "We can't." It was a classic out-of-control movie, and I was unable to get it back under control. I was frustrated, and I took my frustration out on the only person I could, which was Warren, and he did the same with me.

We drove each other crazy until finally, out of complete frustration and desperation, I said to him, "I never want to speak to you again for the rest of my life," and hung up the phone. The filming finally ended, and I didn't speak to my old friend again for six months. What I did do, though, was find a way to protect our astronomical investment in *Reds*.

There were no completion bonds at that time, where you got someone to guarantee a film's budget, but I did find a kind of insurance for *Reds*. There were tax-shelter arrangements you could make on movies that were shot in Europe. They were pioneered by John Heyman, who had been a famous agent in the 1950s and 1960s, representing people like Elizabeth Taylor and Richard Burton. He then became a producer. We had made *Divorce His/Divorce Hers* together with Burton and Taylor at ABC. When I started at Paramount, Heyman wanted me to buy an already completed film biography of Josip Tito, the unifier and dictator of Yugoslavia, called *The Battle of Sutjeska*, which starred Burton. He said, "You have to go see this movie."

I said, "I'm never going to buy it, John. Please don't make me."

He said, "I got the Yugoslavian government to put up all this money and I just have to have somebody like the head of a movie company at least come and see it."

So I flew to gray and dreary Belgrade and sat in a cement-block screening room, where they said, "We very much want to show you the film, but we haven't been able to marry the film and audio track together, so we'll show you some footage without sound and then go into another room to hear some of the soundtrack." I thought this was insane, but there I was. I had no choice but to spend the next three hours first watching and then hearing this mess of a movie. I was fuming, but I had John Heyman's everlasting gratitude. He told me he thought my visit kept him from being assassinated by the government for wasting a fortune on this fiasco.

Anyway, Heyman made a deal to tax-shelter a series of movies for Paramount. I insisted *Reds* be one of the films in that package, because if you would ever want to shelter anything, it would be *Reds*. It turned out

that the tax-shelter deal was in British pounds. We always had a conservative position on currency, and we hedged so that we wouldn't bear risk if
the pound went down and it was devalued.

But the pound skyrocketed over that two-year period, and when we
closed out our position, we'd made about $32 million on the hedge. Which
was exactly the cost of *Reds*.

Of course, I didn't tell anybody; god forbid I should let Warren know
that his movie was financially safe.

When I finally saw the rough cut, at around five hours, I turned into
a large mush of love for what I thought was a magnificent film. We ended
up with a running time of three and a half hours and released it with an
intermission. We even had reserved seating. You couldn't present a movie
more prestigiously. The poster featured Warren and Diane embracing at
the train station and came in for criticism because both of their faces were
obscured, but that was by absolute design. It was probably not the savvi-
est marketing decision, but if you had seen the movie, that particular shot
went right to your heart. It was the art and essence of *Reds*. Unfortunately,
in retrospect, it was one of those perfect images that make you want to see
a movie a second time, but not the first.

When the film finally opened, we got the most outstanding reviews,
but not great box office results. We were nominated for twelve Academy
Awards, but David Puttnam, the head of Columbia, had his own competing film, *Chariots of Fire*, and he went all out publicly denigrating *Reds* as
an out-of-control spendthrift production that took jobs away from Hollywood. That clever and craven campaign did us in.

Using the test of time, *Reds* is one of those films that will be remembered forever as a great work of art. And Warren is one of my closest
friends to this day. I will always treasure the "Pro" (the perfect nickname
Jack Nicholson had for Warren).

As the 1980s progressed, technology began to finally thrust its way into
the movie business. We had made a terrific movie, *An Officer and a Gentleman*. Usually a film like that would stay in theaters week after week over
the summer. We thought it'd be an interesting experiment to release the
videocassette of the movie while it was still in theaters. We'd see what

effect it had on the box office and get a sense of how big a public market videotapes might have. Not only did we sell a ton of videos, but the box office actually went up, and off we went as the studio to establish a new multibillion-dollar market. It was rare when technology disrupted the movies, but when it happened, it did so with a roar. First sound, then color. Then nothing, for about fifty years, until this moment when consumers were able to get direct access to the films they wanted to see. These were titanic shake-ups that the Hollywood majors absorbed and eventually controlled. But today, in the final throes of what I believe is the end of Hollywood as we know it, the revolution in streaming has ended that hegemony; all is now controlled and dominated by the tech overlords. That mighty roar of the lion of MGM is now a whimper, a vassal to the retailer Amazon.

Flashdance opened in the spring of 1983. There never was such a thing as "flashdancing." The whole idea was made up, a complete piece of Don Simpson blather. Don was a complex character. He had been our very successful head of production, and we knew that he played as hard as he worked. But one day, at lunch in the Paramount commissary, he was so whacked on drugs that he literally—and I do mean literally!—fell face-first in his soup. That scared us, for the danger both to himself and to the company. Our solution was to take the pressure off him and promote Jeffrey Katzenberg into that position, and have Simpson recuperate as a house producer. Over the next years Simpson went on to be one of the great producers—*Top Gun*, *Beverly Hills Cop*—interrupted by many drug rehabilitations, and a final overdose that ended in his early death.

Staying Alive was the only movie I ever made at Paramount solely because Charlie Bluhdorn wanted me to. It was a sequel to *Saturday Night Fever*, and it was horrible.

Of course, Charlie had loved the first movie, and about an hour after it opened, he already wanted a sequel: the story of what happened to Tony Manero once he crossed the river. Four years had passed since *Fever*, and still no one thought this was anything but a bad idea. Nevertheless, Charlie wouldn't get off this dim sequel horse and I placated him by arranging a meeting with Travolta at the Hôtel Byblos in Saint-Tropez. Charlie romped around the room, trying to talk John into doing it. It was, of course, a stupid thing for John to agree to, but he was overwhelmed by Charlie, and he uttered an incautious yes. For no connected reason Charlie then met with Sylvester Stallone. He immediately called me and said, "I have a great coup! Stallone is going to direct the movie."

Fed up with this Charlie foolishness, I fairly exploded. "This is the worst idea I've ever heard in my life. Sylvester Stallone is not light on his feet—he doesn't know anything about dance, and he has the sensitivity of an ox. This is crazy."

The whole thing was a fool's errand from the beginning. The first danger sign was that Stallone did not like Travolta's slender build, and made John go to the gym every day for two hours with a trainer to bulk up. The next thing I heard was that Stallone did not like hair on Travolta's body, so he made him shave or wax every square inch from neck to foot until he turned John into some kind of oiled, greased Narcissus.

In the script, John was going to lead the dance chorus of a Broadway show and be the choreographer. Stallone thought being a choreographer was the same thing as being the coach for a sports team. I watched the dailies dumbfounded. Stallone had John standing there with a whistle around his neck, holding a clipboard.

It was a horrendous movie, just awful. Not as bad as *Moment by Moment*, the Travolta-Tomlin unlikeliest romance ever made, but horrible just the same.

Looking back on those golden years at Paramount, when practically everything we touched succeeded, I wasn't able to enjoy it as a whole, to live in it rather than just plow through it. Living in the moment, whether high or low, has always been hard for me. I didn't comprehend how we'd changed the entire movie business, or our effect on the culture of the mid-1970s through the mid-1980s. In each of those seven years where we were number one in both movies and television, I was constantly worrying, never fully appreciating just how remarkable an organization we'd become. Robert Woodruff, who controlled Coca-Cola during its great post–World War II growth, said "the world belongs to the discontented." To me that's the greatest single explanation for those who succeed greatly, but it isn't exactly the definition of a happily contented human.

Other than a very few of Charlie's actual interactions with Paramount's business, I had complete sovereignty over the entire company. No one else in the giant conglomerate that was Gulf + Western was allowed to have any involvement in its wholly owned studio. I reported only and directly to Charlie. And while we always had a combustible relationship, he knew I would never lie to him. I always had his best interests at heart and was protective of him. My loyalty was absolute. While it wasn't ever relaxing to be with him, because he was either ferocious or sleeping, I was always there whenever he needed me. He was lonely because he didn't much trust anyone else in the company. But he trusted me unconditionally, and I trusted him equally in return. What I didn't know, what no one outside his family knew, was that Charlie was sick. He was battling leukemia. I was oblivious to the little signs. Over a weekend his hairstyle suddenly and radically changed; he'd gotten a wig to hide the hair loss from chemotherapy. I did not see him get weaker. It must have required superhuman effort to avoid showing anyone what he was going through.

A few months before he died, we were together in San Francisco. Charlie was in the Presidential Suite at the Fairmont hotel, and I was in the suite directly underneath him. We started having what was to be a long and sensitive phone conversation. At several points I said, "Why don't I just come up and see you instead of talking like this?" Very firmly, he said, "No, let's just keep talking," which I thought was weird. It didn't occur to me that he didn't want me to see him wigless or in whatever poor shape he was in.

On that call, Charlie spoke for the first time about the Gulf + Western corporation and his lack of anyone to rely on there. He said he needed someone to trust now more than ever and that he wanted to put me on the board.

I was speechless. Nobody from any of the individual companies Gulf + Western owned was on the board, nor were any of the most senior corporate people. The board was entirely composed of outside directors.

It was probably better that the hotel ceiling separated us. I didn't want him to see that I had tears in my eyes. I didn't know what it stemmed from, but I could hear the vulnerability in his voice when he quietly pleaded with me to keep our conversation secret until after the New Year, when he'd want me beside him at board meetings. It more than touched me that this business-busting titan wanted me to help him, to protect him as he felt more isolated and alone.

We never spoke about it again.

Paramount had been so successful for so long making movies and television shows that I was getting a little bored with all that extremely bountiful bread and butter. Mike Nichols called with a Broadway opportunity. He wanted us to finance his production of *My One and Only*, with songs by George and Ira Gershwin, a book by the veteran Broadway writer Peter Stone, and starring Tommy Tune and Twiggy. I thought it was a great project and would be a learning experience in an arena I had been drawn to since I was eleven and fell in awesome love watching Mary Martin on the L.A. stage in *Peter Pan*. And what an experience it turned out to be. If I'd thought the movie business was an everyday roller coaster, I was about to discover one without any guardrails whatsoever.

The original director was a critical and artistic darling named Peter Sellars, known for his adventurous work on obscure plays and even more obscure operas.

With great anticipation, a group of us went to Boston for the first preview. The house of eighteen hundred was filled with theater lovers who liked nothing more than getting the first glimpse of a big Broadway show.

After three hours, half of them left.

At three and a half hours, we lost most of the rest. And when the curtain finally came down after four hours and twenty minutes, we producers outnumbered the audience. It was a legendary disaster.

We closed the show, fired Sellars, and started over in a workshop with Tommy Tune directing.

It was a flimsy book at best, a silly story that depended on the great music of the Gershwins, Tune's choreography, and the chemistry of the long-limbed Twiggy and Tommy onstage. But we had a terrible time trying to mix this brew into something coherent.

When we finally got out of workshop and onto the preview stage, it was shorter, but even less satisfying. Back we went into workshop. I said that this couldn't go on. We were already the most expensive show ever; we had to either set a firm opening date or abandon ship. No one wanted to let it go, so we announced an opening four weeks later. After the first week of still-messy previews, we were even more desperate and hired the now-legendary Michael Bennett to save the show. Since our brief romance ten years earlier and the giant success of *A Chorus Line,* he'd directed *Dreamgirls* and was considered the reigning genius of Broadway. What we didn't know was that he was sick, using all kinds of drugs to ward off the effects of AIDS. Three weeks out from opening, the drug-addled Michael ordered all the costumes in the second act replaced. He got the act up, and it was so dissonant and so far from what the rest of the show was that we knew he had to go. We were valiantly trying to save the show, while Michael was far more valiantly trying to save his life. Firing him was the Broadway way of doing things, everything for the show, but it was shallowly done and I've always regretted it, just as I regretted not having this dazzling creature in my life all those years after our fevered early romance.

As for *My One and Only*, a miracle, the kind that only seems to happen in theater, happened to us. In the last weeks, Mike and Tommy somehow pulled together all those elements that never fit before and created a seamless, joyous theatrical experience. The music and the dance, and Tommy's and Twiggy's performances, made everything sizzle and click. The show now had style and polish, and with three days to go, we froze it; finally, two years after we started, we opened to a thunderous reaction from all those pros in the audience who had been happily deriding us while we were teething our way through to the finish.

We gave a dinner for all the principals at Mr. Chow, and before I went over, I stopped at the New York Times Building to pick up the early edition of the next day's paper with our review. I waited in the lobby until the side door opened and got the first copy, literally hot off the press. It was a total rave! I danced over to Mr. Chow, where I stood and read it to our little band, who hadn't breathed anything but anxious breaths for so long. The show won Tonys and ran for two years.

If you crave the highest highs and the lowest lows in entertainment life, there ain't nothing like Broadway.

Meanwhile, the very foundations of Paramount were about to shake. We had two great marketers at the company in charge of all our campaigns over the last seven years, Gordon Weaver and Steve Rose. They did more to modernize how movies were promoted and advertised than anyone else in the entire business and were deeply respected in and out of the studio.

One day our CFO, Art Barron, came in with this staggering news: "It appears that our two lead marketing people have been stealing from us."

The illustrious pair had been receiving both hard and soft bribes from almost every vendor we had. They'd been doing it for years. I can't describe my anger over our senior-most executives breaking our trust. Of course, I knew we'd terminate them, but the question was, do we also inform the police of their crimes or try to bury them in the time-honored manner of Hollywood? This is where I found a principle that is bedrock for me. *The clock starts ticking the moment you're made aware of the incident.* From that second, you're responsible for actions taken (or not), as well as the consequences of those actions. Until that moment, you're really not responsible, presuming you have no culpability in the transgression itself. But after that clock starts to tick, every move you make is a reflection of your ethical standards. Despite a few of my colleagues' wanting to find a softer way to handle this, I knew we had no choice. I authorized removing them from the building immediately and informed them we were going to turn the matter over to the district attorney.

In an attempt to stave us off, Gordon Weaver, the person whom I'd faithfully supported over the years, told our CFO that if we informed the DA, he "wanted it clearly understood" that his eleven-year-old son was going to say that Barry Diller had molested him in an elevator. I was beyond shocked by this betrayal and unhesitatingly instructed our lawyers to give all our evidence to the authorities. In April 1990, Weaver was indicted for conspiracy and filing false tax returns. He ultimately pleaded guilty. A further irony is that Weaver, who was married, soon came out as gay himself. It was hard to believe that this person I was so fond of and thought so highly of could commit such thievery. It was morally reprehensible and personally unforgivable to me that someone who was gay and knew its particular vulnerabilities would himself threaten to make such an ugly accusation.

Shortly after this abominable episode I went to the Dominican Republic to celebrate the opening of one of Charlie's Mad King projects. I hoped it would bring him great happiness—which it did—but it was also the last time I saw him alive.

After Charlie had spent thirty-four years building up Gulf + Western, it owned dozens of companies with twenty-one separate business units and one hundred thousand employees. It was one of the most valuable companies in the world, and Charlie Bluhdorn had become one of the world's greatest industrialists. He didn't have his own country, but he came pretty damn close. Charlie had bought a company called South Puerto Rico Sugar in 1967 and had been adding millions of acres to its holdings, which now included 10 percent of the land in the Dominican Republic. It had become one of the largest sugar refineries in the world.

Sugar was the Dominican Republic's most important export and the bulwark of its economy. Charlie had also become the biggest sugar trader in the world. He had convinced the Dominican government that they should pool their sugar with his and let him trade it all.

He singularly moved and manipulated that market for years. There wasn't a day that he wasn't trading huge amounts of sugar; for a few years sugar was the largest profit center in G + W.

He was more powerful in the Dominican Republic than its president.

One day, as he was driving through the brush on a hill above the Chavón River, he got the idea to build an arts colony so that Dominican artists would have a place to create and show their work. He imagined something, in his words, like Saint-Paul de Vence, a charming medieval village in France. But, like with all things Charlie, it got way out of hand. He grandly called it Altos de Chavón, and hired Roberto Coppa, an Italian set decorator he met through Dino De Laurentiis, to take this French classic and turn it into a faux Italian village that made absolutely no economic or artistic sense.

The dirt began flying and stones were laid, and about five years later, at a cost of many millions, in this poor country there stood this fairly deserted, unbelievably opulent oasis, with broad plazas, shops, apartments, and an amphitheater that could seat five thousand people.

Meanwhile, we at Paramount had started to produce a series of concerts for Showtime. We were trying to find a unique location and concept for Frank Sinatra. I thought how great it would be if we set it up in Charlie's otherwise deserted amphitheater. We called it Concert for the Americas.

The date was set for August 20, 1982.

I was staying at Charlie's gargantuan compound, Casa Grande. It had a great room that could seat two hundred and guest cottages strewn about the property. The concert was to start at eight thirty that night. Around seven, I banged on the door to Charlie's bedroom, where he was napping. He groggily opened it and I said, "Please get up. I want to show you something." He grumbled, but I got him out the door.

I had secretly arranged for the helicopter that was doing the opening shot for the show to be parked a few feet from Charlie's house. The planned opening sequence for the show was to have a helicopter fly up the Chavón River and then sweep up to the Altos Amphitheater, which was on the ridgeline three hundred feet above the water. It would then dive down to the floor of the amphitheater as Sinatra walked out on the stage.

My present to Charlie was to surprise him with a preview of the sequence. As we got in the helicopter, Charlie complained that his sleep was more important than tooling around in the sky, but slowly, as we took off and began flying up the mouth of the river, with the sun beginning to fade, the drama of it all swept over him.

Charlie so loved what he had built at Altos de Chavón and was in awe of what we were creating for its inauguration. We flew up and over the amphitheater, already packed with thousands of the country's great and good people, and Charlie began to weep. He told me I had given him a deeply profound experience, and seeing him so happy made me cry along with him.

It was one of Sinatra's best performances. Charlie was glowing at the party afterward. He embraced me close, and whispered how grateful he was for this night he'd remember for what was to be the very short rest of his life.

Charlie died a few months later in the Dominican Republic—the country he more or less adopted—in the house he built and loved.

I was skiing in Aspen, when at five a.m. the phone rang in the downstairs kitchen of the duplex condominium where I was staying. I stumbled down to answer it, and the houseman at my Beverly Hills home said that Martin Davis was urgently trying to reach me. Davis, an executive VP of Gulf + Western, was Charlie's longtime fixer.

I immediately thought, *Oh god, something terrible must have happened.* I didn't want to face whatever it was without a coffee and a cigarette, so I delayed calling him back.

When I did, and with no preamble, his first words to me were "Charlie's dead."

His next words were "When can you get to New York?"

CHAPTER 15

Diane had left me, and now Charlie had, too. Diane and I were living separate lives, and while we saw each other rarely, she was never completely out of touch. She was living between Bali and Paris, and I was still commuting between New York and Los Angeles. Somehow, without prompting and by a kind of cosmic alchemy, we would reach out to each other at critical moments in each of our lives.

Diane sent this letter to me after Charlie died, dated Sunday, February 20, 1983:

Dear Barry:

I felt so strange last night, so unable to express myself and so unable to help you! More than anyone, I know what this sudden death of Charlie means to you. I know how much you respected him and how much you loved him. He was good to you, because he knew you, because he trusted you, respected you, and most of all loved you. You were what his son could never be.

That is the reason I said that the only thing you can do is make sure that his work and his life gets followed through! I didn't mean that you should take over, but I certainly think that you should help through the transition and make sure that whoever takes over does it the way Charlie would have wanted it.

I love you Barry, I am very sad also because I know what you feel . . . I wish I could do something . . . all I can say is I'm sharing your sorrow!

Always, Diane xxx

Through the early 1980s, my career was spinning higher as I was also spinning through various relationships that never really worked out for equally various reasons. They really weren't relationships in any conventional sense, more like crushes turned into friendships with occasional benefits. And almost all of them were shadowed and worse by the AIDS epidemic.

One of the oddest was with Johnny Carson's stepson. Tim was the son of Joanna Carson, Johnny's next-to-last wife. Johnny and I had a difficult beginning. When I first got to Paramount, one of the stranger deals the company had was with Carson. He was midway through his astoundingly long and successful hosting of *The Tonight Show,* and Frank Yablans had signed him to develop other programming. But when I got there, the deal was already two years old and not one thing had been put into development; we were paying him huge amounts for no work. I went to see him, and he told me that he didn't want to get paid for doing nothing, and I left with great respect for what a fair-minded person he was. We stopped paying him, and he promptly sued us. As the years passed I'd see him socially, and we would laugh about the earlier disagreement. And then we started playing together in a monthly poker game that went on for twenty years and we became good friends. That was some poker game—Johnny, Carl Reiner, Steve Martin, Neil Simon, the flamboyant and elegant producer Dan Melnick, and me. It wasn't a serious game—given the players, it was more a comedy fest—and no one lost or gained much money, but we laughed and ate through the proverbial roof.

Tim was a young actor and writer who wanted his sexuality hidden, especially from his mother and Johnny. Ours was something of a high school romance, very intense and fraught, varying between acceptance and denial. It ended without much of a whimper from either of us. The dichotomy in our lives—he was a beginning actor and I was a big-shot head of a studio—made it problematic. During our relationship, I'd see the Carsons at some dinner or whatever and then come home to Tim in my bed. We hadn't seen each other for a year or so when I learned Tim had died of AIDS.

He'd kept his diagnosis a secret as long as he could. His mother refused to accept the fact that he had the disease and insisted it never be mentioned. I had two other close friends with whom I'd had relationships who also would succumb to this dread disease. Like the others, both were never high romance, more like fond hangouts, but both Don Richards and Steve Sager were very much in my life in those years. They both died in their thirties before the drugs came on line that would have saved them. I hadn't seen Steve in a while; he'd moved to North Carolina for work. One day he called to say that he wasn't well and wanted to come back to L.A. I went to pick him up at the airport. This wonderfully energetic and up-for-anything, adventurous young man came off the plane in a wheelchair. I took him to my house, and he lived there until he died just a few months later.

I had another close friend whom I went to see at Roosevelt Hospital in New York; he'd been battling the disease for two years and was in the final stages. It was beyond wrenching to see him for what I thought would be our last visit. But, instead of what happened to dear Steve and Don, the fates were with him; he was given an early trial drug that saved him. Thirty-five years later he's growing into the old man so many others deserved to be. How wonderfully random for him and how awfully random for so many others.

Until 1984 I wasn't much involved in the crisis. After that, I did lead many charitable initiatives and started a group that helped destigmatize the disease in the Hollywood community. I wasn't in the forefront of the battle, though; I should have paid more attention from the beginning. I was shamed for this by several of the protest groups railing against inaction and deserved it, though once I did understand the level of the crisis, I gave and raised great amounts of money to help the afflicted and further the search for a cure. As the number of those stricken with AIDS went up, it did begin to dawn on me that even though I was low risk, I too might not be able to dodge this bullet. I recently saw a startling picture of myself, taken by Patrick McMullan at an *Interview* magazine party at the Limelight nightclub in 1983, where I looked frightened and dissolute. Around that time I was at my doctor's office for a checkup and routine blood testing. He asked if he should screen me for AIDS, and I somewhat nonchalantly said "Sure." He said he could have the results by Monday. That was on a Thursday afternoon. By Thursday night, I was insane with fear.

As the hours went by, I was consumed by the realization that somewhere there was a vial of my blood that was not in my possession, and out of my control. With that blood's analysis, my life and destiny could be changed in an instant. It didn't matter that what was or wasn't present in the vial could not be changed by any actions of mine. I simply couldn't take the threat that a death sentence might soon be coming my way, and it made me close to crazy. I urgently called my doctor, who had apparently gotten on a plane to Central America and was unreachable. By the next day I was consumed with terror.

It was not just that I might have AIDS, it was that something could completely alter my life and was completely out of my control. That never-ending issue, that desire for control, affects and often infects everything around me. I've always thought that I could talk myself out of any bad situation. I called his office again and said I just had to reach him. The next day with some irritation he called me, and, close to hysteria, I said, "I'm sorry but I can't bear this. I need to know exactly where my blood test is right now and I need it destroyed. Will you please promise me that you will call now and make certain it never gets analyzed? You have to do this, or I won't be able to breathe." I was that crazy and didn't care that my ever-patient doctor knew it.

That kind of thinking—pure denial—had governed a lot of my life. As I was growing up, I had much to deny, and I had various strategies to keep it that way, and now this was another new way to bury my head in the sand. My doctor said, "If it's that important to you, I'll do it." The fear of this disease that I'd surely been bottling up was now bursting through as I demanded he destroy the possible prophecy of my demise.

A year later, he said to me, "I didn't do it—the test was negative." Oh, those terrible times.

———————

As the years passed, my parents and I developed a fond but somewhat distant relationship. We still never talked about anything personal or substantial. My mother played tennis and my father swam and golfed through their sixties and early seventies. They, too, loved the water and spent months on cruise ships all over the world. We'd have lunch every month at their club and, with longish pauses, chat amiably for an hour or so. We never spoke of anything other than superficialities—the guard was never lowered to anything emotionally intimate, not ever. Oh yes, they were certainly proud of my success, but from a respectful distance. While it was unvoiced, I always felt their affection, but no, we never discussed any aspect of my personal life. Just like when I was in my teens there were no questions about where I was going, who was I seeing. I always thought "Don't ask, don't tell" was invented by my family.

While my mother was always more than thoughtful and kind to me once I left home, I stopped depending on her at seven that summer at camp, and I could never find a way back.

She battled leukemia, went in and out of remission, until she said she wanted done with it and told her doctor to let her go. I was called to the hospital late that night. I entered her room after she'd gone, and saw the toes of her foot exposed above the sheet. I turned and fled.

Just as I was finishing this book, the PBS show *Finding Your Roots* traced my family back five generations and uncovered some information that rocked me. Mr. Addison, as my mother referred to her father, had not been killed in a trolley accident; he'd shot himself at thirty-one. A conductor on the Boston elevated rail, he'd been involved in a massive strike some time before, one of the many labor actions of the day. The strikers had won, but it seems he was sure he would be targeted and would not be able to support his family. My grandmother had put her two children in the orphanage because she did not have the money to look after them.

My mother told us she had never forgiven her. Forty years after her death, I wonder: Did she not know? Did her mother never tell her the truth about her father? Was she trying to protect her from a suicide's stigma? A never-to-be-solved mystery, but my god, what horrific circumstances.

Shortly after she died, my mother's longtime nurse and my father became lovers, to the horror of all my parents' friends.

By then I'd gotten closer to my father. The distance between us had melted and the switch that so often happens was beginning. I didn't completely become his parent, but it was close. He had never asked me for anything, ever, until one day, a year after my mother died, he called urgently and said, "I need your help."

The soap opera saga began: It turned out that the husband of Janice, my mother's best friend for fifty years, had also recently died. They were the model family I wished I'd belonged to when my parents' marriage was on the rocks. Janice still lived in San Francisco, and after my mother died, my father secretly began seeing her. He was flying up and down the coast, back and forth to San Francisco, to be with her. Every once in a while I'd hear from the nurse about how my father was coping, but one day she called saying, "Your father's acting very strangely, disappearing for days with no explanation."

Yes, he certainly was. The help he needed from me was to somehow get rid of the nurse, which he was afraid to do on his own. "I want to marry Janice," he told me. He was eighty-two years old.

So I had the wonderful job of explaining to the nurse, who was truly in love with my father, that it was over and she had to leave immediately. I made it comfortable for her financially, but it was still brutal. A month or two later my father and Janice got so very sweetly married. She told me she had always been in love with my father, but had to wait almost fifty years for that love to be consummated. They were together for nearly two years lolling happily on the world's most luxurious cruise ships, getting off one and boarding another with maybe a week's pause between.

In those years just before Charlie died, I was very much alone—no one I'd been seeing had come close to the place Diane had occupied. My personal life had pretty much stalled out and I was coasting along on Paramount's success. For me, coasting is no damn good, since I can't grow or develop unless there are challenges. Thankfully, for bringing up Barry, I wouldn't have to wait long for that to change.

CHAPTER 16

That fateful morning when I got the news that Charlie had died, I was staring out the window of my Aspen condominium as it was being battered by a huge snowstorm. The airport was closed and our pilots said they wouldn't be able to get the plane out of the hangar for at least another day. Martin Davis had asked me to get to New York as fast as possible, for what reason I couldn't contemplate. I was still in shock at the news.

Two hours by car from Aspen the weather was clear. So I chartered a tiny Learjet in Grand Junction and figured I'd be able to drive there through the storm. But then—oops!—I realized a friend who was spending the weekend with me was sleeping upstairs. I didn't know what the hell to do with him. I had given Jack Nicholson a ride up from Los Angeles, and Jack had already met him. I called, woke him up, and said, "Will you please take care of him and get him home while I get to New York? Once the Paramount plane can get deiced it will take you back."

Jack said, "What do you mean, 'take care of him'?"

I said, "I'm not telling you to *sleep* with him; just see that he's okay for the weekend and that he gets on the plane back to L.A. Godfather him a little because I can't."

I went upstairs, made what I'm sure was an unintelligible explanation, got my things, and drove as fast as possible to the airport in Grand Junction and on to New York.

That blizzard was nothing compared with what would soon start pelting me from all sides.

Martin Davis asked me to come straight to his office as soon as I landed. It was around ten p.m. when I got there. He shocked me by saying that Charlie had been secretly sick for the last three years. They never discussed it, but he'd found out. Not much of a surprise, because Martin had a detective agency on the side that did all sorts of nefarious things and provided him with god-knows-what information. He didn't know when Charlie was going to die, but he knew he was seriously unwell. He'd used those years to systematically ingratiate himself with the outside directors, waiting for the inevitable opportunity. No one else ever bothered much with the directors because Charlie was so dominant and thought to be indestructible.

At first, I didn't really understand why he had asked me to rush to New York or why he insisted on seeing me so immediately. It was just me and Davis in his dimly lit corner office, where he further astonished me when he said, "I want to succeed Charlie and I need your support."

I'm sure I probably stifled a laugh. I thought it was the silliest thing I'd ever heard. Martin Davis was basically a high-flown clerk; he was called an executive vice president, but he had never in his life had any operational experience; he had simply been Charlie's fixer. His only official responsibilities were overseeing corporate functions like communications, HR, and legal affairs.

Davis and I had an easy enough relationship—he knew that Paramount reported only to Bluhdorn and was off-limits to everyone else at Gulf + Western—but I always thought of him as one of those gray faces you used to see when party functionaries in the Kremlin lined up for the Victory Day parade. The board never met with the operating executives. They knew only Charlie and Jim Judelson, the company's president, who'd been with Charlie since the beginning and oversaw all the industrial businesses that Charlie didn't care about, other than that they made lots of the profits.

The only other senior man the board knew was Don Oresman, a cynical and tricky lawyer from the firm of Simpson Thacher who, as outside counsel for the company, attended all the board meetings. I had no clue then—but came to understand later—that Oresman and Davis, knowing Charlie was sick, had been plotting together for years to take over the company.

Gulf + Western had been so totally dominated by Charlie Bluhdorn that there simply were no strong people on the corporate side. Charlie made every decision unilaterally, and the board acquiesced in whatever he wanted. "Corporate governance" was an unheard-of concept at Gulf + Western. So when Charlie died, the vacuum at the top was total.

The natural choice would have been to promote Jim Judelson as CEO. Though diminished by the overpowering Charlie, he was officially the number two person. He had a good record administering all the businesses, and while not personally impressive, he at least had the requisite qualifications. He certainly wanted the job, but his problem was that Charlie had been so dismissive of him for so long, frequently cutting him down and belittling him before the directors, that he had no standing of his own and little credibility.

So there I sat in Martin Davis's office, late at night on the day of Charlie's death, as Davis calmly and clearly explained how he intended to get elected CEO and how he needed my help to do so. My brain was slowly hardening with the knowledge that he meant to do this, and worse . . . needed me to accomplish it.

Paramount wasn't the biggest business at Gulf + Western, but it had become such a public and shining success that Davis felt that outside of the board itself I was the key player in the transition. He also knew that I was close to Yvette Bluhdorn, Charlie's very long-suffering French wife, and that in Charlie's will he asked that she take his place on the board. Davis said that Judelson's ascension was a terrible idea and that Judelson had no support in the financial markets. Davis made it clear, though, that Judelson would likely have support from the operations and business leaders of all the other divisions inside Gulf + Western who'd been reporting directly to him for years.

While I still thought Davis was a big joke as a replacement for Charlie, it was becoming clear that this wasn't a hopeless goose chase, that he had concocted a serious plan, and was ready for the fight it was certain to become. Davis told me he was sure he'd have the votes in the end, but wanted my support—particularly with Yvette Bluhdorn, who would be elected to the board at the emergency meeting he was going to call in the next days.

I was tired, confused, and not yet living in the reality of the moment. I told Davis I had to talk first with the Bluhdorn family and determine their wishes before I made any commitment. I then went down in the elevator and walked across the park to the Bluhdorn apartment, where the atmosphere was sad and somber, but calm. I had been living with the shock of Charlie's death for about twelve hours, but his family had been living with his mortal illness for almost three years. They were more consoling to me than I was to them. I didn't stay long, because it was already past midnight. I said my farewells, told them I'd come over the next day, and walked wearily and worriedly to my apartment at the Olympic Tower. The magnitude of Charlie's loss and the battle I knew was coming both weighed heavily.

The phone was ringing as I entered my apartment. Naturally, it was Jim Judelson, asking when we could meet. I said, "Tomorrow. For now I'm just going to try to sleep."

So began two days of shrieking stress. I was pulled this way and that by the two candidates, each trying to get me to support and endorse him. All grief was postponed, held captive by the timetable for choosing Charlie's successor.

Judelson came to my apartment and said that having Davis succeed Charlie would be a blasphemy, that Davis was an evil and manipulative man who had no decency of character, no history of running anything, and would destroy the company. He said he had the support of all the operating group in the company other than Paramount and that everyone would desert the place if Davis took over.

After he left my apartment, I sat in my small den with its view of the top of St. Patrick's sharp spire.

I felt as if I were going to be impaled on it.

I actually began to shake. If I made the wrong choice, it could be the end of my career there, despite my success and stature in the industry. But who would be best to lead the company? In the end, I made the winning choice, but it was absolutely the wrong one for the company.

And the worst possible choice for me.

Over that weekend I spent a lot of time with the Bluhdorn family. Yvette had great disdain for Jim Judelson. Not surprising, since Charlie had spoken derisively about him for decades. He had ceaselessly made fun of him as a blowhard of little talent with pretensions of grandeur.

She didn't know much about Martin Davis other than that he'd been Charlie's great defender whenever Charlie got close to trouble. I didn't really know Judelson and was swayed by Yvette's belief that Charlie would be violently against his being the successor. Also, I thought Davis probably did have the votes regardless of what counterplot any of the other executives in the company might attempt. We both thought—and, oh, how wrong we turned out to be—that Davis would be the more malleable choice.

The next days were spent worrying over the coming board meeting and the funeral, which took place on a properly dreary, rainy Monday.

The following day, I was one floor down from the boardroom, with a group of ten pro-Judelson executives who had gathered with the idea of storming the meeting to say that they would *not* work for Davis. I told them this would be a terrible mistake. I said that Martin Davis had the votes necessary and he couldn't be stopped. And when I finished telling them with certainty that Davis would never forget their actions against him, they began to cower and back off.

The meeting began, and the first order of business was, as per Charlie's will, to elect Yvette to replace him.

After that, both candidates made their presentation. Then they left and the caucusing began.

Gulf + Western had a very large board—seventeen members. As the vote finally went around the room, it was evenly split between Davis and Judelson with eight votes each. The last vote was the board's newest member, Yvette Bluhdorn. She was the swing vote, and she paused for a long time before she cast it for Davis—and it was over.

The Charlie Bluhdorn era was finished. The tempestuous Austrian, with all the Sturm und Drang that he always brought to everything, was replaced by a man so uncomfortable in his own skin that he gave the creeps to anyone close to him.

Jim Judelson left the company immediately. Davis, in the first flush of victory, was grateful to me and said he intended to reorganize everything and wanted me to be head of Gulf + Western Entertainment, which was to include Paramount Madison Square Garden, Simon & Schuster, and all the other entertainment assets. By that time I was a wet rag, exhausted by it all. Without any enthusiasm, I agreed to the changes.

Davis was an incredibly effective conniver, but he had no ability to actually manage and grow the unbelievably complex business he was now in charge of. He was very proficient in public relations, very savvy at up-from-the-streets devious scheming. He wasn't capable of devising any go-forward strategy. Charlie had acquired an extraordinary array of businesses; all Davis knew how to do was dismantle the whole thing.

First, he began to sell the stock portfolio, which Charlie had brilliantly built up to almost $1 billion (a huge sum in 1983 dollars). If Davis had done nothing other than keep Charlie's stock investments over the next ten years, they would have grown to be worth more than every other asset in the company. Davis then started to sell off the heavy-industry companies. Next he peeled off the insurance companies and all the other profitable businesses.

And, while he busied himself dismantling Charlie's empire, he began month by month to reveal himself as the rat he was.

Charlie wasn't even cold in his grave when Yvette Bluhdorn called me and said, "Can you find out why my tie-line doesn't work?" She had a phone at her apartment that was a direct line to the G + W switchboard, from which you could dial all the internal extensions, including the dedicated line to the Bluhdorn property in the Dominican Republic. I asked someone to find out what was wrong and fix it, only to learn it had been disconnected on the orders of Martin Davis.

I rang Davis up and he said, "Charlie's dead. There's no reason for her to have it at the apartment."

I said, "Marty, Charlie's dead two months; she uses it to talk to her children in the D.R. Her daughter, Dominique, is basically living there."

And Davis said, "No, it isn't correct."

I told him, "This is just crazy mean-spirited," to which he replied, "It's the right thing to do—she doesn't need it." I hung up the phone and stared at the wall in disbelief.

What kind of person would do that to the widow, especially one who cast the deciding vote giving him the top job in her husband's company?

Martin Davis was that kind of person. He turned out to be cruel and sadistic, just a little man with little talent, in over his head.

With every new revelation of his evil, I felt not only stupid but also guilty for having helped anoint him.

At Paramount, we had almost no politics; we operated in a classic top-down structure with an absolute clarity of roles and responsibilities. Without organizational ambiguity there's little internal political behavior. That was the opposite of the new Martin Davis regime at Gulf + Western, where everything reeked of politics. One day, about six months into his reign, he said to me, "You know, Michael Eisner acts like a clown."

I explained, "Well, he's a good and effective clown and he's my clown, so leave him be."

It was one of those conversations that wasn't designed to resolve anything, but it rattled around afterward in my head. I began to understand that this was Davis's method: over the past months, he had ruthlessly weeded out Charlie's loyalists in the company. And the way he asserted his authority was by forcing the number one person in each division to fire the number two person. Once he had done that, he had the balls of the number one guy in his pocket.

I watched him do it to five or six people, and of course he was now trying to do it to me by saying, "Fire the clown."

I've always said that Michael was goofy and irrepressible, and that sometimes ridiculous things would pop out of his mouth and mind, but it was an extremely original mind that sometimes creatively worked faster than his ability to speak or self-edit. Michael could be excessive, but he was supremely talented, a genius in many ways, and well worth tolerating every eccentricity. I thought he was Paramount's biggest asset.

None of that mattered to Marty Davis, who went after him through me.

I had a revealing discussion a couple of months after that first talk about Eisner. Marty said to me, "You're going to have to remove him."

I said, "Well, you'll have to remove me to remove him, because I'm not removing him."

Davis responded, "I feel very strongly about it."

"You can feel as strongly as you like, but you're wrong, and I'm not doing it."

He said coldly, "Well, at some point I'll have to confront that."

My tart response: "You do whatever you like."

That ended up ameliorating things, because Davis didn't want to have a confrontation with me. At least not then. Paramount was just too successful, and I was still in a very strong position.

For the next months I protected Michael from having to deal with Davis. I never told him that Davis wanted him out; as a result, until the very end, Michael thought that I was keeping him from Davis for my own political reasons. At one point, Davis came to me and said, "The fact that you and Eisner earn fifty percent of Paramount's profit pool is excessive. I don't mind your share, but I don't want any going to Eisner."

"That's absurd."

He said, "I want to be talking about a new deal for you, but I'm certainly not going to want to continue with Eisner in the company."

I shrugged and said, "Then there's no point in talking."

He said, "I'll convince you."

I never told Michael what was going on because I knew there was nothing he could do to change Davis's mind. But that was a mistake. I should have told him that I was the only thing standing between him and annihilation. This pushed us apart, and he became suspicious of me. We began to talk less and less.

When I knew I was going to leave I did eventually tell him. But I'd held the information too close for too long and he'd grown to distrust me.

His reaction was to tell me he thought I'd been keeping him and Davis apart for competitive reasons. Although he slowly came to understand why I was standing between them, he never fully accepted what was the purest of motivations in protecting him, apart from my just not wanting Davis anywhere in my pants.

I kept on fending off Davis's attempts to get control of me and of Paramount, but it was a miserable time.

After Charlie died, I tried to revive the idea of starting a fourth network at Paramount, and my team and I made a formal presentation to Davis, urging him to buy the Metromedia stations. Presentations that formal were a rarity at Paramount, so this was a big deal. We had worked out a very solid plan. After two hours of selling our hearts out, Davis said only a brisk "Thank you," then got up and left the room.

His response—or lack of one—was insulting on so many levels, especially since Paramount was at the height of its success. At the very least he should have complimented the people on the presentation, thanked them for their effort, asked a few questions, and then said, "We'll consider this and get back to you."

But no. Nothing. Zippo. Zero response.

There was no joy to be found at Paramount except for one hot night in July when we put on a free concert in Central Park with Diana Ross and taped it for a Showtime special. An astounding 800,000 people gathered on the Great Lawn. I was both Diana's longtime friend and the "producer" of the event. I had invited a hundred of the New York glitterati to come to the show and to a dinner afterward at the restaurant on top of the Gulf + Western Building. Half an hour before the show started, one of the assistants found me and said the fire commissioner needed me urgently. He said there was a lightning storm coming within the hour and we had to cancel the performance. At that moment the sun was shining, and though a look westward showed ominous gray swirls, I told the commissioner, "You must be mad—look out at that crowd growing so excited to see Diana. No chance we're telling them there's no show." He said that because of the denseness of the crowd, if the coming lightning were to strike the steel towers we'd constructed as light and camera positions, we could kill 100,000 people. I said if it didn't and we canceled the show, 200,000 people would kill us. I said we just had to brave it and go on.

We started and it was a glorious sight as Diana sang the first numbers with a long red scarf blowing ten feet in back of her as the wind picked up. Then came the deluge—thankfully no lightning, but a downpour for the ages. Soaking in my light-beige suit, I clambered up onstage and whispered in Diana's ear that we had to stop. She resisted and went on as the wind and rain pelted down and the mikes for the orchestra went dead, though hers was somehow still working. After I went up a few more times, she agreed, telling me, "Just let me get these people out of the park safely." With the most magnificent artist's instincts, she slow-talked almost a million people out of that park without a single injury. But my god, what a disaster.

We were both wetter than wet and chilled to the bone and went to my apartment to take hot showers to try to warm up. We then got dressed and went up to the party, where all the invited guests had fled from the concert. The place erupted in cheers as Diana and I announced we'd put the concert on the next night, assuming the torrent wouldn't return. All the equipment had shorted out and the massive crew spent the next day drying it out with industrial fans and handheld blow-dryers. That steamy evening, she gave one of the most triumphant performances ever seen and recorded; it's still shown on television. And I still have the photograph that appeared on the front page of the next day's *Post*, showing me trying to get her offstage with a caption that read "Diana Ross's assistant tries to stop the show."

After a year and a half of Martin Davis's reign, even though Paramount continued to lead in both movies and television, I was becoming increasingly unhappy, not at all enjoying my increased responsibilities or having to dodge the labyrinth of politics inside Gulf + Western. Don Oresman, the outside counsel, was now Martin Davis's official on-site henchman. He had joined the company as its senior general counsel. A man who worked every side of every room, he had become Davis's co-snake. Years earlier, Joel Dolkart, Oresman's law partner at Simpson Thacher, had become Gulf + Western's chief outside lawyer. G + W was the firm's biggest account. It turned out Dolkart was embezzling money, and Oresman, on behalf of the law firm, went to Charlie and said, "We have an obligation to tell you this. It's up to you whether you report it or not." Bluhdorn told the law firm to report it.

When Dolkart was told they were going to call the district attorney, he said, Judas-like, "You go after me and I will go after Bluhdorn."

They told Charlie that, and he said, "I'm not going to be threatened by anyone; he's a common thief and ought to be prosecuted." The district attorney had an easy case: Dolkart had stolen nearly $3 million, absolute clean thievery, with no extenuating circumstances. However, Dolkart did indeed go after Charlie, saying that he had committed various crimes of self-aggrandizement and SEC filing errors. Dolkart ended up becoming a government witness, never served a day in jail, and never paid back the stolen money. And Charlie went through five years of absolute, and absolutely undeserved, hell as a result.

Oresman was the survivor of all this, and in his avuncular way he tried to intercede in bettering the relationship between Davis and me.

On a walk in Central Park, he said, "It's just Marty. He means you no harm. Don't let his nasty personality bother you; you just continue to run your store."

I told him, "I don't like the atmosphere. I don't like what this place has become. Marty is destroying everything Charlie built and radiates his poisonous personality in every direction. I can't stand to be around him."

He said, "Let me set it up correctly for you to go talk to him again. All he wants is for you to continue to run the company. I'll try to get this mania against Eisner curtailed." I thought it was hopeless, but I agreed to talk again to Davis.

For a meeting designed to smooth over our disagreements, it couldn't have gone worse. Right away, Davis reiterated that he was very uncomfortable with Eisner and insisted I had to "get rid of him."

"You're totally wrong and I'm not doing it."

We batted back and forth while I began to sweat profusely. I had now become physically uncomfortable in his presence—it went way beyond his feelings about Eisner. I had come to dislike him to the core.

The penny finally dropped—and there was now only one option.

I had to get out.

I left his office on the forty-second floor, got into the elevator, and by the time I got to the thirty-seventh floor, I had decided firmly and irrevocably that I would leave Paramount.

As I emerged from the elevator, my head clear with resolution, I walked down the long corridor to my office. On my secretary's desk were the yellow sheets listing the phone calls received that day.

My eyes zeroed in on the last call—it was from another Davis, Marvin Davis, no relation to Martin. This Davis was the Denver oil tycoon who had recently bought 20th Century Fox. Marvin Davis had never before called me. But I knew, just intuitively knew, when I saw that name that this was going to be the key to my getting out of Paramount with more than my tail intact. I'm not conflating the timing of events here. It happened just this way: deciding once and for all that I had to leave and getting that phone call five minutes later. Somehow the gods must have decreed that I deserved a savior from *Martin* Davis, and he would be named *Marvin* Davis. In a lifetime filled with inexplicably serendipitous moments, this one topped them all.

CHAPTER 17

The two Davises were as opposite as Laurel and Hardy. One was uptight, string-bean thin, with a popping Adam's apple; the other was buffalo fat and over-the-tent-top showy. But, unlike the sweet slapstick of Laurel and Hardy, one secretly and silently crafted every move; the other boasted and conned his way using everyone else's money to get rich. All they had in common was that both were crummy individuals.

At six feet four and weighing more than three hundred pounds, Marvin Davis qualified as a big man . . . except in terms of honesty and integrity. He claimed to all that he *owned* 20th Century Fox. That's the title he took for himself: owner. As if he had put up all the money. In fact, he put up only $25 million, got the fugitive Marc Rich, on the run from an indictment on charges of tax evasion, racketeering, and wire fraud, to secretly put up another $25 million, and borrowed the rest of the purchase price. He fashioned himself as a Denver oilman, but he wasn't the kind of westerner you'd imagine an oilman to be: he was born in Newark, New Jersey, and grew up in the Bronx.

He was a huge, hungry bear of a man, and most people thought him extraordinarily coarse. A story about him in *Vanity Fair* after he died was titled "The Man Who Ate Hollywood."

In the oil industry, Marvin was known as the guy who had invented the "100 percent for three-fourths" formula, meaning that he got people to invest 100 percent of the cash but own only three-fourths of the company.

Marvin got the other 25 percent, plus management fees. He drilled hundreds and hundreds of wells as a result of all those partnerships and was considered the biggest wildcatter in the United States. Like many social-climbing businesspeople, Marvin liked putting celebrities on his boards. He had Henry Kissinger and Gerald Ford on the Fox board, certainly not for their expertise in the entertainment business. Before he called me, I'd had only one actual conversation with him. It was at a dinner given by the Kissingers at their New York apartment. Marvin and I were seated at the same table, and I was feeling sorry for him because he was being ignored by the high and mighty, so I chatted him up. I could tell he was grateful for the attention. That was all I knew until I got that message.

I returned his call within minutes. He said, "I'd like to get together with you." I told him, "Sure, when I next get to L.A." He said, "No, I'd like it soon and privately if possible." We arranged to have lunch the next week at my L.A. house.

I asked my cook to prepare a big lunch for the big man.

Nevertheless, I had never seen anyone eat like that.

I later found out that Marvin Davis kept an immense number of ties in reserve, because food would be all over him within two minutes of beginning a meal. He ate a huge amount of roast beef at this lunch, and between mouthfuls he announced, "Twentieth Century Fox is a disaster. I've owned it for two years, and they make terrible movie after terrible movie."

For the last few years, Fox had been run by Alan Hirschfield, a finance man who'd previously run Columbia Pictures. Davis was very direct with me. He wanted me to take over Fox; he'd give me 25 percent of the studio and anything else I needed. A desperate offer from a desperate man to another quietly desperate man. What I didn't know then was that there was a darker reason for his extremely generous offer. I told him disingenuously that I might be interested and we ought to have our mutual lawyers get into the details. *Might be interested? Please.*

These secret discussions went on for the next several months. I told no one other than my lawyer and accountants, who endlessly negotiated back and forth. Davis and I had a few more big meals at my house, where he fulminated about his terrible Fox executives, who wouldn't listen to him about anything. I wanted him to know politely but with clarity that I probably wouldn't listen to him, either. I told him that at Paramount we operated autonomously from Gulf + Western and made 100 percent of our own decisions.

With the nerve of a cat burglar, I told Marvin, "Since I don't know you very well, you would have to agree never to speak to a single person in the company other than me. And while I'll surely be in touch with you informally about the state of the company, I will formally agree to meet with you once a year." I had been so scarred by Martin Davis's behavior that I wanted these extreme protections, particularly with someone who had already interfered willy-nilly with the people at Fox. He wasn't happy about such distancing, but he did agree.

My contract with Paramount was due to expire in September 1984, and I'd been stalling the other Davis, who'd been saying for some months that he was eager to negotiate a new deal. Marvin Davis was represented by Bert Fields, a very tough lawyer I'd occasionally used for particularly difficult issues at Paramount. My lawyer, Bruce Ramer, was equally tough, but less flamboyantly aggressive. Back and forth they went, trying to write my profit participation with a precision that went against Fox's abstruse accounting policies. That, together with my demands for autonomy—and my insistence that Davis agree to fund the studio's budget personally— made it a particularly complex process. As it dragged on, Davis's desperation pushed his lawyers into caving on every principal issue, and the written agreement moved to closure.

I was surprised—to put it mildly—that they were agreeing to what was the most one-sided employment agreement in the history of employment agreements.

I learned later the real reason he needed me: the banks he'd borrowed all that money from either wanted it back or wanted him to put more equity into the company to protect their loans. I was considered, at that moment, the most successful movie company executive, so he could use my hiring to keep from having to put actual money into the business. Remember, the only cash he put into Fox was that original $25 million.

I don't think he cared whether I was Barry or Harry or Billy or Dopey. Davis hated putting up his own money for anything (it later turned out that he'd even borrowed the money to pay for the paintings on the walls of his house). As for me, I simply needed someplace to go. It wasn't as if I craved running Fox, though I did smile at the thought that not so long ago I'd been a romping teenager jumping over the fence at Beverly High to roam its back lot.

There were only six studios and three networks in 1984, so there were few arenas where I could play. This was an escape, not an exciting new adventure for me. I didn't yearn to keep on making movies and TV shows. There wasn't much new to learn or to challenge me. But this was the only world I knew, and I was at the top of its game, so apprenticing in any other field didn't make any sense, and I wasn't imaginative enough to think there could be possibilities outside show business.

Nevertheless, I kept postponing, finding excuses to avoid finalizing the agreement. I was enjoying keeping a big secret, enjoying the parry and riposte of the endless negotiations, where I seemed to have so much leverage. And, given the almost fantastical fortuity of the timing, I never fully believed this was real. But there was no way the tensions inside Paramount could be contained much longer. Martin Davis was asserting and inserting himself more and more into my business, pestering me constantly to get rid of Eisner and to make a new deal for myself. I'd stretched this all out further than was rational, mostly because I just didn't want to face the final reality of leaving my beloved Paramount. But any thinking that I could stay was purely delusional. And the other Davis kept pushing me harder to sign in order to solve his own Fox problem. Finally, in the week before Labor Day 1984 I fixed my name to the Fox contract and that was that; we'd announce the following week. Surreally, the bad Davis had scheduled a visit to the studio before that Labor Day weekend.

He hadn't once been to the studio in the ten years I'd spent there. Martin had been saying for a while that he didn't know anyone at Paramount and wanted to spend time meeting the executives. It had been postponed over and over again, but here he was the week before my secret bombshell announcement, having meetings with the divisions. The schedule was to end with a dinner at my house for our top fifty executives.

I held my breath that the news about Fox wouldn't break while sliding through the forced civilities between Davis and my Paramount colleagues—which wasn't easy, given that he was the most awkward man on the planet. To have to introduce him to people and try to make them comfortable with him was yeoman work, but my secret and its ramifications kept me inwardly giddy.

The dinner I gave for him was a night of suspended animation, a farce that was about to explode. I wandered around my house detached from the proceedings but knowing the chaos that would soon ensue. I felt great empathy for the executives I had nurtured and supported for a decade. Their careers would soon be up in the air and their lives overturned. But they were all acknowledged best in class, and whatever happened, they would be more than okay. I was sure most of the key people would leave, and I hoped I'd be able to get them to join me at Fox, especially Michael Eisner. A few weeks before, I had taken him into my confidence and told him my plans, saying that I wanted very much for him to join me as president of Fox. He agreed to keep the secret, but he also said he was certain that Davis would name him to succeed me. Thanks to my bungled communication he couldn't imagine any other scenario, even though I had told him that Martin Davis despised him. He was sure Davis would have no other choice than to make him Paramount's chief executive. He did, however, agree to meet Marvin Davis before my formal resignation.

I arranged for Michael and his wife, Jane, to come to Marvin's house for get-to-know-each-other drinks. It was an awful meeting. Marvin didn't exactly jibe with the Eisners. First, there was Marvin's *Beverly Hillbillies*–ridiculous house—an eleven-acre, forty-five-thousand-square-foot mansion with eleven bedrooms and seventeen bathrooms, a huge granite pile that had originally been built for Lucy Doheny Battson and was as formal and proper as the dumpy Davis was ill-suited to be inside it. As drinks were served, out came about three pounds of caviar, two pounds of which Marvin gorged on in the thirty-minute interview.

On the Tuesday after the holiday, Marvin asked Alan Hirschfield to come to Denver, where he told him I'd be replacing him immediately. He asked Alan to keep it confidential until it was announced later that week. My plan had been to fly to New York Tuesday afternoon, meet with Martin Davis at Paramount Wednesday morning, get back on a plane, and fly to L.A. in time for the announcement on Thursday.

But once Hirschfield got the news, he had nothing to lose, so he started telling people he'd been fired. I was in the upstairs bathroom of my house, ten minutes from leaving for the plane, when the news blew up and was all over the wires—and nobody could get news faster than Martin Davis. Ungodly sums of money had been spent on communications at Paramount because god forbid anyone should surprise him with anything.

So I called Davis to tell him my big surprise that was no longer much of a surprise. I said, "I'm leaving. I'm sorry this happened this way, with Hirschfield leaking it, but I want to do the right thing and resign in person. So I'll leave now to get on the plane and will see you tonight or tomorrow morning."

Martin instantly replied, "No need to come. Let me just read you my press release."

I said, "Why are you issuing a press release when we're not announcing this until Thursday?"

He said, "I have to protect my company."

"Look, I'm getting on the plane. Let's do this in an orderly and proper way. I've been at Paramount ten years, and I want to respect that and all the people I've worked with. The only way to do that is to do it in person with you."

"Well, then, why did you put the news out?"

"I didn't," I reiterated. "How would it have been in my interest to put the news out this way?"

He was adamant that he was putting out a release that night, so my trip to New York became academic.

I told Michael Eisner that now I wasn't flying east, and he immediately said, "Well, I'm going. Davis asked me to come in, and I assume he'll offer me the CEO job."

"Don't go," I warned him. "It will just be a humiliation. Martin's never going to make you CEO. He'll probably promote Frank Mancuso," who was head of distribution and the kind of non-Hollywood executive that Davis liked. "He'll fire you," I said. "Don't go."

Michael said, "Of course I'm going. I just talked to him, and he invited me in for a discussion."

Again, I said, "Seriously, don't go," and Michael said, "He can't fire me. We're the most successful company in the film business!"

I tried every which way to prevent this humiliation, but Michael still didn't trust me when it came to Martin Davis.

They met soon after Michael landed. Davis told him he was going to make Frank Mancuso chairman of Paramount and that Michael could leave if he wanted to.

Michael, outraged, told Davis he wanted a cashier's check for his yearly share of profits and wouldn't leave the building without it.

Davis said, "I can't get you a cashier's check at ten o'clock at night," to which Michael replied, "I'll be here at nine o'clock in the morning, and I want the check."

The next morning Michael got the check, went across the street, deposited it, and flew back to L.A. and out of Paramount.

Meanwhile, the news had indeed upended the town. Not since the 1930s had anyone skipped so seamlessly from heading one studio to heading another, and no one had ever been given $3 million in salary (that figure also leaked out). The entire creative core of Paramount was now at risk of leaving, and while the studio had a decent backlog of movies, there was real concern that this mighty hitmaking machine would cease to function. It had been taken for granted that Paramount was the most stable and best-run studio; no one outside a very few knew how unstable the relationship had been between me and the head of Gulf + Western after Charles Bluhdorn died.

After Michael returned, we made an agreement for him to come to Fox as its president. But over the next weeks, as I pressed to finalize it, he kept telling me he was so devastated at being fired by Martin Davis that he couldn't concentrate on his future, that he'd sought the help of a doctor, that he was depressed, that he was this and that.

I'd try to reach him, but he'd be unavailable for days. When I did reach him, he told me he just couldn't face life right now and asked me to be patient. It was a good act, and I dimly and naively bought what was really a delaying tactic for Michael trying to secure a better position than being my number two at Fox. Of course it was devious—but who could blame him.

Michael was at the time secretly engaged in a long-shot effort to be CEO of Disney. The Bass oil family of Texas and Roy Disney's business manager, Stanley Gold, had organized a group to take over Disney, but they wanted to have new management on board when they made their final proposal. They had already gotten Frank Wells, formerly of Warner Brothers, on their team, but they needed a creative executive to work alongside him. They offered Michael the position of president, with Wells over him as CEO, but Michael, in a great gambler's move, said he wouldn't do it unless he was CEO.

Ultimately, Wells graciously agreed to be president, but those complications were what had kept it all up in the air—and kept Michael unreachable. He didn't want to risk his one firm job offer by telling me he was after the Disney job. I was at home on a Sunday morning when Warren Beatty called to say that Michael was going to Disney. The pieces in the disappearing puzzle of Michael now fit. Shortly thereafter Michael called me from his car to say that he'd just left the Disney board meeting and it was going to be announced that he was its new CEO.

I was angry that he hadn't told me the truth about his maneuverings, and I was terribly disappointed that he wasn't coming with me to Fox, but of course he was right to take the Disney job. Even though Disney was a much smaller operation at that time and had been moribund in the last few years, it was also an extraordinary opportunity and Michael was right to do it.

And what a beyond-spectacular success he was to make of it.

I really was on my own. For ten years I'd built up an organization where I knew everyone and everything in it down to the studs, and now I was all by myself. Every encounter I had with Davis made me trust him less. What the hell had I gotten myself into? I'd been out of my element going from staid ABC to Paramount ten years before, but now I was entering an even wilder West. During our negotiation, Marvin said to me, "You know, I have this grand house in Beverly Hills. It'll be great because I can have Hollywood stars stay there when they come to shoot a movie for us."

I tactfully said, "I don't think that'll work." Unseen, my eyes were rolling to the back of my head. I knew my contract made him manageable, but his huge bulk of a personality and some of this talk made me anxious.

Before I arrived, Davis had been having a good time at Fox. He liked lording his status over everyone on the lot, and liked Hollywood and all the extracurricular stuff that went with it. The Davises were very socially ambitious, and they had an interesting technique to attract celebrities: they would send them elaborate flower arrangements or gifts, invite them to some event, and then send a thank-you gift afterward. I said to some of my friends who received this graft, "Rather than accept these gifts, why don't you just get paid directly in cash for coming? Why don't you say, 'Ten thousand dollars a pop for drinks, one hundred thousand to come for dinner'? Because, you know, this is not about being social. This is about being bought, so you might as well get paid in cash without the froufrou."

It quickly became clear to Marvin that I was no fun. He tried hard to woo me, using his general tactic of gift giving. On my first day at Fox, he took the big gold watch off his wrist and gave it to me. I tried to say, "Oh, no, I don't want your watch," but of course he persisted.

What a shit I was, being so ungracious, but his lord-of-the-manor behavior made me cringe. He didn't seem much interested in the actual business; he only wanted to use it for bluster and social upsizing. I began to think that there really was something dodgy about this character.

I had told the outgoing CEO, Alan Hirschfield, that he could stay in his office, that he didn't have to leave right away. I hadn't emotionally let go of Paramount and found it hard to get up much enthusiasm for Fox. Another day, another studio to run. I was still officially at Paramount for the three-week interregnum before I was to begin the new job, but I regularly went over to Fox to meet some of the executives. All their offices were in this three-story art deco–style building that Darryl Zanuck had erected. Huge wide hallways from one end to the other, with even more cavernous offices on the first floor for the top four executives. Each one had a private staircase going down to the basement, where there were two private projection rooms, a gym, a cold pool, a sauna, and a massage room. Zanuck, who reigned from the 1930s to the 1950s, would have a daily massage, a jump into the cold pool, and then a further jump onto the starlet of the day. Zanuck's office had a trophy room with a bed next to the fifty-foot-long main office.

Paramount had old-style Hollywood glamour, but it was all concrete and soundstages on a relatively small plot in the heart of actual Hollywood. Fox was a sprawling campus smack up against Beverly Hills.

By the time I started, it was clear I wasn't going to bring Michael Eisner with me, and because Disney was so alluring, Michael was able to get most of the Paramount executives over with him. I wasted weeks trying to convince them that Fox would be better for them, but by then Michael was able to show them that Disney had these extraordinary hidden assets that hadn't been tapped since Walt Disney died.

So now I was alone, in what I was soon to learn was a failing company. Although my lawyers and accountants had spent months in negotiations, they'd been outwitted by the wily Bert Fields, who plied them with endless data that was designed to disguise the dire situation at Fox.

I was really a novice about running a stand-alone business. I'd been part of the huge Gulf + Western conglomerate, where all the financial reporting and accounting was done at the parent-company level. All I had to worry about was creating hit movies and television shows. There wasn't even a balance sheet at Paramount, and I wouldn't have known what it meant if I saw one. After my second year at Paramount we were cash positive, and over the next eight years poured billions of dollars of profits into Gulf + Western. When I was at ABC, and had my own store, my mini studio, I'd understood every number down to how much film stock we used. But that was on such a small scale compared to the complexity of Fox.

This is where better schooling would have helped me. I'd never taken an economics course—let alone any accounting—and never even had to balance my own checkbook. I couldn't add beyond simple math and was basically financially illiterate and here I was the CEO of a company that had $600 million in debt.

I had no choice but to jump in the deep end and—as always in my career—*fake it until I made it.*

We had a board of directors that was simply a prize show horse for Davis. I had a nice conversation with President Ford, who graciously said he never understood what he was doing on the board anyway and resigned immediately.

I told them all I saw no reason why we needed a board and abolished it in my first week.

About a month in, I was told I was going to have to make a presentation to the bankers about how I was going to turn things around.

Bankers, me? Jesus!

But I could tell a good story, so I went up to our huge second-floor conference room to greet twenty-five bank representatives from the loan consortium that had financed Fox. I told them I thought it would take me about eighteen months to two years to get the company on the way to being a consistently profitable studio. With confidence I said, "Give us a little time, and I'm completely sure we'll get there."

After about an hour of this, the senior bank representative said, "That's all very nice and aspirational, and you're clearly capable of pulling it off, which is why we haven't called in the first tranche of the loans due last month. However, the company needs an urgent infusion of equity to keep it afloat."

Equity? Infusion? What the hell are they talking about?

I really didn't understand the words they were using to describe the situation. It was like they were speaking in tongues. I finally translated their jargon and understood that it was a simple demand that more cash be put into the business.

I asked, "How much?"

"At least one hundred and fifty million dollars."

It was all beyond me. Apparently, new cash—and not the bank's cash—would have to be brought in to justify and balance the bank loans. Otherwise, the banks weren't going to extend the credit. That much I grasped. The only way the company could be financed—the only way I'd have any ability to build anything, was by Davis—or *someone*—putting up more cash, and more than six times what Marvin had put up to "buy" the whole place.

I walked dazedly downstairs to my office, closed the door, and sat at my desk, my head in my hands. It hit me with such force what a monumental fool I had been not to have fully understood Fox's underlying financial structure and debt. I'd been the most successful executive in the film and television business over most of the last ten years, and yet I'd just been duped into joining a soon-to-be-bankrupt company.

I had thought I'd protected myself by demanding Marvin Davis sign a personal guarantee that he would put up the funds necessary for the company to make new product, but what I had been so naive about was this: *How would I be able to enforce it?*

I called Marvin and said, "I just had a meeting with all the bankers, and we need to discuss the terrible condition we're in."

He was fairly dismissive about bankers being able to do anything other than shove money at him, but he said I could come down to his Palm Springs house if I wanted to talk.

I got in my yellow Corvette and arrived two hours later at his house, which bordered Frank Sinatra Drive on the Tamarisk golf course. I approached the big white columns in front of a huge door, which was opened by a gloved butler. He took me down a shiny white marble corridor to the great room, where Davis sat in the most oversized chair I'd ever seen. Then his two daughters came in, chirping, "Daddy, we want to go shopping!"

Davis said, "C'mere," somehow got his hand in his pocket, and pulled out the biggest wad of hundred-dollar bills I'd seen anywhere outside Las Vegas. He peeled off half an inch, and the girls exited. At the same time, a huge platter of caviar was wheeled into the room.

He wanted to banter, but I got right into it, telling him the bankers wanted at least $150 million in new equity to be put in or they'd not renew the loans. I told him I resented having to come to him for this and was gobsmacked that he hadn't disclosed that the loans were in trouble.

Although I was angry about having to sit there and ask for money, I had no reason to assume he wouldn't quickly affirm the contract between us that said he would fully fund Fox personally.

Instead, he put down the caviar, looked up at me for the first time, and slowly said, "I'm not putting any more cash into the company."

Astonished, all I said was "What?"

Another mouthful and he repeated, "I'm not putting up any more cash."

I sputtered god-knows-what until I was able to croak out, "But you have to, you signed a personal guarantee to fund the company."

Long pause.

And then, his jowly face turned decidedly mean, and he said, "Yeah, so? What are you going to do about it?" He followed that with "Instead of bothering me, you ought to go out and raise the equity funds yourself. With your record, you should easily be able to get the money."

And that's when it fully hit me: *Marvin Davis gave me this extraordinary deal for 25 percent of the company to get out of having to put in any new cash.*

It was certainly check if not checkmate. "Patsy" was not an adequate word for how I felt. "Fucked" was a lot closer.

I stood up without a word and got in my car with a face redder than the desert sunset.

My brain was going as fast as my Corvette on the way back, finding each terrible option and then tossing it out.

What do you do when you realize you've made an agreement with a con man?

Davis had correctly calculated that the only option I realistically had was to go out and raise the money. I couldn't exactly quit and say, "Uh, sorry, I didn't bother to look under the covers of the company I just joined." The contract I thought I'd meticulously worked out was worth about as much as the paper it was written on. Quitting after what was trumpeted as such a wizardly deal would reveal me to be the biggest imbecile in the world.

I would go instantly from triumphant to pitiful.

All the way from Palm Springs I was banging on myself for getting into this ridiculous situation. I was a child; I was gullible, stupid. I could blame my lawyers and accountants for not delving deeper into the company's financials, but I knew the fault was mine. Relying on the simple words of a Davis guarantee had been foolish. I had no recourse other than a lawsuit. But I also knew he'd been sued multiple times over the years, swatting each of them off his elephant hide like flies.

Now I understood the reason he never wavered from that huge deal he'd offered me at our first meeting: he really didn't care. He had a far simpler motive for hiring me: *Get Diller in place and my debt will be his problem to solve.*

I was just part of his long con.

I had never been betrayed before, not like this, but Marvin Davis was a master betrayer. I'd been so protected and cosseted all through my business life that I was something of an innocent at forty-two years old. I stewed and stewed, hated that I'd been so easily and sloppily taken in. Time to grow up and deal with hard realities. Time for me to take charge of this awful situation. I was innocent no longer; I was in the big leagues now.

I called Davis, who was still at his house in Palm Springs. With as much ice in my voice as I could summon I said, "I'm not going to go out and raise any money. Zero. Either you put it up as you agreed, or I'll sue you for fraud."

Davis responded to my declaration of war by saying in the mildest tone, "I've been sued many times, son. Good luck to you," and hung up.

CHAPTER 18

A few weeks later, while I was preparing for litigation, Marvin Davis called me—without any preamble, no hello, no reference to our last conversation—and said with brio, "I've sold half the company to Rupert Murdoch."

Now, that was a stunner. I guess I did get his attention.

At that time, all Murdoch owned in the United States was the *New York Post* and a few other papers and magazines. I had met him socially, but didn't know much about him. Davis said that before Murdoch would agree to the deal, he wanted to meet me.

Rupert and I met secretly at Hillcrest Country Club across the street from Fox, where Davis was a member. It was just the two of us. Rupert is gifted with great charm whenever he is after a goose, and it was on full display. He wanted to know what my plans for the company were. As I told him, he was completely enthusiastic, and the hot bath of Rupert Murdoch's enthusiasm is something quite extraordinary. The only issue that worried him about buying into Fox was my agreement with Davis. He said he'd be very uncomfortable if by contract he could talk to me only once a year and couldn't speak to any Fox executives. I said that was a purely defensive move on my part toward Marvin Davis, and that I thought with him I'd enjoy more collaboration.

Not surprising given his great ability to seduce, I left the lunch liking him. He was so smart and engaging and heart-ticking ambitious. He was also fun to talk to, a great gossip, and quick to laugh. He did about two days of due diligence—very, very little. Rupert didn't care. He would have climbed over seventeen mountains to get Fox; he wanted into the United States, and he wanted a seat at the big studio table.

Between our lunch and the time Murdoch finalized buying into Fox, he'd gone to Australia, and then on his way back to New York stopped for two days in L.A. He called and I invited him to come over to the studio for a chat. And, here's where my North Star of serendipity once again showed up: three seemingly disparate events threaded themselves into the opportunity of a lifetime—at least my lifetime. First, that particular day was Michael Milken's annual investors' conference, called by some the Predators' Ball. Milken was at that time the biggest financier of companies in the United States. He had previously called to say he had just financed John Kluge's buyout of public shareholders at Metromedia, which owned six blockbuster television stations. They wanted to have a reception away from the place where the conference was being held, and Milken asked, as a favor, if I would give them a soundstage to have it on. The afternoon of that day, Murdoch arrived in my office. And finally, as soon as Rupert sat down in my conference room to talk, my assistant buzzed me to say that Mike Milken and John Kluge were in my reception room to say hello before their party.

I said to bring them in and introduced them to Rupert, and we all sat down for what I thought would be a few minutes of niceties. Milken was raving about the historic fundraising for Kluge he'd just completed to take his company private. He announced that now Kluge ought to consider selling the stations that made up the bulk of their company's assets. He couldn't have known Murdoch would be there, or that I'd be in my office at the moment they wandered by. Some celestial force seemed to be driving things as Kluge rhapsodized about how reluctant he'd be to ever sell the stations he'd been building up for twenty years—mesmerizing us except for that seller's gleam in his little Germanic nugget eyes.

Having whet the beast's appetite, they got up and went to their reception.

Outside the three networks, Metromedia had the best station group in the United States, covering 25 percent of the U.S. population. I was astonished that it might be for sale. I told Murdoch that when I was at Paramount, we had tried to launch a fourth network and that, aside from the economics, our biggest hurdle was not having a big broadcast group to be the backbone of a network service. I told Rupert that if we could ever buy these stations, they could be the catalyst in my longtime dream to compete with the big-three broadcasters.

There is no dog with hearing as sharp as Rupert Murdoch's when opportunity calls. It took him less than a second to say, "Ha! Let's go after this!"

I called Milken, who said, "John wants a billion seven fifty. But he thinks he could sell the Boston station to Hearst for six hundred million. So it's a billion one for the other stations."

I called Murdoch and reported all that. Rupert wasn't fazed and just asked how much the whole effort would cost.

I called my friend Marty Pompadur, a very senior media executive who had been a key ABC executive and knew everything about broadcasting. An hour later Marty was in my office, and we began chewing over how to build a fourth network.

It's hard to believe now, when there are zillions of networks, but at that time cable was just beginning to do more than deliver a clear picture; there were still only enough high-power stations with coverage across the United States to support three networks. The rest of the stations were lower power, and only a few had meaningful viewership. The only way we could ever hope to compete would be to build up these not-even-fourth-rate stations with great programming and promotion. We could do only guesstimates about what all this might cost.

With nothing more than scrap sheets, I called Murdoch and told him we would have to spend about $200 million before breaking even. I added, though, that there really wasn't any way to actually know the costs, because no one had tried to build a new network for thirty years, and that attempt failed miserably.

Despite having been presented with that flimsiest of a business plan, Rupert was ecstatically on board. He didn't flinch about the costs; he saw only the opportunity.

And, with that, he had me. There's a great thrill in working with Murdoch when he sees a daunting hill to climb. He's never happier than when there are huge obstacles to overcome in pulling off something wildly ambitious; he's a warrior when fighting to establish something in enemy territory—usually against the Establishment.

Marvin Davis was still a 50 percent partner when all this happened, so we had no choice but to tell him about this opportunity. He said, "Okay, I'm in, but I don't know enough about the broadcast business, so I'll just take an option until I know more." Typical Davis bullshit, but I didn't care, because at least it got us going.

I returned to New York the next day and called John Kluge. We went back and forth a little on the terms, but I essentially said yes to his proposal. Kluge said, "Done! Come right over to my apartment at the Waldorf Towers and we'll drink to it." I called Rupert, who was at his *New York Post* office, and said, "We have an agreement. Kluge wants us to come up and toast to it."

Rupert said, "Pick me up."

So I went way downtown to the historic New York Post Building, where Rupert worked in Dolly Schiff's original mammoth office, which had been designed to intimidate the men around her. In a taxi on the way back uptown to Kluge's apartment, Murdoch let out a gleeful "What a great adventure! We're betting the company!" and slapped the seat for emphasis. Honestly, what sheer fun it was to be with him and his master gambler's enthusiasm.

Kluge opened the door to his huge apartment with a big welcoming smile. We thought this meeting was just to shake hands on the deal privately. We had made an oral agreement an hour ago and hadn't yet done any due diligence or any of the legal work necessary to announce a transaction. We were in the midst of some small talk about how excited we were to acquire the stations, about all the work we'd have to do, and after five minutes Kluge stood up and said, "Okay, let's go tell the news to everyone."

Given that there were only the three of us, I couldn't understand whom he thought we were going to tell. John then steered us across his vast living room and opened the double doors to his dining room, where there were about thirty journalists and their television crews. He marched us to the head of the dining room table, greeted everyone, and announced that we'd bought all his television stations. There was no way he was going to let us escape from this deal.

As for Rupert, the grand risk-taker, with only a verbal assurance that we could actually start a fourth network from someone he'd just met— me—he'd agreed in a flash to buy these stations for more than $1 billion. And this was all done before he even officially owned his one-half of Fox and without any regard for the stringent rules about foreign ownership or any other of the endless details that would have to be worked out.

I had definitely left the farm for the big city.

By now, I had zero relationship with Marvin Davis and began to play by the strictest interpretation of the joint venture. I disliked the way Marvin had mixed his personal life with the business of Fox, so I called him up and said now that the company was a joint venture, he would no longer be able to dictate or authorize any expenditure on his own. He couldn't have his Carousel Ball charity dinner paid for by Fox, or have his children officed at the studio, or any of the myriad nonbusiness items he'd been charging to the studio.

He said, "I'll do what I want."

I told him, "I want to be very clear—listen carefully. You own fifty percent of the equity of this company, and you have fifty percent rights with the other owner, News Corp. I'm the chief executive officer, and I have all operating powers. All you have is your half vote, so you can literally do nothing in the conduct of the business other than vote your shares, which unless you have the vote of Murdoch means you can't do squat." Fox wasn't going to be any more fun for Marvin Davis. I was finally learning how to play by big-boy rules.

He called Murdoch right away. "We have to fire Diller. He's no good. We've picked the wrong person. We should've gotten Michael Eisner."

Rupert told me everything Davis said. And he told Davis he wasn't inclined to fire me. That created a stalemate that went on for a few months, until Davis informed Murdoch that he wasn't going to exercise his option to join the Metromedia buy. "You can do what you want with the network," he said, "but you can't use Diller in any way not associated with his duties running Fox."

I told Murdoch that as messy as this was, maybe I should resign, that they could get someone else to run the studio. That didn't make much practical sense, but it was a chip thrown on the table during the months before the station transaction was finalized. These low-light skirmishes continued back and forth between Marvin Davis and me, all designed to show him that as far as Fox was concerned, his only involvement was going to be a slip of paper noting his ownership. Given that he had fraudulently misrepresented the state of the company and then reneged on his commitment to finance it, I had zero sympathy for his position.

Finally, Davis gave up. He called Murdoch and agreed to sell him his 50 percent for $350 million. I was thrilled to finally be done with him.

But my thrill was stayed by one last gauntlet.

After all the details had been ironed out, weeks went by, and Davis began braying around town that he wasn't sure he was going to be out of Fox, because Murdoch probably didn't have the money to close. I had no idea why he would trash Murdoch, other than he didn't want people to believe he'd been forced out. It was just nasty.

He held on to the final signing papers for days without returning them, crowing publicly that the deal might never happen.

Finally, I called and asked why he wasn't signing the papers. He said he'd get around to it soon. I said soon had to be now. He said, "Okay, you can come by the house tomorrow and I'll give them to you." I drove up the driveway to that mega-mansion on Schuyler Road and parked in the vast forecourt, a hundred feet from the doorway. His massive figure appeared, and he walked down the steps toward me, the signed papers in his hand.

I took them, and as I turned around and walked back to my car, he said, "Well, kid, you made me a lot of money."

Those were the last words ever spoken between us.

CHAPTER 19

With Marvin Davis gone, and Rupert Murdoch's grand ambitions directed at Fox, we were ready not only to revive a great old Hollywood studio but also to revolutionize television. Big talk indeed.

But what I had to do right away was stabilize the film company. Fox had been run like a candy store for a sweet-toothed con man who was in it for all the wrong reasons. Everyone was out only for their own good, spending most of their time on the internal politics of pleasing the boss. At the senior levels they were all toadies. One of those was the brilliant and very young Scott Rudin, whose talent even then sent sparks flying, some of them ricocheting right back onto him. And at the other end of the age spectrum was Larry Gordon, the wisecracking filmmaking pro I'd known at Paramount.

We'd inherited one good movie, *Romancing the Stone*. I also saw a rough cut of a little movie Ron Howard directed called *Cocoon*, which I thought was lovely and if distributed aggressively might have a chance. I argued with the producer Dick Zanuck, the studio's ex-president whose father founded the damned place, that we ought to release the film that coming summer. He felt it was too small to compete with all the big films that had already been scheduled, but I thought it was perfect counterprogramming. And it worked. We'd also made this movie called *Commando* with Arnold Schwarzenegger. Despite his success in *The Terminator*, I considered Schwarzenegger just a hulk who pushed his overbuilt body into the movie business with little acting talent. But the film, a fairly ordinary action flick, was an out-of-the-box hit.

One day early in its release, I got a call from Arnold asking to see me. He came bounding into my office saying, "I want a billboard on Sunset Boulevard."

I told him, "We don't do that. I don't believe in billboards. It's a waste of money."

He said, "No, no, no. I *have* to have a billboard. It's *very, very important* to me. I must have a billboard on Sunset Boulevard."

I said, "Well, you ain't gonna get it from me."

He then proceeded to do an utterly impolitic and unactorish thing, which was to call me every week for the next two or three months, always saying the same thing: "I have to see you about my billboard!" And every time, I said no.

What did I know? I thought, *Here's this dumb-fuck oaf who wants a billboard, and I'm not giving him one.* I told him, "Look, the problem with stuff like billboards and full-page ads is that it becomes a precedent. The next person who wants one will just say, 'But you gave it to Arnold—why aren't you giving it to me?' I don't want to do any of that stuff. I don't believe in it. I'm never giving a billboard to anyone."

Even though Arnold kept at it and at it and at it, I never gave in to him. But from the first, I knew he was someone with both real smarts and granite ambition to get his way. It was then no surprise to me that this thickly accented Austrian non-actor became Arnold Schwarzenegger the movie star, and later the governor of the state of California.

Just as I had with the *Movie of the Week* at ABC, I was again starting all alone to try to establish a new television network. There I was with my big idea, my theory that there ought to be an alternative to CBS/NBC/ABC. I knew instinctively that there should be more options than three look-alike networks and wasn't daunted by how many tries before had failed. I just knew it was time to try this. But how to turn that blue-sky idea into an actual plan? We now had this backbone of Metromedia stations, but how would we find enough other stations to be viable, to cover the rest of the country? What kind of programming would work? It wasn't as if anyone was clamoring for a fourth network. Even though the three networks had basically morphed into one bland blob, there wasn't any factual evidence to support starting one. But I was sure it could be done.

I didn't see, as I usually don't with a new idea, how difficult and expensive it would be to get such a project up and running. The only business plan created before we started was truly written on scratch paper with roughly estimated figures I pulled from the air. I also had never researched how many independent broadcasters would be needed to reach the entire country. I was going to follow my usual process: one dumb step forward, two back, course-correcting as I went, bouncing off one wall then the other, finding my way. Deeper examination would have doomed the network from ever starting. PowerPoint decks with all their worthless forward projections would have said it couldn't be done. Instinct and grit were all we had. So we began. Again, a pure start-up with me as the only employee. The first three we hired were Garth Ancier, who was twenty-eight; Kevin Wendle, who was twenty-seven; and Jamie Kellner, the oldest of the three at thirty-eight.

Garth looked twelve, and Kevin looked even younger. I'm naturally disposed to hiring people who don't necessarily qualify or have lots of prior experience; it comes from my own history. I like to give people "too much" responsibility because I took on "too much" when I was at ABC in my early twenties. I liked my process of drowning until I could figure out where the current was moving.

By the time I got to Fox at age forty-two, I had learned the hard way that the odds of hiring qualified people based on résumés and brief person-to-person meetings were pretty poor, and the worst way to populate a company. Especially at senior levels, where I would say the odds are so much against it working out.

I much prefer hiring people who are relatively blank slates, but who have sparks of energy and smarts. And some edge. If you do that consistently enough, which we did at Paramount and at Fox, you end up with a very strong group once they've had a few years to marinate. Maybe it's a simplistic formula, but it works: Give them responsibilities before they are considered ready. Drop them in the deep end and see who struggles and who survives. Keep promoting those who survive.

Garth was a kind of idiot savant about television—a native program-mer with the history of television at his fingertips.

Kellner was a key hire in making Fox an actual business. He had a ter-rific ability to sell, which was critical in getting affiliates to join us. And he knew how to set up a top-notch advertising operation.

I look for people who I think get it, and getting it is relatively rare. I put them in the cauldron with me to solve gnarly creative problems. I can help them grow, help them hone their instincts, remove excess baggage. I hate the word "mentoring"; it's too pretentiously formal a word and has become far too formulaic for a process that best works naturally. God knows, I've paid millions of dollars in fees to headhunters over the years, but I find it to be generally a bad investment. What I always used to say to headhunters, until I finally stopped saying it because I stopped talking to them, was "Find me the number four, number eight, number twelve, number eighteen person in an organization, the person who is unique be-cause of his energy and edge. Go by the theory that under a rock is a good thing rather than a bad thing, and turn the rocks over." I've learned that most of the people who are supposedly qualified with big prior positions are mostly retreads.

At first, we were going to call the network FBC—because ABC, NBC, CBS . . . and FBC sounded just like the others. There are even photos of us at one of our earliest press conferences with an FBC logo. But just as we were to painfully learn in programming, aping the others was never going to work.

It should have been obvious: we had a brand called Fox, which (a) was not simply three letters that stood for three words and (b) actually had a known history.

After such dull thinking, we very quickly, and ever after, said, "We're FOX."

I had one philosophy about new ventures: If you like the idea, get on with it.

Don't overanalyze it, don't waste time making decks and projections where it's absolutely certain, *absolutely*, that they will be wrong, high or low. Don't do anything other than shake the idea back and forth until you resolve that the only known is . . . it's a *good idea*. And then, just *get on with it*! Make mistakes and correct them as fast as you can, and eventually there will be fewer mistakes. This is the way non-geniuses succeed, and I'm very squarely in that camp. I don't see things clearly in the beginning; I can't see around corners. It's process I prize—the rocky road from idea to implementation. The consternation and the thrill of pulling it through to success is the most gratifying work. Once that's done, I lose interest and want to find my way to the next gnarly process.

I'm drawn to things that don't conform to the standard, which is, in some way, a rejection of the concept that normal is good. Normal is average, and I learned very early that concepts of normality not only didn't apply to me but weren't going to produce anything original. We were going to find, unfortunately not in the beginning, that all our successful shows were "different" from what the three networks offered. We learned not to program in the mainstream and instead be an alternative entertainment experience.

But before we got that figured out, we needed to sign up hundreds of stations across the United States. We put together the slickest and best presentations, but we were selling spit. I was out there making speeches, meeting with heads of station groups, trying to persuade them to give up their independence for networked Fox programming. They later all got rich and built big businesses off us, but we had so many doubters at the beginning it was like pulling teeth to get them to sign on. Conversely, selling advertising was never an issue for us. Advertisers were tired of being held hostage to the three networks' yearly cost increases. Plus, we were going to guarantee that our shows would reach the ratings we'd projected. In the early days those actual ratings were so anemic we were called the make-good network, because we had to run commercials over and over again until we made good on the guarantees. During that first year, there were endless stories about our folly. Larry Tisch, the venerated industrialist who owned CBS, said he wouldn't give "a plugged nickel" for Fox.

I'm relatively thick-skinned about what is written about me and my projects. It's far better to be discounted than to be seen as anyone's sure thing. And the perception in media circles was that we would fail resoundingly. While we did get stations and advertisers to join us, we were all just holding a deep breath until we got on the air. And when we did, it was hardly with a bang.

Meanwhile, we had these very powerful stations that we owned outright, and they all needed their own programming. That's where Michael Eisner came back into my life. He showed up at my house one Saturday shortly after we bought the Metromedia stations. One of his first big projects in reviving Disney was to launch the Disney Afternoon, a two-hour daily block of cartoons from four to six. I thought it was a good idea and wanted to support Michael in his early days of building up Disney, so I agreed to buy it for our six stations. It went on to become a huge success for us both. After two years the deal came up for renewal. Jeff Katzenberg, who'd gone to Disney with Eisner, was designated to call and say, with undisguised competitive glee, "By the way, next year, we're going to take the Disney Afternoon block from your L.A. station and put it on the one we just bought, but we'd still like to renew for the other five stations."

Outraged, I said, "We gave birth to this fucking thing, and you're going to take away one of our key stations?"

He said, "Yes," and I was beyond angry at the lack of loyalty for my having backed it on pure faith in the new Disney team. I told him if you do that, you can take the whole Disney Afternoon and shove it.

Shove it they did, taking the whole block to our competitors. I so hated that my old colleagues would do this and hated more that I then shot myself in the foot for revenge. Thankfully, our Jamie Kellner came to the rescue with the idea that we ought to start our own children's network and go head-to-head with Disney's. We blew them out of the water with our much more adventurous and original cartoons, and the Disney Afternoon was soon toast. Then Disney, in malicious reaction, sued us in federal court for antitrust violations, saying we were an unfit broadcaster. They went for our very throat and tried to destroy us. It failed, but I didn't speak to Michael Eisner for three years. So much for our own non-animated children's games of friendly and brotherly competition.

It would have happened eventually without me, but I did start the concept of voyeuristic television, which evolved into the endlessly repetitive "reality" shows that are now everywhere.

I began tinkering with news programming at our L.A. station. When you're in the newsroom preparing for a broadcast, everything is of the moment. It's exciting, tearing from the edit bay to get something to rip and read on the air, searching for a graphic or racing to get experts to speak. It's all so urgent, hyperfast, and compelling—*in the newsroom*. But there was a cavernous difference between being there and being the viewer. All the excitement and urgency were missing. If you're making a movie or a show, you're always searching for rhythm: you know what a scene has to be to lead to the next scene. But with a news show, nothing is connected; the rhythm you're creating and experiencing as you're building the broadcast has an energy that isn't transmitted to the viewer. It began tugging at me—what was real and of the moment versus what was packaged and smoothed out for viewing. I searched for a way to fuse the two, something raw. I came upon a gawky, small in size but big in ambition production assistant named Mike Darnell. I told him to take a crew and find an opening of *anything* where there are celebrities. I said, "If a limousine door opens, and they get out of the car and trip, *that's* what I want you to find." I didn't want anything that was programmed and "presented." I wanted real life. "Just keep the cameras rolling until something unexpected happens," I told him. So, Darnell went out and started shooting at all hours of the day and night with all sorts of people and brought back these real nuggets. Out of this came the Fox hit *Cops*.

Getting the network landed was a glorious mess. In the early years I made almost every decision down to the paper clips, and my process was not as easy or neat as my paper clip policies. While I never lost conviction, everyone thought we were a folly, my folly, and our terrible early ratings almost lost us our biggest advertiser, as well as the support of one Rupert Murdoch.

Coca-Cola was the first one to sign on with us. They liked the idea of having an alternative to the big-three networks, and they liked our spunk.

It was their initial order that got other advertisers to give us a shot long before we started airing anything. Don Keough, president of Coca-Cola, called me up a few months after we went on the air and said, "Look, I'm your biggest supporter and we'll stay with you until you figure things out, but you've got to stop running our spots. Because of your low ratings, it's embarrassing to see so many of them. So forget the guarantees—just stop running our spots so often."

That's not the kind of call you want: *Stop running our ads!*

A few years later, after we'd become a big success and were overdelivering everywhere, I called Keough to say that another company had made a commitment for the next season and would replace Coca-Cola as our biggest advertiser, and I just thought he should know. In an instant he responded, "Let's be clear: We *are* your biggest advertiser and will remain so. Just tell us the number that gets us there and that'll be that." This became a rule of the house between Coca-Cola and Fox, lasting for the next six years. Some ten years later, I joined the board of directors of Coca-Cola, and I've been serving now for twenty-three years. I don't think there's a business like it in all the world. It operates in 196 countries and has been doing so since many of those countries were founded. It's usually the first commercial business that gets formed in emerging markets, and its worldwide political sophistication is unrivaled. It's also the greatest distribution system conceived by man.

At Fox, though, the eighty-seven weeks it took for the network to break even felt like eighty-seven years, the last months of which almost felled us. The ever-impatient Rupert Murdoch thought we took too much time to get the programming right, and this led to the one serious argument in our eight years of working together.

The eruption took place in my car on our way to Warners to see its leaders, Bob Daly and Terry Semel. Rupert had the incredibly gutsy idea of starting a satellite service in Britain to compete with the already announced and funded government one. Hollywood movies were going to be the backbone of both services, and I was helping him buy movies—you never completely put your old job behind you!—for the new channel. We were on our way to shake hands on the deal we'd negotiated.

On the way, Rupert abruptly turned to me and said, "This television thing is a mess. There are all these horrible programs you're putting on." Then he said, "I think you should really consider giving up the television side. God knows you're rebirthing the studio, the film side, and you do that great. But you have these two programmers"—he meant Garth Ancier and Kevin Wendle—"these young, inexperienced kids who have no idea what America wants to watch."

I fought back and said, "We *are* making progress. It's a process and I can't do it faster." He said, "You're costing me a fortune." I was by then confident we'd pull it off and the value of his stock would increase enormously. I snapped that instead of grandstanding about what it was costing him, he might consider that it really was me making a financial sacrifice for his eventual gain, since every dollar we lost at Fox was deducted from my 5 percent of annual gross profits. This went back and forth as we descended into the Valley, and I was so angry I almost told him that I had real work to do and he ought to just *go in there and buy his own fucking movies*!

I did have a higher tolerance for "temporary failure" than Rupert did. (Although my revulsion at the prospect of *ultimate* failure may be even greater than his.)

We got to Warners, where we had to smile and be nice to each other through the meeting. Then we got back in the car and went right back at it, all the way up the other side of the hill and down to Fox. We got out of the car with nothing resolved.

One of the things I've always said about Rupert is that if he's on-site with you and engaged, he's the most stimulating collaborator. But at that time, Rupert was mostly in Australia or London or New York. He wasn't focused on our actual business, only on our immediate failures and losses. Once again in my career, I was running out of time and thought the rug might get pulled any minute. Dick Sarazen, the CFO of News Corp, called me soon after our venomous car ride and said, "Fox is getting to be a real problem. We've put in over one hundred and twenty-five million dollars thus far, and it's hurting News Corp's overall performance. These losses can't continue." They didn't, but it was another very close call. The cat again escaped its demise.

CHAPTER 20

I was hurling and holding multiple balls in the air, building up Fox movies while starting the new network. Still bouncing my way back and forth from Los Angeles to New York. I had moved into an apartment in the Waldorf Towers in New York City, at the time the most rarefied housing in the city. I was on the thirty-ninth floor, two floors below where the U.S. ambassador to the United Nations lived and where U.S. presidents stayed when they came to New York—and also where I once ran very much afoul of the Secret Service. I was coming home from the Fox office in midtown just as the Secret Service was beginning to close down the side-street entrance to the Towers because President Reagan was shortly arriving. In the commotion of getting out of my car while dodging security, I'd left my old battered briefcase on the steps to the entrance. Up I went to my place and took off my clothes to shower. Suddenly, there was a pounding on my door. When the Secret Service discovered a lone briefcase right in front of where the president's limousine was about to disembark, they immediately cleared the entire area and called the bomb squad. The doorman said he thought it might be mine, as I was the last one to enter the building. Three Secret Service men bundled me down the hall, into the elevator, and pushed me out into the street, bathrobe flapping and half naked, to identify my briefcase before the truly bewildered hundreds waiting for the president to arrive. Thankfully there were no iPhones then, or that picture would have become the one that pops up first in any Google search.

In our first regularly scheduled season, all our early attempts at programming flopped. No one in the production community was paying any attention to us. All we got offered were shows rejected by the big three. We believed, completely incorrectly, that we had to take these castoffs, as that was all we had to choose from. Those early shows were no different from what the other networks were airing. I wish I could say it was otherwise, but my contrarian nature wasn't much in evidence, and it took too long for us to look and feel like the alternative network we needed to be.

Finding our own vein took some false and painful poking about. Finally, in the nick of time came a script that lit my contrarian spark and came to define what Fox was. The title on the first page woke me up: *NOT THE COSBYS*. At the time, *The Cosby Show* was the most successful program on television, a gentle sitcom about an idealized, decent, and loving family (just how idealized we now know, given the revelations about Mr. Cosby). *Not the Cosbys* was about a dysfunctional family saying and doing every impolitic, incorrect thing possible. And it was hysterically funny. We'd found our edge. We were going to be an *alternative network*! We had to change the title, of course—it became *Married . . . with Children*.

The one producer/writer/director I wanted to bring to Fox from Paramount was Jim Brooks. I'd helped start his film career way back at ABC, and he'd made some great movies at Paramount, particularly the Academy Award winner *Terms of Endearment*. The Paramount diaspora now at Disney went after him hard, but we got him, and apart from making the very great movie *Broadcast News*, he agreed to help us develop television programs. The result was *The Tracey Ullman Show*, a sketch and music variety series that turned out to be far too highbrow for Fox. But inside it were these little animated one- or two-minute interstitials about a family called the Simpsons. Short though they were, Brooks and his co-creator, Matt Groening, thought they could make a half-hour series. It was expensive—a huge gamble. But more than any other show, it built Fox. *The Simpsons* is probably the longest-running, most successful show in the history of television. Ironically, we scheduled it directly opposite that number one series, *The Cosby Show,* and we beat it that first night out. That cemented Fox Broadcasting firmly as the fourth network.

In our eighty-seventh week, we defied the odds and broke even. We'd spent about $1.3 billion to land an asset that's worth easily many multiples of that. We'd go on to beat the three networks and become the number-one-rated network in all of television.

While battling everything and everyone to establish the network, I needed to keep the studio bustling with successful movies. Our big hits in 1986 were James Cameron's *Aliens* and David Cronenberg's remake of *The Fly,* which starred Jeff Goldblum. I loved *The Fly* from the first moment I heard the idea—a time-transporting experiment gone wrong, resulting in a fly's head on a human. I thought the movie was both stupid and great. The ad—"Be afraid. Be very afraid"—entered the zeitgeist, and audiences came out in droves. It was a nice, juicy, totally unexpected success.

Aliens was a big, square hit for us, and Jim Cameron wasn't even Jim Cameron yet.

In 1987 we released both *Broadcast News* and *Wall Street.* Despite the pedantic names, they were seminal movies of those times. *Wall Street* defined the moment with a line from the movie ("Greed is good") and *Broadcast News* had what I think is one of the all-time great speeches.

Albert Brooks to Holly Hunter about Bill Hurt, the blond-haired vanilla news anchorman Tom in the movie:

> I know you care about him. I've never seen you like this about anyone, so please don't take it wrong when I tell you that I believe that Tom, while a very nice guy, is the Devil. What do you think the Devil is going to look like if he's around?
>
> Come on! Nobody is going to be taken in if he has a long, red, pointy tail. No. I'm being semi-serious here. He will look attractive and he will be nice and helpful and he will get a job where he

influences a great God-fearing nation and he will never do an evil thing . . . He will just bit by little bit lower standards where they are important . . . Just coax along flash over substance. Just a tiny bit. And he will talk about all of us really being salesmen. And he'll get all the great women.

An observation for all time, certainly for our last thirty years.

Fox's 1988 movie slate included *Die Hard*. God, that movie was great, but I mostly remember what a nightmare making it was. Right at the start I got in a big fight with my head of production, Leonard Goldberg, my old boss from ABC. He told me, "We can get Bruce Willis!"

I said, "What do you mean we can *get* Bruce Willis? Who cares about Bruce Willis? No one really likes Bruce Willis!" ABC's *Moonlighting* had turned Willis into a TV star when it debuted in 1985, but before *Die Hard* his first two attempts at movie stardom, *Blind Date* and *Sunset,* were flops. Len said, "Oh, no, no, no-no-no. He's perfect for this part! There's only one problem. We have to pay him more than he's worth: five million."

I *screeched*. "We are *not* doing it."

The next thing I knew, Len called me, and he said, "Look, we have no choice. We're starting the movie. We don't have our actor. He's the *only* one." Len just battered me until I gave in and we hired Willis.

The next little problem: the film had a scene in which a whole floor of the building the terrorists have seized blows apart. We owned that office tower; it's still standing on Avenue of the Stars in Century City, and with angles that suggest the folds of a paper airplane, it's really quite a beautiful building. At the time we were shooting *Die Hard,* it had just been finished. Fox Broadcasting was still losing money, and that building was important to us.

The producers, Joel Silver and Larry Gordon, came to see me and said they wanted to use it for this blowout scene. Silver, one of the great bullshit artists of all time, said, "We just need it for a night." He had been told that I cared about the building, so he added, "We won't hurt anything. We won't damage anything. We'll have all this prep. It'll only be one night."

He went on and on: it'll be this, it'll be that, until finally I said, "Yeah, okay, fine. Go do it."

And the afternoon of the shoot someone from our real estate division called and said, "They're destroying our building."

"What do you mean, they're destroying our building?"

They told me to go over there and see. It was winter, and at five p.m. it was dark already. The whole street and surrounding area looked like a disaster zone.

The first five stories of the building's windows had been boarded up. I saw Joel, and said, "What the fuck are you doing to this building?!"

He admitted, "It's a little more complicated than I said."

"A *little* more complicated? You've destroyed our thirty-story building! And you said you'd be out of here in one night!"

He said, "Actually, I think it's going to be about two weeks."

I was insane with anger, but there was nothing I could do. They'd already wrecked it. The penultimate shots of the first few floors of the building were an explosion that blew out all the windows. I had thought they were going to fake it with a miniature, but no, they did it for real! It took us a year—and cost us a lot of money—to fix the damage. All our tenants also demanded reductions on their rent.

When the rough cut was ready, Len Goldberg said to me, "Look, it's unbelievably long, so it'd be better if you waited, but if you want to see it, just know that we're going to cut forty to fifty minutes out of it."

When you're told that, it does create much lower expectations. I started watching the movie, and within five minutes I was totally hooked—not as a pro, just as an audience. I was in the projection room in my house, all alone, loving every minute of it. I mean, I'd never seen Alan Rickman before! He was the most delectable villain. I called up Goldberg and said, "Don't touch a fucking thing. This is not a good movie. This is a great movie."

That was one good thing I did, keeping it from being cut. And the next good thing I did was to say, "You can't advertise Bruce Willis."

Len said, "We paid him five million dollars!"

I said, "Yes, *wrongly,* but you cannot advertise Bruce Willis, because no one likes him. After they see this movie, they're gonna love him, but coming in, they don't like him." And if you look at the ads for *Die Hard*, there was the title and the building.

It lasts to this day as one of the great thriller disaster movies. And Bruce was great in it. And very likable.

Home Alone was number one at the box office for twelve weeks. The cash that poured in came along exactly when Rupert's News Corp was technically on the verge of bankruptcy. Rupert had been going around the world to bank after bank to persuade them not to call in the huge loans he'd taken out over the years to finance his acquisitions. Of the many things I do respect him for, the biggest was his handling of the seminal crisis in his career. He was under tremendous pressure for more than a year, but he never complained or tried to lay off the blame. He was humbled but stalwart throughout; a real mensch is the only way I can describe him.

If not for Fox and *Home Alone,* his whole company would have gone down. It really was the cash, almost five hundred million, from *this* one film that saved him. Think of that—a little Christmas comedy saved Rupert Murdoch and allowed all that followed.

Ted Turner was in a squeeze. He'd bought MGM at exactly the wrong time, and his major owners, Time Warner and Liberty Media, had vetoes over anything he wanted to do. He was demoralized, and unused to being caged, so Rupert and I thought he might be feeling weak enough to sell CNN. We flew down to Atlanta to have dinner with him, and Rupert was at his most charming, which makes him immensely hard to resist, but Ted mostly just stared back somewhat dully, not completely comprehending that anyone would dare try to take his jewel network away from him. It was clear that Ted would stop breathing before he sold to Murdoch, and the dinner meandered to a close. If there had been a whiff of an opening, Rupert would have bet the company again to pull that deal off.

Rupert was always a better and bigger risk-taker than I was. I may have taken a lot of career risks as well as product risks, but the big, betting-the-store risk is not something I was constitutionally able to do. Rupert was, always. It excited him, while it hobbled me.

Over the years my risk appetite has grown a lot, but I'll never be in his league. He's a gambler at heart, always calculating just how far he can push to get the opportunities he hungers for. Sometimes he overreaches, and usually overpays, but he's always been saved by his ability to pull out of his hat whatever profits are needed to pay off the debts. Over and over, he's been the great media disrupter. He changed British television by launching Sky satellite service, committing billions of dollars he didn't actually have for a market that didn't exist. I'll be forever grateful that he backed me with Fox Broadcasting against such huge odds.

He did, though, deprive me of being surprised at my own surprise birthday party. My close friend Sandy Gallin had spent months planning it and invited people from all over to come to Los Angeles for my forty-fifth. Rupert rather callously mentioned that he couldn't make it, saying, ". . . oh, I suppose it was going to be a surprise—oh, well, hope you enjoy it anyway."

And oh, I did, though my one memory is that Diane called me in the middle of the party from wherever in the world she was and we had a bittersweet moment. I still so missed her not being in my everyday life.

CHAPTER 21

How do big changes come in the life of someone who isn't introspective? Someone who doesn't philosophically and pragmatically review where he is on any timeline of his life's progress? Someone who's never had any actual goals, other than to "count"?

There wasn't any great epiphany. Why would I ever want to leave the corporate life, where I'd been so successful for so many years?

There was this one moment in 1991 when, completely unpremeditated, the jack came out of the box. I was at a regular board meeting of News Corp and got into a lively argument with one of the other directors on a minor matter. It was about doing what I thought was the right, rather than the expedient, thing. I was having a good time demolishing the director's arguments and thought I was making an important business as well as moral point. But Rupert impatiently shut me down. It was, of course, his prerogative to do so, but the rebuke began to swirl and stew in the back of my mind.

That night was the annual Met Ball.

I found myself stuck in this slow, snaking receiving line with Anna Murdoch, Rupert's wife at the time, who was also a News Corp board member. She casually asked me what I thought of the meeting, and out of my mouth flew, not without some surprising and uncalled-for vehemence, "What difference does it make what I think? I'm just a hired hand." Anna laughed it off, but I didn't.

Those words escaped before I knew I was even thinking them. It was such an unusually unguarded moment that a bell rang in my head, one that not only was overpoweringly loud but couldn't be unrung.

I had been thinking something I hadn't yet acknowledged to myself: that Fox wasn't really mine, that however I acted as if it were, it wasn't.

I thought then and think now that a good employee does believe and act as if the company belongs to them. But of course that's an illusion, one I'd been able to keep full faith in with the three companies I'd worked at for a quarter century. But suddenly the reality that this was an illusion couldn't be denied.

Once it was gone, I couldn't retrieve it. Something had cracked open, and the true condition of my situation at age forty-nine was seeping out, and I couldn't rationalize things back to where they'd been. I realized that if I went on this way for long enough, bitterness would follow, and at some point Rupert would, whether cruelly or politely, get rid of me, because that's what employers do when employees become either obstreperous or obsolete.

As that feeling swelled, I went to have lunch with Jack Welch, the chairman of GE, which owned NBC. He was deeply unhappy with the network's performance. It was a disaster, and I thought it would be fun, even exciting, to try to turn it around. And Jack was encouraging, as he was toying with the idea of selling it. I wondered if I could raise the necessary money, but quickly realized I couldn't pursue that while being an employee of one of its competitors. The truth was I couldn't pursue anything without quitting Fox, without being independent. But that prospect frightened me into inaction. How could I turn from my exalted position to standing out in the cold without the protection of a big company behind me? The very thought froze me.

But I had one other I couldn't get out of my head: *Either you are, or you aren't.*

It's a harsh and binary concept, and not subject to equivocation. Either you are the principal or you're not. The rationalizing powers of a good employee are endless. Good employees make decisions on a company's behalf as if they own it. I'd been doing that since my earliest days at ABC. I acted like a principal, but I wasn't one. I was an employee, and whatever position and power I had could be revoked at any time. I had gone about as high as a corporatist could go. I'd run two studios. I was making more money than anyone else in the entertainment business—I was on the cover of *Business Week*. But as rarefied as all that was, it could be taken away in an instant. All that power I flexed so naturally was devolved from real power. I was craving independence and had a need to stand on my own. And the only way to do that was to take action. But, at such risk.

To be truly independent, beholden to no one but yourself, unprotected by the mothering of a corporation—for a lifelong employee that's a daunting proposition. And thus those words—*Either you are, or you aren't*—were banging around my head with increasing force. You can do all the things executives have done since executive-ing began, fantasize and rationalize all you want—and I was a most practiced player at all that—but that binary about independence rules: *Either you are, or you aren't*.

Most people in the entertainment community are living a kind of pretend life. Most of them talk all sorts of big games: they talk about going out on their own, they excuse away their status, they act big and important. Of course, there's nothing wrong with being an employee. I was a productive one for thirty years, and it served me better than well. Being protected is a good thing, often the only way to accomplish what you hope to accomplish. But if you yearn to be on your own, untethered, then you must take action, or disappointment with yourself and bitterness will grow unstoppably inside you. It was beginning to happen to me. I wasn't bored, and I had done a lot in those Fox years. I'd succeeded in putting a new network firmly on the entertainment map; our movies were doing well, and the company as a whole was thriving. I was comforted and cosseted by the luxuries it provided in my life: houses, boats, company jets. I really didn't want to leave, but there was this imperative gaining urgency. *You either are or you are not capable of being on your own.*

I've never thought in terms of goals. Yes, if you want to be a doctor, you've got to get a license; a lawyer's got to pass the bar. But if you're in the entertainment business, setting an absolute goal such as "I want to be head of a studio" is antithetical to ever getting there. One of the things about the executive side of the entertainment business is that you don't really need to *know* anything to prosper. You need smarts, mostly of a particular street kind, but what you truly need are instincts and willfulness. It's that alchemy that makes for a significant career. Having specific goals on that path forward are often detriments. Better to just take opportunities whenever they come and not overplot. God knows that's what I did for all it was worth, but now I couldn't get around the idea that there was someone's thumb on my neck.

I had almost no frustrations with Rupert. I made every material decision while I was at Fox. Although I talked to him about our progress or lack thereof, I didn't ask him about the movies we should make or get his permission. I always *acted* like a principal.

My original five-year contract with Fox had ended, and when it expired I told Rupert I didn't want to enter into a new contractual relationship. I thought it better for us both to just have a six-month mutual termination clause: either of us could end things with half a year's notice. We had stability and confidence in each other, and my compensation was fair. We both thought that if either of us wanted to stop working together, all we had to do was push a cease button. As my frustrations and aspirations rose in the summer of 1991, I went to Rupert and told him I wanted to be a principal. I remember saying to him, "We both know I *act* like it, but I want to actually *be* it. I want to be some kind of a partner in this enterprise."

He said, "Give me some time to think about it." A few days later, he came back to me and said, "There's really only one principal in this company. I mean, you make decisions, and that's been fine for me and for you. But this is a family company and you're not a member."

With that, whatever delusions I was still holding on to crumbled.

I hadn't contemplated that there would be consequences to that conversation. I hadn't thought this through to any practical action. Our offices in L.A. were next to each other. When Rupert was there, he would always come into my office through a side door. He'd wander in and out, and I would do the same throughout the day. But over the next few months—from October 1991 to January 1992—after that partner conversation, I noticed that he wasn't coming around much anymore. At first I didn't think anything of it—nothing had really changed—but eventually I sensed that Rupert the Sun God was shifting his glow away from me. He'd gotten what he'd needed out of me and now we were on cruise control—a dangerous place to be in Murdochland.

I didn't see the strain that was developing between us. He was in the final stage of reorganizing the debt that had been hobbling him for the last two years. The ending of his debt crisis was a national road show to sell bonds to a new bank consortium.

During that period cash was still in the shortest supply, and I was personally caught up in trying to help with these cash flow problems. My own compensation arrangement was that I had 5 percent of the gross of Fox, which came to $12 million that year. It was supposed to be paid to me on the first of the year. I kept postponing the payment, telling Fox's CFO not to write the check. This went on for almost a year.

News Corp was running on fumes, and every dollar that Fox made was going to bolster it. I assumed that my altruistic act of not taking my 5 percent would be noticed. At least remarked upon, an acknowledgment that I was indeed a partner in the company. It was part of the illusion I held on to, of not being *just* an employee. But no one seemed to notice my sacrifice. I think Rupert was somehow resentful that Fox—and even me personally—was helping prop up his company. He had been so damaged in the financial community that the banks didn't trust him. On the other hand, I was the symbol of Fox's success. When Dave DeVoe, the News Corp CFO, said, "You have to go on this road show with Rupert and help him sell the bonds," I replied, "I hate making speeches. I'm not going."

He said, "Please do this. Fox is a big part of whether we'll be able to get the money."

I reluctantly agreed. It was a hard slog. We repeatedly humbled ourselves as we performed before dour-eyed bankers while they ate their overcooked chicken breasts.

We were on that road show for more than a month. Although Rupert never said anything to me outright, I think he felt envious because my presentations were greeted so positively, while his were received with niggling, skeptical queries like "What are you going to do with our money?" or accusatory ones like "Are you going to blow this money and buy something terrible like *TV Guide* again?"

By Christmas, though I couldn't put a finger on it, I felt something fundamental had changed between us. In the first week of January, I went to New Orleans to give a speech at the National Association of Television Program Executives; it was a big deal, and an important speech for me because I was arguing for a second stream of income for broadcasters. Broadcasters received revenue only from advertising, not from cable systems, where consumers were paying directly for that programming. I believed they/we were entitled to a share of those cable revenues. That, of course, was anathema to cable owners. I got cheers for that speech, but it took another few years for cable to cough up a share of their revenues to the companies that made the programs.

After the speech, I flew back to L.A., and Rupert asked me to come to his office. He said something like "Sooner or later I'm going to want to change things." Thwack.

I had set the dominoes in motion in my yearning for independence. I had pushed Rupert and now he was pushing back. He wasn't firing me, but he was telling me that at some point he wanted to take over Fox. But I hadn't worked it all out yet, hadn't thought my actions through to an endgame. I wasn't ready and felt blindsided. My reaction was to go berserk.

"You fucking asshole. You used me to save your fucking company and go on that road show and sell my little ass off for *this*?"

Rupert had no idea how to respond. I went on and on about what a bastard he was to use me and then want to discard me. He just stared at me as I railed on, and then I stormed out. He hadn't really said anything that enraging, but all this stuff had been washing around inside me, and I felt rejected. I drove to an appointment with my psychiatrist for life, Dr. Aronson. When I recounted my confrontation with Rupert, I went berserk all over again.

He was never simply a passive listener. After I finally ran out of steam, he just looked up at me and said, "Well . . . seems like you got what you wanted."

And he was right.

It was a long, contemplative journey back to Fox, though only five minutes in actual drive time. I went straight to Murdoch's office and said, "Okay, fine, I resign. Here's how I want to do it. We should keep this an absolute secret until we decide to announce it. You tell no one and I'll tell no one. No leaks. There's nothing actionable because we have this six-month notification agreement. We don't need to do anything legally, as we'll just pull that trigger as of today."

"What's your plan?" he wanted to know. "Where are you going? What are you going to do?"

I told him I didn't have a clue. He said he was traveling to Australia for the next three weeks, and we worked out a date in February, after he returned, to make the announcement. I walked out, finally feeling totally and irrevocably in charge of myself and my situation. I have not had a harsh word with Rupert since.

Either you are, or you aren't.

I had my answer.

CHAPTER 22

I was leaving Fox with a clean and blank slate, and not a bad report card. I'd been incredibly lucky. I didn't have any serious enemies. Not any declared ones, anyway. Yes, over the years some people have done me wrong. But it was always about little things, nasty gnats to swat away. I have a very poor memory for the details of being mistreated. I generally forget them; literally, I can't remember. I think it's because I have no appetite for vengeance.

During the next few weeks, we managed to keep my departure from Fox a complete secret. I'd written a multipage version of the press release. Diane made fun of me because one of the lead sentences was pretty flowery stuff: "As the winter turns into my fiftieth year . . ."

A day or two before sending it, I showed a draft to Rupert. He read it and said, "Do you mind? I'm a good editor."

And he plucked every flower, every petal, and cut it all down to just the facts. I wish I had kept his version, because there was a blue pencil through 80 percent of it. He left in a quotation from him and one from me.

I said, "Rupert, that's nice, but I think I'm going to keep it the way I wrote it."

I so wanted to get my leave-taking right. I knew it was going to be a surprise to everyone at Fox and in the industry and provoke all kinds of speculation. What I wrote may have been somewhat overwrought and overwritten, but it was everything I needed to say about my long-simmering yearn for independence.

And here it is, as published:

THE NEWS CORPORATION LIMITED
25 FEBRUARY 1992

Barry Diller announced today that he was resigning as Chairman and Chief Executive Officer of Fox, Inc. Rupert Murdoch, Chairman and Chief Executive of News Corp., Fox's parent company, will assume the direct responsibility of overseeing the Fox Companies.

Mr. Diller said: There is a time for change, and after an endless amount of thought and consideration I believe now is that time for me. Rupert Murdoch and I began discussing last summer my growing desire to become an actual principal in the business activities with which I was associated. Clearly, since Fox is a wholly owned unit of News Corp., that was not a practical or possible ambition within the company.

After being at Fox for seven and a half years, the present status of the company was also a consideration. All four operating divisions have key leadership in place and are performing well. The depth and quality of the executives throughout the company are remarkable. The Creation of the fourth network that I had dreamed about for more than ten years was now a landed reality as Fox Broadcasting Company.

I've essentially been an employee my entire business career. I don't want to denigrate that. Far from it. Since the beginning I have had genuinely amazing opportunities, great good luck and real satisfaction being just that. But, I have also yearned to have my own company in whatever shape or size I am comfortable or capable of creating or acquiring. So, as summer turned to the approach of my 50th birthday, I became convinced that I really did want this kind of career change, and that there was no excuse at this point in my life not to act now.

This is completely amicable. Rupert Murdoch and I have no disagreements. I have had no direct conversations about any potential future activity. I thought it inappropriate to do so while running companies for others. To be fair, the kind of activity that has oc-

cupied my thoughts could only be pursued practically following a
clean break of this kind. There is no perfect time for this . . . in the
end the only way to do it, is to do it. And to the probable surprise
of everyone, especially me, I irrevocably have.

My Colleagues will now understand my gradual disengage-
ment, in my fashion, over the last several months. Technically,
my original contract with the company expired June 30, 1990. At
that time we extended the agreement, cancelable on six months
notice, which I have this day given. Notwithstanding that, Rupert
Murdoch and I believe that as a practical matter the transition will
be completed in weeks not months, and neither of us can imagine
it will take longer than April 1. I will, of course, be available to
help beyond that date and probably, given my feelings about this
place, long beyond anyone's interest in hearing from me. About
Mr. Murdoch, I would say that if you're going to work for somebody, work for him. He's the best . . . straight, supportive, honest
and clear. And I would add that if you want to be an entrepreneur,
a better example for inspiration and aspiration could not be found
anywhere. My gratitude to all of the people of Fox for joining
with me and putting up with me in the creation of a unique company is immense.

Mr. Murdoch said: We are all extremely saddened by Barry
Diller's decision. He has been a great and visionary leader for the
Fox Companies and has achieved extraordinary success. I have
known for a long time his intentions to make this move and respect his decision. Barry Diller's thirty-year career in the television and motion picture industries marks him as one of the all time
great figures of the entertainment business. Our policies will continue unchanged. Namely, to build Fox into the world's best and
most integrated film and television company. Fox has assembled
a magnificent group of people with the talent and determination
to achieve this goal. We have all learned enormously from Barry
Diller and have much for which to thank him in bringing us this
far. We wish him more than well.

I spent that Sunday on my PowerBook, writing to everybody I knew, hundreds of personal notes—I scratched in the margins of most of them, "Wish me luck." On Monday at six in the morning, my office faxed them all out.

The reaction was utter shock. I insisted that Rupert and I spend the day together collegially answering every question so everyone would know we were completely aligned.

Rupert and I had separate exits from our offices that went out to the street, where our cars were parked next to each other. Around seven that night we came out at the same time, and with a big and gracious smile he said that no one in history had ever handled their leave-taking this well. I smiled a crocodile smile back, got in my car, and drove off.

For the next two days it was as if I had died—the press gave me as great a eulogy as I would ever get.

Just as I was preparing to physically depart from Fox, I was awakened early one morning by a call from my stepmother, Janice, saying my father had died.

They were on a cruise ship in the Bahamas just outside Nassau. Janice told me, "We had the most wonderful last night: he made love to me and we slept in each other's arms and he simply never woke up."

I got the plane organized and raced down to meet the boat.

I was still officially Fox's chief executive, so I called Rupert to tell him I'd be away for a few days, and why. All he said was "Oh, sorry." He was not disrespectful, but he was not particularly interested; he had moved on.

When the boat docked, the Bahamian authorities wanted my father taken off so they could go through their legal procedures. I wanted him to stay on the boat, because it was leaving that afternoon for Florida. That way I could fly him to Los Angeles once the boat docked in the United States. The Bahamians were adamant, and the captain of the ship said they were sailing that afternoon; if I didn't get permission, they would have to put him ashore.

We had about five hours to override the local authorities, who were interested only in the many fees we'd have to pay local undertakers before the body would be released.

Luckily, a friend of mine, Henryk de Kwiatkowski, lived in Lyford Cay in the Bahamas. He had a lot of influence, so I called him, and he called the prime minister, and with ten minutes to go, we got permission for my father's body to stay on the boat.

When we finally arrived in Los Angeles and the doors to the plane opened, there on the tarmac was Warren Beatty, who silently embraced me—a lovely act of friendship.

My father felt an existential unrest and tension most of his life, but he had been truly happy and content the last twenty years, first with my mother and then, after she died, with her best friend. He was a good, decent, and honest man, and I wish we could have really known each other. The formality of my relationship to both my parents still astounds me. Was it me or was it them? That they never, all my life, ever, asked me a personal question seems unbelievable, but is true. It's equally true that I never asked for advice or ever shared anything about my inner life with them. They set the initial rules, but I never pierced through them, and to this day, it's still so difficult for me to be open and emotionally available. It's both a continuing mystery and a sad testament that I'm still mostly incapable of easily sharing my inner life.

It was around this time that Diane came back in my life. It had been almost ten years we'd been separated. We'd never lost complete contact, but we saw each other little and weren't in each other's orbit. Diane had been living in Paris conducting her literary salon life with her boyfriend, Alain Elkann, an eminent Italian novelist and journalist who'd previously been married to the daughter of Gianni Agnelli, whose grandfather was also the great-grandfather of Diane's children. Euro circles encircle. Her friends were high left-bank intellectuals and mine were on the other side of the intellectual planet. She had tired of that life and moved back to the U.S. to start up her fashion business. I was on the brink of leaving corporate life and finding an independent way. We'd both had relationships with others that didn't come close to standing the test of time. Hers were deeper and more complete, mine were mostly superficial and incomplete, but each of us had lived a lot of experiences in those ten years, a lot of the wildness had ceased, and we both were at a kind of midpoint, both with fresh careers, and more maturity. Without plot or plan we began to tack back into each other's lives. It was not the *coup de foudre* of our first ferocious love—instead we came back together gently, month by month, then day by day, until we coalesced into the couple we are to this day. We never discussed what was happening or put a definition to it. It wasn't about our age or any desire to "settle down." Not then or now could that ever be a consideration for either of us. We're both too restless. Until our hearts stop beating, neither of us is capable of letting a day go by without some purpose. Our purpose with each other was that we finally knew we fit only together. It couldn't be any other way for either of us. We had met our match long ago and no one or nothing was ever going to replace or displace that. I'd never for a single day stopped loving her and we had both kept a pilot light on for each other in all those out years.

Diane moved back to New York, and I was spending more time in the East as my work at Fox was ebbing. Diane and I, and Alexander and Tatiana, lived at the Carlyle Hotel. Diane lived on one floor and I took an apartment three floors above, and the stairways began to connect us more and more. Our lives revolved around our careers during the week, with weekends spent at Diane's farm in Connecticut. I bought a sailboat, a white furled ketch, and we sailed it together in the Caribbean and the Mediterranean. The children were beginning their adult lives and came on the boat with their flirts, and the word "family" began to not be too far off to describe us.

Aside from that gentle but terrible breakup lunch, we have never had a relationship conversation. Ever. And we made no declarations to ourselves or anyone else. We were still independent states—we've always been well with ourselves on our own, but when we are together there is such comfort and complicity that neither of us can imagine life without the other.

As the years went on, the children were having children, and the knit-ting together had gathered momentum. Diane was always grown-up, but I spent the decade we were apart finally moving on from my emotional immaturity. I had always thought it was in the stars that we'd be together again, and while neither of us said, *Oh, now let's*—we understood without any resolutions or declarations we now were, and would always be, our very own version of a loving couple. It was destined.

ACT THREE

CHAPTER 23

I turned fifty in February 1992. It was a turbulent, pivotal time. I'd lost my last connection to blood family; I was officially an orphan. Free and newly born, I was open to all possibilities and without a job for the first time since I was nineteen, with no clue what I wanted to do next. All I had was a steely firmness about what I *didn't* want to do.

But, just as the digital opportunities were coming online, everyone and their mother was calling me about this or that opportunity in old media.

Kirk Kerkorian came to me and said, "Let me buy CBS and you can run it."

Bill Cosby even called and asked if we could team up to buy NBC!

I was offered the chance to run both Universal and Columbia, but heading another studio had zero interest for me.

I didn't want to repeat myself and wouldn't allow myself to be under anyone's direct control. But two negatives don't produce a positive. I liked this period of suspended animation, but I also felt stuck. I couldn't see any kind of adventurous future, since all I knew was the entertainment business; I had pretty much perfect pitch in that world, but I had no reason to think I could function outside of it.

I decided to tell everyone I didn't want to make any quick decisions, that maybe I'd take a break for a year, even though I didn't really mean it. My plot was to reduce the pressure of figuring out my future as close to zero as possible. I wanted to create a vacuum, where only something fresh could whoosh out.

Finally, I came up with an idea how to begin, how to start off my new life: I'd see the United States, and not from the air. I'd been flying across it for decades, but never set down anywhere in the middle. I wanted to flee both coasts because I knew I couldn't create a void in either place. I love to drive and I love open air, so I bought myself a red Mustang convertible and, starting in Seattle, with the idea of diagonally crossing the country to Miami, I began to explore.

The summer before, in 1991, I met Bill Clinton at Pamela Harriman's house; she had invited twenty or thirty people for a day retreat to help revive the Democratic Party after twelve years of Reagan and Bush. I flew overnight to Pamela's and landed at her house at six in the morning. I'd never met Clinton before, and he and the other candidates spent the day meeting with us in groups of six. It was clear to me after five minutes that he was a star. He oozed every quality you'd want in a politician—every aspiration you'd had about politics was blazing away in him. He had not declared his candidacy yet, but I thought he was our great hope. A few months later he came to see me in my Fox office and asked me to support him. I said, "Absolutely—to the finish line."

At that point, everyone believed George H. W. Bush was going to be reelected. A few months later I was in New Orleans on my car odyssey when Governor Clinton called and asked me to come by for lunch in nearby Little Rock. He was depressed because the media had started attacking him mercilessly, and the polls were very much saying that while he'd be the nominee, he had little chance of being elected.

I was confident he would win, really sure of it, and told him so, and that seemed to melt away his bad mood. After lunch, George Stephanopoulos walked me to my car and said, "The governor and I would like you to be our liaison to Hollywood and play a major role in the campaign."

I thought, *Well, that's an interesting idea,* but I gave my usual vague answer about how difficult it was for me to figure out my next step.

As I drove back to the airport, I thought, *Wow, this would be a totally different thing to do,* but I decided, *No, I'm not doing it. I don't like asking people for money, and I don't want to do the work of corralling pain-in-the-ass celebrities.*

During this interregnum, Steve Jobs asked me to fly up to San Jose so I could see a movie he was in the middle of making for this unknown company he'd acquired called Pixar. But first he wanted to show me what he was doing with a "revolutionary" computer system at another new company of his called NeXT. It hadn't been going that well because its complex yet elegant design couldn't find a market, given the absolute domination of Microsoft.

I went to the NeXT office, where Steve showed me a few scenes from *Toy Story*, and asked if I would join the Pixar board. I said I'd have to think about it. I didn't want to commit myself and didn't want to insult him, but I'd never been much interested in animation and had never made any animated movies. I don't really understand the form and I thought this new Pixar work was awkward, and, separating me from most of the world, I didn't get any of the charm of *Toy Story*.

I ended the night saying, "Look, I'm being really shy about making commitments to do anything."

Steve said, "This is ridiculous. This is going be a giant hit. Pixar's going to be a very big company. You'll own a really nice slice of it. Why won't you do it?"

I said, "I don't know, please let me think on it."

I got back on the plane adamant about keeping my mantra of independence for as long as possible, so a few days later I called him and said, "Thank you, but I just don't want to do this."

I completely underestimated the company and the man.

What a dunce.

By the summer of 1992, I hadn't made any progress and was worried the world would pass me by. I'd soon just be the forgotten man—a once high-flying executive, sidelined.

Nothing filled my head but negatives.

Here's all I knew:

I wanted to count. Which is all that's ever really driven me. I wanted to do something that mattered.

Of course, that means different things to different people, and it meant something different to me at fifty than it had when I was twenty-five. It didn't have to be grand, but it did have to excite my curiosity.

People say I'm competitive. I'm not really, at least according to the standard definition, which is wanting to best another person. Competing, for me, is simply wanting to succeed. I have no need for anyone else to fail in order to consider myself a success. I don't have to be the first at the finish line. I just have to get there.

Growing up in the kind of family I did, with parents and a brother to whom I never mattered, what became necessary for me was to count in whatever world I found myself. I couldn't be cellophane. Or a cipher. Feeling invisible for me was death. After six months of driving across this vast country, and taking meaningless meetings with people in whom I had no interest, I still had no idea what I was going to do. I was increasingly worried my career and life had peaked. The days ambled by aimlessly and anxiously.

Until, that is, one momentous day when Diane told me about a television shopping channel called QVC, the acronym for Quality Value Convenience. It sold all sorts of merchandise directly to viewers. I'd never heard of it before. She said since I was stuck in this limbo, I ought to go to the wilds of Pennsylvania, where it was located, to see the operation and report back if it would be worthwhile for her to sell her clothes on the channel.

It is no understatement to say that trip gave me one of the purest and most powerful epiphanies of my life. I didn't know it then, but it would turn out to be my way forward.

CHAPTER 24

At ABC, Paramount, and Fox, I had known what could be done with video screens: we told stories on them. But when I went to QVC in that eventful year of 1992, I watched a screen do something I'd never realized it could do. It wasn't just a passive one-way delivery system of content. At QVC I witnessed the primitive convergence of telephones and televisions and computers all working together. They were interactive. There was a little video monitor on the set that showed the number of calls coming in when a product was offered for sale. The vertical lines representing the calls rose during the period of the sales pitch, and then, when it ended, they subsided.

I was thunderstruck. To me, those calls were like watching waves coming to shore. I thought, *Screens don't have to be just for narrative, for telling stories. Screens can interact with consumers*—that was the epiphany. It was clunky and rudimentary and I had no clear idea how to turn that revelation into action, but it sat there for a while warming up on the back plate of my brain.

For now, though, I went back to wandering around, seeing more people who were interested in talking about my future, but who were really only trying to repackage my past. I was beginning to despair of the whole process; every opportunity seemed to be one that was a repeat of something I'd already done.

At the end of that summer, I unenthusiastically flew to Philadelphia to meet Ralph Roberts and his son Brian. They had a midsized cable company called Comcast, but a big desire to grow beyond that.

I'd avoided the meeting because I couldn't see what little Comcast could possibly have to interest me, but Brian was tenacity and persistence itself, so I flew off to have lunch with them. Brian was tall, but nowhere as tall as his ambition, and he was whip-smart. His father, Ralph, was a good-looking Philadelphia country gentleman with white hair, a bow tie, and, as I was to learn, a spine of tensile steel.

I sat down and my attitude was *It's just an hour of my time—no worries.*

I knew what their agenda was: they wanted their small-time cable company to get into the program business. They were floating the idea of building a production company and having me run it.

I didn't respond directly, but all I could think was *How do I tell them in the least rude way how uninterested I'd be in having anything to do with production?*

I changed the subject.

I turned to Ralph and asked, "So how did you start this cable company?"

He said he had been a suspender and belt salesman, and in his wanderings he'd found a tiny cable company in Tupelo, Mississippi. He bought it and then he bought some more. And then some more. And then some more.

At some point in the tale, which I enjoyed because I really do love hearing people's stories, Ralph mentioned, "And then I founded QVC with this friend of mine, Joe Segel."

The match had been struck! Serendipity über alles! I instantly perked up and stopped him short. "QVC, really?" I said, leaning forward, suddenly completely engaged. "I was just there last month and was amazed and excited by the interactivity of selling on television." Ralph looked astonished. While he was proud of it, it was a small-time operation and way outside mainstream media. They both were looking at me weirdly, and then at each other. *Why would Barry Diller be interested in a home-shopping company?* Until then I had been utterly passive and now, suddenly, my eyes were lit. "Tell me more about QVC. I want to know everything."

All I've ever needed was pure curiosity, and here it was, raging. I was rapt—my divining fork was twitching furiously.

QVC was a successful concern, making around $60 million a year. But it was not something the Robertses thought would be their ticket into big-time media. Ralph then mentioned, mostly as an aside, that Joe Segel was soon going to retire, and he planned to sell the 15 percent of the company he owned.

"I want in. Can I buy it?" I blurted out.

They looked at me as if I were a Martian.

"Why *would* you?" Ralph asked.

"Because I know in my bones it's the ground floor of something, that electronic screens and interactivity will change everything."

Brian asked me, "What would you do with it?"

I spluttered, "I don't know, but QVC is this primitive clay I want to get hold of and use it to pursue *interactivity.*" That was mostly babble, because all I really knew was that this was the first time in months I'd been intrigued by anything. Ralph and Brian knew they'd just hooked the big fish, but were bewildered by the small stream it wanted to inhabit.

As I got up and walked out of that lunch, I knew what I was going to do with the rest of my life, and it wasn't going to be just selling oversized dresses to oversized women.

I was finalizing my deal to buy and run QVC when Diane went on air to launch her first selling event. In the first hour, she sold $1.3 million in merchandise, and *Vogue* called it a "fashion phenomenon."

I'd told Ralph and Brian that I'd promised myself to never again sign an employment agreement and that I'd report to a board, but not to an individual. QVC was a public company, and the other major owner was John Malone's Liberty Media. Malone had become the overlord of cable media. He controlled the largest cable network, and with Liberty, he owned most of the programming. He was known both as the Cable Cowboy and, in a swipe from then–vice president Al Gore, as the Darth Vader of media. He was and always has been the smartest person in media, with

an extraordinarily subtle and ingenious mind in the body of an outdoors-
man conservationist libertarian who's never met a tax he wanted to pay.
I didn't want to ever be stuck between them and would only agree to a
three-way partnership where any two members could decide an issue, as
long as I was one of the two. This made them more than uncomfortable,
but I was adamant—I'd never do anything again where I wasn't in some
position of control.

I began to confide in a few people about going to QVC, and heard only
one response: "Have you lost your mind?"

The first to say it was Mike Ovitz, then at the height of his Ovitzdom.
I remember going for a walk with him where he said, "This is the dumbest
thing I've ever heard—and you'll never be heard from again."

I completely understood that other people did not see why I was so
interested in this new use of screens. They were coming from the insular
and passive world of television and movies, where you just sat there and
watched.

The more they told me how crazy this was, the more I wanted to go
for it. Diane was the only one who said unequivocally, "Do it." She knew.

My taking over QVC was announced in December 1992. I agreed
to purchase $25 million in common stock, or 3 percent of the company
(with options to buy another 15 percent), and to form a partnership with
Liberty Media, which would hold 21 percent of the stock, and Comcast,
which would control 14 percent. *The New York Times* said, "People who
know Mr. Diller and are familiar with the deal said that . . . he plans to
turn the shopping channel into an on-line entertainment and merchan-
dising service in which the subscriber and the cable company can freely
interact."

This generated a lot of excitement, without anyone in the media and
entertainment world having any understanding of what interactivity was.
But it sounded shiny and new and suddenly everyone and their mother
wanted to come to bucolic West Chester, Pennsylvania, to see if the emperor really had some new clothes. I finally shut the door on most of
that because showing all those visitors around and explaining how it all
worked, I was hardly getting anything done.

At first I was staying at the Four Seasons in Philadelphia driving forty minutes to QVC's offices in the morning, then back at eight or nine at night. It was winter and bleaker than I could have imagined. I wondered what the hell have I done.

The people in West Chester thought of New York and anyone associated with it as inherently untrustworthy and most likely amoral. They treated me like some sort of alien who had suddenly plummeted into their staid and steady lives. They had been working in that utilitarian building for more than ten years, and everyone and everything had become inbred. Joe Segel, the founder whom I had replaced, spent an immense amount of his time inspecting people's hands to see if their fingernails were clean enough for demonstrating products on air.

Nevertheless, they had built up a rigorous and disciplined method of buying and selling merchandise, and they were total pros at it. The shows looked as if they were produced in Poland in the 1950s, but as far as understanding their customers, and being disciplined about catering to them, they were damn good.

I especially found their jewelry operation fascinating. There was an assembly line where thousands of little shiny, sparkly things moved on conveyor belts to be packaged and sent out all over the country. It was the scale of it that was so impressive. They bought thirty or forty thousand of each item and wouldn't put anything on sale they didn't have in-house. Shipping the next day was a big part of the appeal—instant gratification. The logistics—the cost and weight per package, how the complex machine worked—was something I wanted to learn from the ground up, though I was never to master the art of being a merchant.

I soon left the Four Seasons and moved to the Sheraton in West Chester, one of those three-story, workmanlike hotels built around suburban malls, and commuted back and forth on the weekends to New York. Sometimes I'd go by train. I'd work late, then wait in the vast hall of the Philadelphia train station, in the cold, wearing my overcoat. For a Californian, an overcoat is a terrible thing.

There was always a line to get on the train. I'd stand there, with my briefcase on the ground in front of me, kicking it a foot forward every few seconds as the line inched along. Then I'd get on this train from Bleak House to the Evil Empire, and think, *What has become of me?*

But learning a new trade overruled any of those feelings—I loved every newfangled second of it. I wanted to expand the market by telling a large general audience how convenient and efficient it was to buy goods through e-commerce. I came up with a great ad that said in big type BUY UNDERWEAR IN YOUR UNDERWEAR, and took out full pages in *The New York Times* and *The Wall Street Journal.* QVC stock shot up. I was trying to upgrade everything at once, particularly the on-air look, which was drab and dowdy. QVC had been steadily growing from its first days as a television retailer. It was always profitable. I came with the simple idea that if you upgraded the merchandise and everything around it you could easily expand the audience of buyers from one that had been mostly ordering quadruple-X stretch pants. I was wrong. I just barged through with my expansion plans without respect for QVC's relatively narrow audience, which ranged from women in their forties to their seventies with a lot of time on their hands. I soon realized the QVC audience wasn't as elastic as the apparel we were selling them. I was pushing it too far too fast. I was certain the revolution in electronic commerce was coming and I wanted to move it forward before anyone else. Nevertheless, QVC's momentum was so strong that its high-flying stock made us a darling of Wall Street.

Most people leaving high positions in media companies either hang a shingle outside their door waiting for their previous reputation to produce corporate opportunities or get a production deal to keep them minimally relevant. Usually they never again attain the power or influence they had in their corporate life and just slowly fade away. I understood there was no way to replicate my previous center-stage life unless I was prepared to go back to being an employee. While everyone else was misunderstanding what I was doing in the wilds of Pennsylvania, I knew just how much a real advantage it was to go from having a big position and big profile to one that, while so much smaller and less jazzy, had the most solid of profit foundations and a public currency. That's so much better than starting out from scratch with just a shingle out front. And here, for the first time, I could legitimately claim I was a principal.

My need for independence and for not re-stomping old ground had forced me out of the entertainment business, but far sooner than anyone thought conceivable the value of our soaring stock gave us an invasion currency that would lead me right back to the old media world I'd just left.

CHAPTER 25

It was only a few months after I'd bought into QVC that Enrique Senior, an investment banker at Allen & Company, called to say he had a big idea for me, one that needed total secrecy. He wouldn't say anything more over the phone and wanted me to come over to his office. Intrigued, I canceled my next meeting and went over there. He took me through a slide presentation about the growing value of QVC and its possibilities—the most exciting of which was that we should . . . wait for it . . . buy Paramount.

I was flabbergasted. My new entrepreneurial life was just starting and this was all happening much too soon, but I also thought, *Jesus, this isn't completely crazy; it actually makes sense.*

The value of Paramount was much, much bigger than ours, but we were moving up and they'd been going down for a long while. That gave us a financially sound opening, and while it was so early and unexpected, I was straining at the leash to see if we could pull it off. The Robertses, with their extraordinary ambition to be big-time media players, were instantly on board, but we needed our third partner, John Malone, to be with us. We couldn't make this big a move without it being unanimous. We flew out to Denver to see John. Unbeknownst to us, he had been trying to persuade my old foe Martin Davis, Paramount's CEO, to sell the company to *him*. Malone said he liked our plan to use QVC's stock to buy Paramount, but I was later to find out that right after we left the meeting, Malone, in a not very partnering way, called Davis and said, "Well, Marty, unless you want Barry Diller to buy your company, you'd better sell it directly to me."

One can imagine Davis, hearing that it was me in the hunt for Paramount, clutching fiercely at whatever pearls he owned, as he realized how humiliating it would be for him if I became his boss. Seeking the only safe harbor he could find, he quickly made a Faustian bargain to sell the studio to Viacom, controlled by the voracious Sumner Redstone. In this deal, at least he'd survive and keep what little dignity was now on offer. Even though he'd have to work for Redstone, the roughest of the roughest, he'd still remain Paramount's CEO.

When they announced their deal we knew we'd been given an opening. They'd made a huge mistake by offering a low price to Paramount's shareholders, arguing that the synergies the two companies would create was worth much more than the initial cash offer. On its own that was a good rationale, but if anyone actually came in with a higher price, it would be unlikely the shareholders would choose Redstone's high-flown speculation about synergies over receiving more cash. Our strategy was to make that higher bid, and for that we'd need a ton of financing. We had an introduction to Jimmy Lee, a leading banker at Chase Manhattan, and told him our idea to overbid Viacom with both QVC stock and cash. Lee, who would go on to become the preeminent banker of the boom 1990s, liked the idea and said he would finance it. Just like that. I was shocked at how quickly this was coming together, with spit and a ball and not much else. Amazing everyone with our audacity, particularly Martin Davis and Sumner Redstone, we announced our offer. And the rockets went off.

It was a dramatic story: me and my Paramount history and upstart QVC buying that fabled old studio. I was twenty-four years old when Charlie Bluhdorn barged into my office to save his recent acquisition of Paramount from going bust, and here I was twenty-five years later bidding to buy the whole company.

The afternoon we made the offer, I called Martin Davis to tell him an official letter would soon arrive on his desk.

Now, *that* was truly fun.

In the years since leaving Paramount, I hadn't much spoken to Davis. He knew I had no respect for him, and I knew he felt threatened by me. It was a short and curt conversation. I said, "We're going to make an offer this afternoon that will top the Viacom offer."

He said, "Viacom and I have a closed deal."

I said, "Well, we're going to reopen it."

"We have a signed merger agreement," he said, "and you can't make a bid." Without getting too far into the weeds here, the deal they struck was reliant on a previous Delaware court ruling that a merger (between Warner Brothers and Time to form Time Warner) could be upheld against a cash bid (ironically by Paramount) if the parties had a valid argument for creating value by combining. The board could then make the decision accepting the lower bid. Here was Davis justifying the legality of his deal by citing the precedent from his previous loss in trying to break up Time Warner. I cannot count the number of ironies here.

The first battle would be in court to determine whether we could even top their bid.

This dippy, diving thrill ride of a deal took the next six months of my life.

Paramount refused to negotiate with us, citing their closed agreement with Viacom, and we sued them in the Delaware courts to reverse the previous ruling, arguing this wasn't a merger but a pure acquisition by Viacom, and therefore the shareholders ought to have the right to choose between the two offers.

We prevailed. We had the high bid, and Paramount was ordered to accept it. This set new landmark law in the Delaware Supreme Court. For the moment, we had bought Paramount!

It was early evening after the court victory when I got a call from our lawyers; they were finalizing the agreement and wanted me to come down to their offices to sign it. I walked down Second Avenue, shaking my head in amazement that it was almost ten years earlier when I'd left Paramount for Fox, then left Fox to go off on my little own. Now here I was returning to the movies, but this time as a principal, actually *owning* Paramount. When I arrived, all the lawyers were scrambling about, papers flying between different floors of the building. I was put in an office to wait for Martin Davis to arrive, because we had to cosign the agreement.

He was utterly defeated, and when he came in he looked it. He'd made a devil's deal with Redstone just so he could nominally remain head of the company, but our intervention had tossed that out the window. We signed the papers and spoke minimal and polite monosyllables. I put a steady stare on him, but he never looked back at me.

We both thought it was over, but it was just the beginning of the war. The court had set up an auction between us and Viacom, with the highest cash price prevailing.

For Davis himself, though, it *was* over. Whichever way this turned out, he'd be gone. That seemed fair justice to me given the cruelties he imposed on so many people.

I went off to a Christmas cruise in the Caribbean with about ten pounds of Paramount internal data to study. The bidding process had given each side the ability to top the other with a three-week pause between bids, and I was prepared for Viacom to raise the stakes. Which they did. Over the next months the bids went from $62 a share to $95, and the transaction now approached $9 billion. We both had to raise more equity. Redstone got Blockbuster to inject $500 million into Viacom, and we got Advance, the parent company of Condé Nast, as well as BellSouth, to come in with us. It was a grueling process, and the media followed each bid as if it were the longest horse race in history. At one stage, when Viacom had the leading bid, *New York* magazine put me on the cover with the headline MOGUL IN A MESS.

For the umpteenth time I was so in over my head—I had zero experience in big-game dealmaking and was only months into running a publicly held company. I was also embarrassingly naive about what drove investors. I had lunch with a group of twenty or so institutional shareholders of Paramount. I was doing my passionate sell about why we were the better buyer—why I'd do a better job running the company than old Sumner. I was going on and on and could tell I was losing my audience as they dolefully picked at their food. Leon Cooperman, a legendary stock picker who had a big position in Paramount, interrupted my monologue. "I don't care about how you're going to run this better than him—just pay me a dollar more so I can go home."

I shut up and sat down, deflated.

By this point both sides were stretched to the max. Sumner was quoted as saying that I was his great friend who'd betrayed him and that little "crummy" QVC was no match for the great Viacom. I responded, "This is about the future of Paramount—which I led for seven straight years when it was number one in the industry. So do you want this fifty-year-old person or this seventy-year-old? I'm young, I'm vigorous, and he's old." Oh, do I now rue trashing a seventy-year-old for his age.

Then Redstone had his PR people put this out there: "Well, what about AIDS?"

Geraldine Fabrikant, a writer for *The New York Times*, who was on the story regularly, called and said, "I feel bad, but I have to do this because this is what I've heard: How is your health?"

"My health?" I said. "My health's fine! What are you talking about?" When she told me what the Redstone side was implying, I was truly shocked. She couldn't report that I had AIDS, because I didn't, but she could have printed that "questions have been raised" about my health. She didn't.

Low blow for sure, bringing my sexuality into the fray. And here's what I felt: that anvil that so terrorized my early years was never going away!

There were so many people engaged on both sides—arguing, analyzing, and positioning. Our side now had more than six principal investors, and each one of them had their own advisers and lawyers. The meeting rooms got bigger and bigger, sometimes with sixty or more around giant conference tables. In the middle of all this, Sumner Redstone sued John Malone and Liberty Media, our biggest investor, on antitrust grounds, and they had to withdraw from our group. That almost finished us, but we were able to replace him, and the competition continued unabated.

Ted Turner called me a few times to say he wanted to get in, insisting I should do this with him instead of those other people. "They won't have your interests at heart. I will," he told me. One night, when we were both scheduled to attend a charity cable event, he called me from his suite at the Waldorf Towers, where he and Jane Fonda (his wife at the time) were staying. "Why don't you come down and we'll talk before we have to go to the dinner?" I didn't think there was any way for him to participate, but he was adamant, so I went down to his suite.

Ted began stalking around the room, shouting, "You've had bad parenting. All the people you've worked for were bad parents, and you should be with a good parent. I'm a good parent and you're a battered child." Periodically, I'd look at Jane cross-eyed. She could see his rants and parenting rap weren't exactly resonating with me, and she tried to get Ted to sit down and shut up. He finally ran out of steam, and we went off to the dinner, never to discuss it again.

Our investor group began falling apart. Donald Newhouse, the head of Advance, called and said his family was uncomfortable the price was getting this high and wanted out. I argued with him, saying that if he did so, we'd be finished. I assured him that if he stayed in and we won, we'd take him out and pay him off after it closed. He finally agreed, but said he wouldn't do "one penny more." We were still the high bid when Tom Sherak, my old head of distribution at Fox, called—as a "friend"—to say, "I just talked to Sumner, and I think he's really finished. You've won. You've driven him crazy." Of course, Sumner had put him up to it; he just wanted to fake weakness.

The night before the final deadline for Sumner to counter, I went to a birthday dinner for James Wolfensohn, the chairman of Carnegie Hall. It was on the stage at the hall. All night long, people came up to me, saying, "Congratulations, looks like you've got Paramount!"

In the middle of dinner, I decided to call the office and see if there was any news. I found a pay phone and was told that Redstone's primary adviser at Bear Stearns had come up with the idea of adding a CVR, a contingent value right, to the pot.

The CVR was a new Wall Street invention. It meant that if Viacom stock didn't rise within a year after purchasing Paramount to a certain price, then the shareholders would get a stock dividend to make up the difference. This was valued at $2 a share higher than our offer. It was a gimmick, but theoretically had dangerous consequences I didn't want to risk.

What we didn't know was that Ace Greenberg, head of Bear Stearns, had guaranteed to Sumner that he could manipulate the stock during that one-year period so that there would never be a loss—it would never go below a certain level, so there would be no risk. And eventually that is what happened. It wasn't entirely legal, but I was too Rebecca of Sunnybrook Farm to even know about, much less consider, such a manipulation.

I wobbled back into the dinner. At the first table I saw Larry Tisch, the billionaire head of CBS. I whispered in his ear, "He overbid us." Tisch came back with "You paid too-too much, and now he's paid *over* too-too much. Let it go." We had three weeks before the next bid deadline, and I was struggling mightily with whether to go up one more time.

We'd both bid the price up to almost $10 billion! The CFO of QVC insisted that was ridiculously high for the assets we were buying and we'd be crippled by the debt. But what was weighing even more heavily on me was the coalition I'd put together. There were now multiple partners with differing and sometimes conflicting agendas, and I'd have to give up my voting arrangements, which meant I'd again be essentially an employee of a consortium of investors. I sure didn't like that prospect and was certain they'd toss me at the first bad turn. I felt boxed in by all the compromises I'd made, and inside me there was a growing voice crying, *Just get out!*

On a strict economic basis I shouldn't have listened to that voice because on a purely economic basis we *absolutely* should have bought Paramount. The assets would have far exceeded the cost. But . . . I choked. I stopped bidding. In retrospect, thank god I did as I'm sure our group would have eventually fallen apart because there was no real alignment of interests. Most important, it would have put me squarely back in "old media," when I was the only one in media aggressively pushing interactivity and technology as the path forward. Despite the starry allure of going back to Paramount in such a dramatic way, it would have been a distraction from the gutsy course I'd been on in e-commerce. Nevertheless, this had become a game, and the momentum of the chase was pushing me forward, maybe brainlessly.

One day before the final bids were due, Jerry Levin, the head of Time Warner, who didn't want Redstone to get any bigger, called me. "We have to find a way to get you the money to make this bid!" I half-heartedly agreed to meet, and we thrashed around several ideas for more funding.

But in my heart I was finished.

On the last day before the bid was due, we didn't raise our offer. We folded, and Viacom and Redstone got Paramount.

Sumner Redstone went on the *Today* show the next morning, crowing that his ex-friend had cost him $2 billion, but that was okay since he now owned this great studio. He triumphantly boasted about it on every media outlet he could find. I was asked endlessly for a response. Our PR people drafted the usual bromides about how QVC had weighed all the factors and why we didn't make another bid and how QVC would survive just fine. I hated all of them and came up with my own statement: "THEY WON, WE LOST. NEXT." And that's all I ever said publicly. That quotation has stood the test of time. Even now, thirty years later, those five words are often used to describe moving on from some setback.

They won. We lost. Next.

CHAPTER 26

Bent but unbroken, I returned to the quiet suburbia of QVC in West Chester, Pennsylvania, where business had meanwhile been booming along without me. We'd ignited this spark for home shopping, but I believed we could do even better and wanted to develop a more aspirational and sophisticated service that would appeal to younger urban viewers. We owned a second channel that wasn't being utilized, so we came up with the idea of launching a new service called Q2. It was an ambitious upgrading of the whole concept of shopping from home, and we took over the famed Silvercup Studios in Queens to build this new network from scratch. It had a completely different, more contemporary look and retailed more upmarket goods, for an audience that I never thought would shop on staid and steady QVC. This got me out of the desolate winters in West Chester. I loved biking over the bridge from Manhattan to our new studios. It felt like Fox all over again. *One dumb step in front of the other.* Just as I liked it. And I liked sliding into a northeastern axis—all my current interests in a hundred-mile radius: Pennsylvania to New York, over to Queens, up to our farm in Connecticut on weekends with the family, and then in the summer taking a place in East Hampton on Georgica Pond, a sweet little guesthouse at the edge of a very large pond with a small dock and a tiny sailboat, where I'd often skim across to the other side to the houses of Calvin Klein and Steven Spielberg.

That summer of 1994, the writer Andrew Sullivan, a new friend of mine, came over one morning and asked if I'd heard about AOL. It was just beginning, and he showed me how it worked. I was smitten with this new way of communicating. A few months later, who would turn up at my office but Steve Case, the founder of AOL. He was talking to people about buying Microsoft cofounder Paul Allen's stake in the company and thought because of my interest in interactivity I was a likely prospect. He didn't enjoy dealing with the generally uncommunicative Allen and had persuaded him to sell his 25 percent controlling shares. I was intrigued and said, yes, the QVC group would be very interested in buying the stock. I still didn't know enough about stock market values, so I called my partner John Malone. He, too, liked AOL, but thought the price too high and that we should wait for it to settle. The stock quickly went into the stratosphere, and our window of opportunity vanished, along with my chance to own 25 percent of AOL. Several courses of history would have been redirected if I had. Instead, I was again jolted back to old media with a phone call from Martin Lipton, who told me that Larry Tisch, who controlled CBS, was frustrated at the state of the network. Lipton had told his friend Tisch that I was his best bet for reviving the network. Old media was stalking me again. *Once more unto the breach.*

CBS was number one on the dial when there actually was a dial that tuned your television set. Though a bit dowdy, it was still the stylish and dignified fine old lady of broadcasting, and a company I'd long admired. Tisch had built a huge enterprise with his brilliant mind and a trader's mentality. He never looked back with any sentimentality on a transaction. Some years before, he'd exploited CBS's low stock price and become its largest shareholder and then chairman of CBS's board. He enjoyed heading this great media institution, but was tiring of its ratings travails and his inability to find someone to lead it. He also had been cutting costs—he was never a broadcaster, and cutting was all he really knew how to do—but he hated the negative media attention he was getting and now just wanted out. He thought I could at the least get the stock price up as I had when I joined QVC. And then he'd gracefully exit. Like everything with Larry Tisch, it all happened in a lightning-quick stroke. He called and offered to merge

QVC into CBS with me becoming CEO of the combined company. He said, "I'll move out of the building. And I'll turn the whole thing over to you." Those bright lights of mainstream media hadn't yet dimmed enough for me, and I agreed. He wanted me to meet with some of his board members, the oldest of old-line New York grandees, to convince them I wasn't "a Hollywood fruitcake." I guess I succeeded, because when he finally asked me to come over to CBS and lunch alone with his most influential independent board director, he'd already set the wheels in motion. As soon as the lunch was finished, Larry walked in and said, "Okay, it's done. Let's go downstairs and announce it." I asked, "What do you mean?"

He told me, "I called a press conference."

I said, "You could have told me."

He said, "I'm telling you now." It was almost an exact repeat of my experience when Rupert bought Metromedia from John Kluge—get the news out fast before anyone changes their mind.

We took the elevator in the CBS Building down to the lobby, where there were two hundred press people and employees already gathered in the forecourt. A microphone had been set up, and Larry announced the transaction. I said a couple of awkward words. And that was that. CBS and QVC would merge in an all-stock transaction, and I would become chairman and CEO of the combined company. On the front page of *The New York Times* the next day, there I was again, the man of the moment. If only it had turned out to be as simple as the headline.

I had told both John Malone and the Robertses that this merger might happen. Despite the cross-ownership rules that precluded a cable company from having a controlling ownership in a broadcast company, Malone was completely enthusiastic, believing those outdated rules would soon be changed. Brian Roberts was much less excited, because until the rules changed, it meant he'd be a silent owner without a board seat.

"We don't like being told we can't directly participate in any business we're invested in," he told me.

I understood, but reiterated what an incredible opportunity it was. I explained that he needed to have patience. "To be able to take little QVC and end up controlling CBS is an opportunity we can't let go."

"How long will I have to wait until the rules change?" Brian kept asking. I thought the opportunity was worth the short-term sacrifice of Comcast not having a seat at the table. That turned out to be prescient when a few years later the cross-ownership bans were lifted, and Roberts's company, by then the biggest cabler in the world, bought NBC.

Finally I said to Brian, "Look, you're thirty-five years old. Waiting a few years isn't some big tragedy. John Malone and I want to do this, and our agreement says two out of three votes rule, so let's proceed with unanimity." He and his father reluctantly conceded. But the situation left them dissatisfied. They rightly believed QVC was their company, they'd founded it, and here I'd come along and was going to use *their* company to further my own ambitions. This was percolating in the background as I was busy getting to know the CBS executives, and while Larry Tisch, in his fashion, began nibbling away at the edges of our deal. First he said it would be better for him to stay as chairman for the first year or so since he'd still own 20 percent of the company. I'd be president and CEO. Then he told Marty Lipton that his translation of my stock award at QVC into CBS stock would mean I'd get vastly fewer shares in the combined company, cutting me from 5 million to 800,000. I didn't much like that, but I'd never let money dictate a decision for me. Besides, Marty sensibly told me that the only thing to do was to get this done and get inside the company—everything would work out from there. I was beginning to sour over Tisch's finagling, but the momentum had taken over, and I feared that after the Paramount debacle another opportunity for that proverbial big time might be lost. Even though I was adventuring in this embryonic arena of interneting, I was somewhat pathetically still drawn to getting back onto that center stage. I didn't have enough internal "self" to realize how superficially shallow it was to still feel stung by no longer being at the top of the Most Important People in Entertainment.

After lunching with the entire senior echelon of CBS News, who'd been budget-brutalized by Tisch and greeted me as the great savior of a great institution, I left for a quick trip to L.A. to meet with more CBS executives. Twenty-four hours later I got back on the plane to fly to a CBS board of directors' dinner that Larry had set up to welcome me as their new CEO. En route to New York, Marty Lipton called. He had just gotten off the phone with Larry, who said the board felt strongly that the chief financial officer and the general counsel should report to them instead of the CEO. "That's outrageous, I'm not doing that," I said. "You really have to," he replied. Again, his mantra was: *Just get in, get control of the company, and worry about everything else later.*

"Marty, again, I am not going to do that. It'd be crazy to have the two aides to the top job reporting to the board. That's nuts."

"Well, that's their position," he said.

I hung up the phone glassy-eyed. We were landing in half an hour. I felt so stuck and hopeless. How could I call it off at the last minute because I didn't like the final terms for me personally? It would be more than an embarrassment if I couldn't pull off my second big-time media deal. I was trapped, and the thought of becoming an employee again gave me a black heart. I didn't see any good way out of this as we landed and rolled down the runway in Teterboro, New Jersey. As we came to a stop I noticed two men in suits approach the plane. How very odd. As they came closer I recognized Ralph and Brian Roberts. Now, what the hell were they doing there? There was a helicopter whirring nearby that was to take me to the board meeting in New York that was to begin in forty minutes. The noise prevented me from hearing what Ralph was trying to tell me. He motioned me into the hangar so we could talk. Completely discombobulated, I followed them. Once inside, I stared at them dumbfounded. Brian broke the silence: "We know this is going to make you very angry. But we're going to stop the CBS merger. We came here to personally tell you that we're going to buy all of QVC at a twenty-five percent premium to today's stock price." Wowser.

All I could think to say was "You can't do that. You gave your word. And besides, we have the two-out-of-three rule, and Malone and I have agreed to proceed." They coolly said that, nevertheless, they had a separate right to make any offer they wanted for QVC, and the shareholders could decide to buy into this merger or just sell out now for a high price. They handed me a formal letter with the proposal, repeatedly saying they were "really sorry." Not sorry enough to have held off making the letter public. They had released a copy of it five minutes before my plane landed. I don't believe they did it maliciously—they needed to put CBS on notice before they formally voted on the merger.

I called a very angry Martin Lipton, who said they reneged on their word that they would go along with the merger. He insisted we'd prevail in a fight with the shareholders over which deal they'd want. *Oh Christ*, I thought, *another day, another fight*.

I then called Larry Tisch. "Congratulations, Barry—you just made a lot of money," he bellowed at me with his booming voice (the QVC stock I had bought for $25 million was now worth $125 million). He must have gotten their proposal over the wire a few minutes before. Now I was doubly stunned. I quickly said we could easily compete with the Comcast offer and I was sure John Malone and Liberty would back our deal instead of just selling out. Tisch interrupted me, saying, "If you think I'm going to overbid them, you're smoking something. I'm going to the board dinner right now and I'm going to tell them we should authorize a one-point-five-billion-dollar dividend instead of doing this deal because we're not going to get caught up in some bidding contest for a home-shopping company."

I said, "You don't have to bid against anyone. This merger makes more sense to QVC shareholders than being bought out for a premium."

Tisch, without a pause, snapped back: "I don't get into contests, and I don't look at what might have been." He announced that night that the QVC deal was dead and buried and he was going to give a dividend of a billion-plus dollars to their shareholders to make them happy. It was over—my year and a half since storming out of the Fox gates with so much heat and moment was ending in ignominy.

CHAPTER 27

I was now a mogul manqué. I'd made two attempts at the big time and failed at both. And lost QVC in the bargain. *Congratulations, Barry, you are now really and truly independent and under no one's thumb other than your own. Yes, you presciently forged your way into the beginnings of e-commerce, but now you've got no job and no prospects.* I was back where I started after leaving Fox, except now I was nationally known damaged goods. With a stone-cold blood oath I resolved I'd never do anything again where I didn't have hard and absolute control, even if it was owning a corner delicatessen. And that wasn't too far from what was in my future.

The thought of hanging around New York that summer gurgled. As for being at our farm in Connecticut, while it had been a great and glorious refuge from the city while I'd been its up-and-down media darling, now I just felt lost in the woods. And I had no place in the company town of Los Angeles. I was totally deflated after these two bruising back-to-back battles.

I needed solace and I needed to explore something outside myself. Just as I had years earlier when Diane left me, I turned to the water to get myself and my ambition back together. I'd always wanted to sail from Florida to the Chesapeake Bay and visit the small towns along the waterway where time had stood still for a hundred years. I went out and bought the biggest boat that I could run by myself. I didn't want company, and after the teams of advisers and handlers of the last months, I wanted to do things for myself and by myself. I wanted to be solely responsible for the outcome, which was occasionally scary going up the narrow Intracoastal

Waterway; the shoals at every turn made it a navigational nightmare. This was before there was GPS guidance, so I'd often run aground and have to rock and roll the boat off the bottom to deeper water. Running up and down from the flybridge trying to dock on my own meant constantly hauling out the first aid kit for my banged-up bloody shins.

But I loved every moment of every day and the freedom of being unmoored and afloat with no timetable. For the first time in more than thirty years I didn't have people taking care of me and running interference. I made my own bed and cleaned my own (boat)house. I took lazy rides on my bike to the nearest market in these small southern towns, just as dusk was settling over the somnambulant streets. Having not been inside a market for many decades, I'd wander the aisles of groceries like a wide-eyed alien from another planet. Carrying every cheesy snack and comfort food I could, I'd hop back on my bike, precariously balancing the bags on each handlebar. Day after day I inched and snaggled up the waterway, not thinking about much more than where to shelter before it got too dark to steer. Whether I wanted to or not there weren't many practical future possibilities to think about anyway. I had set such stringent guardrails in place about never, ever being subject to anyone else's governance that the two offers I received to run movie studios were very short conversations. By now it was clear to me where this more than mania for control came from. I had wanted so desperately to alter my sexuality as a child and teenager and I had tried so hard and failed. I was left with an unquenchable need to be vigilant about every other aspect of my life. Whatever I could control became mandatory to control. But now I was constrained by the straitjacket I'd put myself in, and worried if I didn't start something again soon I'd be discarded like yesterday's fish.

I was close to hopeless as I neared the end of my meandering up the Intracoastal. Could I end my career with such a whimper? Where could I find the match that would light my next move? I was down to less than a matchstick when I spoke with John Malone early in 1995. I told him the trouble I was having finding something to get me off zero. Joking and dismissive, he said, "Well, I control Silver King. You can have that if you want."

Silver King? What the hell is that?

It turned out to be a string of UHF television stations that didn't actually broadcast anything; they were repeater stations for the programming of the Home Shopping Network. HSN was the forerunner to QVC. It actually invented the interactive-shopping category. Silver King had revenues of only $40 million a year with no prospects other than its income from the Home Shopping Network.

I got the idea I could take these spindly local stations, get them off Home Shopping, and begin networking them with original programming. They covered about 25 percent of the United States and I had dreams—as usual, without much deep thinking or awareness of how difficult it would be—that all these low-power channels could morph into a national broadcasting cooperative.

It was kind of pathetic that this little toad of a company was all that seemed to fit my minimum conditions. Hoping he wouldn't laugh at the idea, I told John Malone I'd take Silver King, but only if I could also get control of HSN itself (Malone's Liberty Media owned a controlling stake in it, too). I still believed home shopping was the entrance to e-commerce. QVC had steadily taken market share from HSN, which had been mismanaged for many years and was losing money, but I knew enough about the category to be sure I could turn it around. The problem was that HSN had been accused of various fraudulent practices and was in a legal mess with the Justice Department. That asset was frozen for now, so my only option, pitiful as it was, was to take Silver King and await HSN's unfreezing.

The prerequisite for my agreeing was that John Malone would give me a bulletproof lifetime proxy on Liberty's controlling interest in Silver King as well as a large ownership stake in it and eventually HSN. Control, my hard-ass mantra, would be hardwired, but it sure was small beer. Once again, everyone thought I'd lost my mind and relegated me to the dustheap of media history. Silver King was located in Clearwater, Florida, on the second floor of a strip mall. The only job its ten or so employees had was to collect money from HSN. There was nothing to run. The day I made my obligatory visit to meet Silver King's "president" was utterly depressing. All I could think of was that Edward G. Robinson line from the end of *Little Caesar* as his hopeless character lies dying: "Mother of mercy, is this the end of Rico?"

After some few months, the legal entanglements came unstuck, and I also became chairman of the Home Shopping Network. I was definitely humbled, but I was back in business and I liked being back on the attack. I also more than liked being discounted again. I was in firm control of two public companies, and while of no size or circumstance, I had enough clay to get going. First up, though, was fixing the forlorn and broken-down Home Shopping Network.

QVC was a place where people were superb at their jobs and took pride in what they did. HSN, on the other hand, housed a lot of cheesy hacks who were just fine, as they themselves said, selling "junk for chumps." Even with my limited experience running QVC, I was a giant among pixies in my knowledge of this new form of retailing.

You do get lucky when you buy a company that has been mismanaged and yet is still running. Running on fumes is still running, and if you're compelled to be willful and tough minded it doesn't take a rocket scientist to figure out the few simple things needed to turn one around. Within a year of me taking over, HSN went from losing $70 million to making $60 million.

In 1994 people were beginning to use computers and the early laptops to communicate, to interact, but on phone lines that were woefully slow. It was the earliest days of the internet, but I was again lucky: I was there at the dawn of the internet revolution with just enough experience and curiosity to be able to take advantage of it, and just enough cash to fund its early growth. While the often ego-inflated executive class would disagree, much of business success is circumstantial; no one—well, certainly not someone without a genius brain—could have artfully prearranged to have a front seat at the technological revolution that was just beginning while also controlling a profitable business that had all the tools, rudimentary as they were, to exploit that revolution. Picture that time: the World Wide Web had just gotten its running shoes on and there I was, fifty-two years old, prepped and peppered by adversity and ready for the race. James Carville had once famously coined "It's the *economy*, stupid" as his mantra in electing Bill Clinton to the presidency. I say "It's the *timing*, stupid" for most great business careers.

If I had succeeded in buying Paramount or CBS, I know two things for certain. One is that I would never have been able to control either—I'd have still been an employee and most likely been thrown out at some point. And I'd never have become an internet entrepreneur. Big word, "entrepreneur." I wasn't a natural one. I was a tried-and-true corporatist with more than a master's degree in managing large enterprises. It had been decades since I'd started anything from scratch and my first moves were pretty mundane. We had these two dreary assets, HSN and Silver King, and while turning around HSN wasn't going to excite anyone, it did give us cash and some credibility to think about expansion. I wish I could say I saw the possibilities of the internet in some full-blown prophetic way. I didn't. But inside the humdrum reason I wanted to buy Ticketmaster was the seed of what would consume me for the next twenty years.

I thought there were synergies with HSN's call centers. It had 2,500 people taking phone orders for merchandise, and Ticketmaster had 1,000 taking ticket orders; we thought combining the back office of the two businesses would save money and be much more efficient. It was a basely pragmatic move, hardly inspired or aspirational.

Ticketmaster was a public company controlled by Paul Allen and run by a blustery caricature of a loudmouthed but incredibly effective lawyer named Fred Rosen, who had brashly led it to total domination of the ticketing business for live events throughout the world. Thank god he was a Luddite, or we wouldn't have gotten the chance to buy it.

When asked about the idea of putting ticket sales online, his reaction was "We'll do it after everybody else does it. Right now it's just a waste of resources."

Of course, coming from cofounding Microsoft, Paul Allen thought the opposite, but he was shy and abhorred confrontation. He had a brilliant mind, but was absolute torture to engage with. If you sat with Paul he would stare at you silently for so long that you began to sweat out of every pore. Talking to him was like thawing out a steak that had been frozen for years. If you asked him something, he would respond in monosyllables.

He was an odd duck, yes, but a smart one and worth about $20 billion.

Anyway, it was not a surprise that Paul, a Presbyterian with a librarian mother from Seattle, and Fred Rosen, a noisy, Bronx-born Jewish lawyer, didn't get along.

I didn't know any of this when I cold-called Paul, thinking he might find the idea of a combination of Ticketmaster and HSN compelling. He told me of his frustrations with Rosen, and how he believed the company should jump-start online ticketing. Eureka—that was the seed and . . . suddenly I did see the future and got so excited about the online possibilities that I couldn't race fast enough to get a deal done. I told Paul that if he traded his stock in Ticketmaster for stock in HSN, I'd deal with Rosen and he could get out of that tortured relationship. I'd dealt all my life with far more obstreperous characters.

Paul Allen quickly agreed and ended up with 11 percent of my company and joined our board. A year or so later he sold his shares, doubling his money (not that he needed it, but if he'd kept his shares, he'd have become far richer than the Midas he already was).

Ticketmaster was so early in online activity that it caused the only fight I've ever had with Bill Gates. He accosted me as I was walking on a path at the Sun Valley Conference. He snarled at me that he was going to destroy Ticketmaster. I said, "Huh—what are you talking about?" He told me Ticketmaster had filed a lawsuit against Microsoft for stealing their web pages. It was so early in the internet game that the litigious Fred Rosen believed no one should take Ticketmaster's copyrighted content without paying for it. Monopolistic Microsoft wanted to show everyone's content.

I said to Gates, "Hey, stop this threatening—the ink isn't even dry yet on this deal—I don't know about this lawsuit."

He shot back, "I'll set up a competitor in every city and put you out of business unless you stand down and give us the right to display your content." He was playing for the biggest stakes and I knew we couldn't stop the tsunami of internet adoption. It was going to roll right over us, and while Rosen's was a principled stand I told Gates we'd withdraw the lawsuit. It was my excitement about the internet and desire to get it going that governed my expedient decision to waive our copyrights—the same issue that today has publishers suing AI on the same basis, with probably the same result.

Ten years after we bought Ticketmaster we merged it into Live Nation, a perfect combination of production (producing the events) and distribution (getting the tickets to consumers). It was a controversial deal, which took us almost a year of negotiations with regulators to get approved. It was also, for me, a new lesson in the perfidy of man, where I made one of the single worst mistakes of my career.

Ticketmaster over the years had become something of a monopoly powerhouse. While it didn't have much competition, the executive I'd chosen to run it as CEO, Irving Azoff, had been telling me for some time that our position might be eroded by Live Nation, the leading producer of live events throughout the world. I would also place hiring Irving high in the mistake category, because he was renowned as an untrustworthy snake of snakes. But this wasn't a children's story being told by a sweet librarian; ticketing was the most cutthroat of businesses, and Irving was a master throat cutter. He had been a leading manager of live acts like the Eagles, and he'd originally come to us to make an investment in his company. We thought that might help our leverage in keeping our ticketing sovereignty, and it did that. We soon made him head of Ticketmaster, because we thought his muscle would keep our clients glued to us. He kept worrying me with his concerns about our long-term competitive position, since Live Nation had begun offering ticketing services, too. I warmed to the idea that a merger with Live Nation would make us an incredibly strong player in all the services related to live concerts worldwide. We'd have the monopoly ticket broker, the monopoly live-event promoter, and a large chunk of live-artist managers; with those elements combined, we'd have a powerhouse with no rival. I also believed we would have the most efficient machine to develop new artists. Live Nation thought so, too, and we began negotiations.

Ticketmaster was larger than Live Nation, so I thought we ought to get a premium for our shares. They of course thought otherwise, and after the usual haggling I decided that the combination itself was more important than arguing over percentages. Then I got the highfalutin idea that we should really make it a merger of equals and neither side should have an edge against the other. Extraordinarily naive, especially if the other side didn't have a millimeter of morality in their bones. The final concession from our side was a trade we made on the name of the company. We agreed to call it Live Nation as long as we had the absolute right to name the combined company's chief financial officer. I was righteously insistent that every other issue be split right down the middle, with six directors from each side. After a lengthy government review we finally closed in January 2010.

Our first board meeting soon followed. All was pleasant until I asked, as the new chairman, "What's happening with the search for a new CFO?" Michael Rapino, who was chosen to lead the company, having previously been the Live Nation CEO, said, "Well, I'm not sure we should really do this. We have a perfectly competent CFO, and it's really not needed." I said, "That's not the deal we made." To which Ari Emanuel, a board member on their side, said, "Who cares what deal we made?" I said, "What the hell do you mean? We had a firm written agreement on this point. Balance and good faith are the cornerstones of being together, and in our first meeting you gleefully renege on a key contractual point?" His disdainful reply was "Who cares? We have the votes." I said, "Votes? What are you talking about?"

Well, little Irving—and his height was at the same level as his morality—had switched sides and was now voting with them. I later learned that Irving and Live Nation had a wink of an agreement that once the merger was completed, he'd be the swing vote on their side. I walked out of that meeting like Wile E. Coyote having been bonged by the Road Runner.

A week later I called a board meeting and began to read a very long statement about their dastardly acts, with a call to return to the clear spirit of the transaction. Ten minutes in, Ari Emanuel interrupted and said, "Why do we have to listen to this? It's just boring." That was followed by various cries of "Hear! Hear!" from the other Live Nation directors. What a monumental dope I'd been. They'd taken over the company—in a merger I'd created—with venality and duplicity. Because I thought good faith would govern, we'd never put in any protections beyond having an equal number of directors. That afternoon, after returning home in a complete funk, I resigned as chairman. The next day I sold all my stock.

About a year later, both Michael Rapino and Ari Emanuel called me to apologize for their behavior. I accepted it as sincere. The skunk Azoff was the real betrayer. I've never spoken to him again.

I'd rather be guilty of naivete than cynicism, but I should have protected us against this rank treachery. In my fortieth year of business, I sure should have known better.

As I was racing around in those early days trying to build up our assets I was also planning to turn the television stations we'd bought with Silver King into a national network. It was unbridled, brainless ambition. Hauling endless bricks of programming up such a steep hill just wasn't worth the toil. Thankfully, a better brick, a gold one, got thrown over our transom. Jerry Perenchio, a truly great entrepreneur and generous gentleman, had just bought Univision, the Spanish-language network, and he thought our stations would further his distribution. He offered us a whopping $950 million. I cashed the check as soon as it arrived. This ended our very short-lived experiment in programming local television stations, and I was relieved to be out of it. I was just learning the difference between extremely difficult business models and internet-enabled virtual ones that flowed fast from idea to adoption. I was also learning to take advantage of luck and circumstance, which made a lot more entrepreneurial sense than trying to pull off an old media idea born only out of my native optimism.

As the internet exploded, you could go from zero to hundreds of millions of consumers in the stroke of a computer key. And now, thanks to the Perenchio gold, we had some real dollars to invest.

It was around then I bought a sailing ketch called *Mikado*, the first boat of mine that needed a crew and that started our now decades-long cruising and adventuring around the world. Diane and I often try and calculate, in the thousands, how many miles we've swum, how many hikes we've taken, how many places we've traveled, both inhabited and not, with friends and family and not. Boats for us aren't for keeping in marinas or sitting in one placid place to entertain guests and have parties. If we have guests, that's nice, too, but we're in the most contented rhythm when we're on our own. We often look at each other across our twin chaises on the bridge deck after a day of swimming and hiking and count our endless blessings.

CHAPTER 28

There was no straight line to my late-stage career. It made no linear sense. Opportunity came from the unintended consequences of disconnected situations that reconnected in serendipitous ways, as if some cosmic hand had been at work. That's about the only explanation for how events that began to grind way back in 1977 would become one of my greatest, zigzagging-est adventures. It took almost two decades for all the disparate pieces to come together into opportunities I never could have imagined. It's also a grand illustration of how the meandering paths of media have crissed and crossed in bewildering ways throughout my life.

This saga began when Gulf + Western, the conglomerate that also owned Paramount, bought Madison Square Garden. To diversify from just being an event space, the Garden started one of the first cable sports networks, called USA. I said to Charlie Bluhdorn, "Let me have it and we'll reprogram it for general entertainment."

So Charlie with one blunt finger transferred USA to Paramount and gave me control.

I thought HBO, which had just begun to program beyond offering movies, could help us and took them in as an equal partner. Then, dumbheadedly, I gave Universal the right to buy into it, too. We were partners with them on our worldwide theatrical distribution and theater ownership outside the United States, and when they heard about our getting into cable television programming, they wanted in. But we were a dysfunctional partnership—three equal, unwieldy players, with different agendas, fighting all the time. At one lunch I watched Universal's president call the leader of HBO a liar. He grabbed the HBO guy by his tie and hauled his scrawny neck halfway across the table before I was able to pull him back. Soon after that incident, HBO sued for peace and agreed to be bought out, leaving Universal and Paramount equal partners in USA and our newly started Sci-Fi Channel. Over the next ten years they were wildly successful, with USA becoming the number one cable network, and an important asset for both of us. That was all good until Universal eventually got sold to Matsushita Electric, and then it got really complicated. The Seagram Company, owned by the Bronfman family, bought Universal from Matsushita, and that brought them into conflict with Paramount (which had been bought by Viacom). If that isn't all that dizzying, just wait.

The reason for the conflict was the way the original agreement had been written, with one critically important paragraph. It stated that all future cable channels owned by either Universal or Paramount were to be equally shared, so when Viacom bought Paramount, Universal took the position that it was entitled to own half of Viacom's cable networks, which included MTV and Nickelodeon. Sumner Redstone, who controlled Viacom, went bonkers when he heard this extreme claim and countersued Universal, saying *he* ought to own the USA Network. As lawsuits tend to, this one dragged on for some time, and the final settlement gave Universal sole ownership of USA.

Edgar Bronfman, Universal's new owner, thought I would be the best person to run USA. He was my old friend, and we'd talked at various times about my coming in to run all of Universal. In 1997, soon after getting total control of USA, he called me and said, "I have no idea what to do with these networks. I don't know anything about television. I don't care about television. You should really manage these assets." That was an unexpected but nice thing to land on my plate, but as much as I was excited by the idea, I told Edgar I wouldn't give up the HSN company we'd been building into an internet powerhouse. So the deal we made was to merge USA into HSN; Universal owned 45 percent of our company, and Edgar joined our board. I loved the name USA Networks and quickly changed our parent company name to something far more aspirational than HSN. It was a totally opportunistic move. I didn't really fancy going back to old media, but I couldn't resist taking this gift basket of assets that had been given to me.

Everyone in the industry was shocked that our little meaningless toad of a company was going to own USA and Sci-Fi.

Sumner Redstone called me, outraged, asking how I got Bronfman to give me control. "That is the *dumbest* transaction I've ever heard of in my life," he yelled in his usual dismissive way toward his competitors. "You never, *ever* give up control." This was classic Sumner. He was a maniac for control, something I wasn't exactly shy about, either, but Edgar really had done a smart thing. He wanted to concentrate on the movie studio as well as build up a record company, and he thought I'd do a better job developing his television assets. In a few short years, we built up USA and Sci-Fi to a value of more than $10 billion. Edgar also got the stub value of our growing interactive businesses. Sumner fumed, which made me doubly overjoyed.

USA, when owned equally by Paramount and Universal, was a classic dysfunctional joint venture. Two equal and usually competitive owners can rarely manage to do something positive together. Joint ventures usually develop into civil service–like operations where no one really is in charge. They also usually lead to tears and are eventually disassembled. Despite all the progress USA Networks had made, I thought it was stuck in a kind of bureaucratic limbo.

What I wanted to do was make contrarian, unique shows—*Monk, Silk Stalkings, La Femme Nikita*. These began to better the image of USA, and the network prospered.

Then we turned our attention to Sci-Fi, which was filled with reruns of *Stargate* and had no buzz about it. I went to Steven Spielberg for advice. We had breakfast one morning in Santa Monica, and I proposed we rename the entire network Steven Spielberg's Sci-Fi.

Steven wasn't up for that. I then suggested we find a good story for him to tell in a miniseries. He came up with the idea for *Taken,* which was a giant success for Sci-Fi, although I'm not sure I could actually tell you what it was about.

As part of the deal with Seagram, in addition to USA and Sci-Fi, we got all of Universal's television library plus their television production company. They had one great series: *Law & Order,* a mainstay on NBC for years. I went to the revered and singularly dominating Dick Wolf, whose show it was, and asked him to stop making pilot after pilot in other genres and just concentrate on making lots of *Law & Order*s. Out of that came *Law & Order: SVU,* which I've been butchering ever since by calling it *Law & Order: SUV,* and many other spin-offs. I think Dick Wolf may be the most successful producer ever of hour-long dramas.

I joined the board of Universal's parent company, Seagram's, which had been founded by Edgar's grandfather in Canada and owned a huge variety of businesses. I found myself going up to Montreal regularly for board meetings, which were mostly about liquor (Seagram owned the largest liquor company in the world) and Tropicana fruit juices. For several years Edgar and I were in alignment about the direction of USA and Seagram's businesses. I was supportive of Edgar's desire to unload many of the non-media assets that had built the company, and his father, the chairman, let him have his way, despite his own brother's conservative disdain for all things Hollywood. I encouraged Edgar to expand into the record business, his first love, and he purchased Polygram, one of the largest music producers.

I remember his uncle coming to me, worried that his nephew was selling off all these classic Seagram liquor businesses to dive further into show business. I knew how rough the music industry was, but stood up for Edgar. We were growing bigger and bigger at USA, and I was happy to cheer him on. But then Edgar started believing he couldn't compete in media at his size. This was the year AOL and Time Warner merged, and the whole media world was convinced that size was the magic solution to slowing profits. Size and scale are what media people talk about endlessly. It's their number one concern. I don't get it. No matter what your size is, as long as it meets minimum conditions (enough capital to roll over the tough years), you can always compete in this business because it always has been, is now, and always will be a business of hits. Or lack thereof.

Nevertheless, Edgar decided to put Seagram up for sale. He worried I might be competitive or would somehow stall his desire to merge with a bigger player, so he never included me in their secret deliberations. A few months later, to the world's shocked surprise, it was announced that Vivendi, a French water company that was being transformed by the ferociously and irresponsibly competitive Jean-Marie Messier, bought Seagram for nearly $35 billion.

I liked the little emperor—JMM3, as he liked to call himself. USA was doing fantastically well at the time, with huge earnings and cash flow, so he liked me, too. But I knew, and he knew, that we would eventually find ourselves in conflict because it only made sense for him to consolidate the television businesses we co-owned, and that had been separated at birth by Edgar. I understood he would want to get our entertainment assets under his sole control, but I didn't like the dubious methods he used to pressure me to do it. As an example, we at USA had come up with an innovative idea to buy $2 billion of Amazon's debt. The stock market tech bubble of 2000 had burst, and people were worried that Amazon wouldn't be able to meet its obligations. The bonds had sold off for twenty-five cents on the dollar. We thought either it'd default and we'd be able to take the company over, or in the worst of the best case we'd make a potful of money if it survived. We wanted to act quickly, but needed Vivendi's approval to spend that much. JMM3 turned us down. He did it just to frustrate me. If I didn't agree to sell them our media assets, he'd just freeze our ability to grow. Frustrated I was. All our interactive assets were booming, and despite so many others flailing in the sector, we had emerged as an internet darling. I wanted to supercharge that growth and didn't want Vivendi holding us hostage to their machinations. I thought the only option was to let them have their way and buy USA.

I was on my boat in the Caribbean when I called Messier to tell him I would agree to sell him USA Network, the Sci-Fi Channel, and Universal Television for $12 billion. I knew he was desperate to consolidate, but didn't believe he was desperate enough to accept my opening number.

But he did, in an instant, asking only that I agree to serve as chairman and CEO of all his U.S. entertainment businesses. I agreed if I could do it part-time—my "night job," as I called it. A week later, we made the announcement to an astonished media scrum. Edgar Bronfman, whom Messier had pushed aside after assuring him they'd run the company together, sat with forlorn dignity in the first row of the press conference.

It reminded me of Sumner Redstone's fierce dictum: never cede or sell control. When you sell you give up being on center stage. Edgar's uncle Charles, after they sold out to Vivendi, said, "All my life wherever we would go, when the plane landed there'd be a Seagram representative at attention on the tarmac to greet us, and we'd roll into the city royally. Now all I am is just another rich guy." I was very grateful to Edgar for having given me the chance to build up his television assets and was really sorry we'd become estranged. Thankfully, over time we repaired our relationship and will always be good friends.

For the third time in my life I was again running a major studio as well as theme parks and god-knows-what-else I had no time for. What no one realized was that Messier was out far ahead of his skis in making these huge helter-skelter commitments all over the world. He was dangerously close to not being able to pay the interest on his debts. His was a giant ego straddling the world like a colossus. He asked me to be the principal speaker at a retreat in Deauville for all his worldwide employees, and I remember him striding across a giant stage like Napoleon (yes, he was a short fellow) in front of the million-dollar video screen he'd erected. It reminded me of the last time I'd been in Deauville back in the late 1970s. It was early in my new relationship with Diane, and we'd taken the children to the elegant Royal hotel for a holiday. One night, DVF and I drove to a famous fish restaurant in Normandy, and I ordered the lobster bisque. It was the first time I was in Europe with her, and of course I didn't speak French and was totally dependent on her language skills (she spoke four different ones). As if I wasn't feeling insecure enough, in the door walked the über-glamorous Yves Saint Laurent, his partner, Pierre Bergé, and several of their darlings. They swooshed by and said their supersized, flamboyant hellos to Diane. I stood up to be introduced and through some wondrous revenge à l'américaine I threw up a quart of that bisque all over Saint Laurent's perfectly white suit.

It soon turned out Vivendi was running on fumes and facing default. The French government and the grandees of France threw Messier out and replaced him with an establishment bureaucrat. They badly needed stability while trying to sort out how to dispose of all of Messier's far-flung financial adventuring and pretty much begged me to take responsibility for all the entertainment assets worldwide, including the largest music business in the world. I felt sorry for their predicament and agreed to this expanded role, though I said I doubted I could do it for long. They wanted to give me lots of stock options, but I declined, telling them I'd do the work for nothing so long as either of us could call it a day on a phone call.

I moved into the Universal Tower on the top floor that used to be solely and majestically occupied by its founder, Jules Stein, the boss of the fabled Lew Wasserman, whose office, one story below, was where I had been humbled as a young ABC executive some thirty years earlier. The movie job this time was the least productive work I'd ever done; the business model had become bureaucratic and gone backward, or at least I thought so. Companies were "budgeting" total costs for making movies; Universal's that year was $700 million. I thought there should be no budget, just start at zero and build up from there only when a movie and its individual cost made sense. Macro numbers and forward projections are fine for accounting, but anathema as a decision tool in making movies, which are and always will be onetime, one-off projects.

The Universal executives were justifying making a terrible and very expensive movie called *Van Helsing*, about the vampire hunter from *Dracula*, saying that they'd come in short of the $700 million if they didn't make it. I said, "That'd be fine with me," and they said if they came in under this year's budget, the next year's would be cut back. I said, "Who cares? The only 'care' is that the script for *Van Helsing* is unreadable," and they said I didn't understand the modern movie business. Also that they had "green light" authority for making films and I shouldn't stand in their way. I hate this term, "green light"; I believe that the final call on filmmaking decisions should always be made by the chief executive.

I never should have agreed to run Universal in this part-time way, being Vivendi's shepherd and just trying to keep its assets from getting into trouble. I felt it was the least I could do, after selling them $12 billion of our properties they couldn't afford. Fatuously, I did like the idea of again being a big-time Hollywood executive. That was lame, vain, and foolish because I had much better prospects in the tech revolution. While the internet was in the doghouse after the dot-com bust of 2000, we, the newly named IAC/InterActiveCorp, came out of the bust with thriving businesses because we had so much financial discipline, while so many others at the early internet feast had overgorged on bad ideas like Webvan and eToys.

Thankfully, my night job at Vivendi Universal Entertainment ended within the year when Vivendi sold those assets to NBC and Comcast. The timing couldn't have been better. IAC now had billions more to invest at exactly the moment when the internet began to take off and be center court in everyone's lives. That detour back into entertainment media, though wildly profitable, was just a way station before becoming something of an internet entrepreneur. Eventually, I probably did qualify for that overused term. Over the next twenty years we feasted on 155 separate internet business transactions. A more apt description of me might be "internet opportunist." I didn't have any great foresight. I wasn't a "visionary"—another overused term. I had no overarching plan. Everything emerged organically from my first visit to QVC, when I realized screens could *and would* be used for something other than telling stories. And then out of thin air—or more precisely, thin wire—came the internet to supercharge it all.

I had such a hothouse beginning after I left Fox, from the high of being on the front pages of *The New York Times* with the announced mergers of Paramount and CBS, to the low when they both failed to materialize. Presumed dead afterward. Taking tiny Silver King like a sad consolation prize and tossing and turning it into a mountain of assets.

My one and constant partner since I left Fox has been John Malone and his Liberty Media company. Over thirty years we had only one disagreement, but it was a monster. Had I lost I would have forfeited the control of the company I'd fought so hard for. Liberty filed an epic lawsuit against me that resulted in one of the few times I've actually been in court in a witness box, other than when I was eleven years old and accused of using my bicycle to run over and scar a defenseless little girl (I didn't do it!). Anyway, after we had started our spin-off process with Expedia in 2005, the market began to discount IAC's prospects, and we went through a couple of years of poor stock performance. One of Malone's executives started to take public pot-shots at IAC and me personally, saying maybe I'd stayed at IAC beyond my sell date. Trust between us began to fray, and Malone was quoted in *The Wall Street Journal* as saying that the "Diller Premium" that the stock had enjoyed for ten years was now becoming the "Diller Discount."

I decided our next spinout would be done in common stock rather than the high-vote stock that gave Liberty and me control. Liberty disagreed and said I'd violated the terms of my proxy (the means with which I con-trolled the IAC companies). We went to high court in Delaware for four days of a very public trial with both John Malone and me testifying. I was the last one on the stand, and after a grueling five hours it was clear to the courtroom and the judge that I hadn't violated anything and that several of the Liberty witnesses had lied in disparaging me. The only one who told the truth was Malone, who had been misled by his executives and wasn't willing to lie to support their claims. The judge quickly ruled in our favor, and that trauma ended with a handwritten note from John apologizing for starting the whole mess. I'm grateful to him for so many things, for being my almost ever-faithful partner, but for that one brief moment, and for being so steadfast in his encouragement and support. Oh, and for my great good luck of being often in the room with by far the smartest man in media.

During the 1990s and early 2000s, I hopscotched my way across every internet opportunity, not that we didn't plow money into some glorious dead ends. We put hundreds of millions of dollars into Citysearch, be-lieving it was a great organizing principle for local businesses to have a web page that connected them to internet users. It was, but it was also an impossibly hard slog at a time when not enough people were online to support it. We struggled for years until Google's monopoly tossed City-search into the dustheap of online history.

That wasn't the only thing Google manhandled us out of. We bought Ask.com for $1.8 billion because we thought its search interface far superior to theirs. It was the first to get away from showing ten blue links and was innovating with what it called "smart answers" to search queries. What we didn't factor in was that Google could simply copy all our innovations and push us into irrelevance. We still own Ask.com. It's a bit of a lemon, but for almost twenty years we've been able to squeeze enough profits out of it to get us way past breakeven on the original purchase price. As usual for me, we made our mistakes early and course-corrected from there.

Some of our ventures led, some fizzled. But the ones that led were block-busters. One that still leads is Expedia. I thought travel was the perfect business to be colonized by the internet. We found and bought a fast-growing but still small company called Hotel Reservations Network based in Dallas. It owned the name Hotels.com, and it was our first foray into online travel. Microsoft had also started an online travel service called Expedia, which by 2001 was getting some traction. After the dot-com bubble burst, I went to see Steve Ballmer, then CEO of Microsoft, on a mission to persuade him to sell it to us. It was still losing money and Steve felt Microsoft shouldn't be in these internet verticals anyway and quickly agreed to let us have it in exchange for $1 billion of our stock. We were set to close the deal in October 2001 when you-know-what happened on September 11 and travel ceased to exist. We had an out clause in our deal for a "material adverse change," and 9/11 was certainly that. We thrashed around for weeks asking ourselves how we could pay $1 billion for a travel service when there was no traveling. One day, as we were stewing around, someone in the room said, "If there's life, there's travel." That rang loud enough for me to say, "That's it—we're betting on *life*," and we closed the deal.

How a person who never dated in the conventional sense came to dominate online dating is another odd one. My stepson, Alexander, had told me about a Canadian online dating service called Friendster. I was curious. It was filled with prostitutes, and I told Alex thank you but no. I couldn't get the idea of online dating out of my mind, though; it was so obvious online technology would be great at matchmaking. Soon after, we found a small Texas company called Match.com that was on the legitimate side of connecting people for dates. We snatched it up and in depth and breadth grew the category into a huge business. Around the same time I agreed to start an "innovation lab" inside IAC to develop ideas from scratch. I never thought much would come out of these internal groups, since stand-alone innovation rarely innovates inside a large enterprise (mostly it just copies what happens next door), but we birthed a giant exception to that rule. Tinder was the name assigned to a screen-swiping technology the innovation lab came up with, and within a year—with zero advertising—it became the biggest hit in dating. Our total investment was about $750,000, and it went on to be worth $15 billion.

I started with no business model other than liking companies that had some actual revenue and profits as opposed to sexy-sounding ideas and big talk. I turned an icy eye on the early schemers and hustlers who spent huge marketing dollars to build audiences but had no path to actually making any money. We survived all that because of *our* values of fiscal prudence, but we were also always willing to take a flier on a good idea, though we would never bet the company on a single transaction.

Over time, and again with no foresight, we did evolve into a unique business model: the anti-conglomerate conglomerate. If you own dozens and dozens of disparate businesses, you're certainly a conglomerate. And we've housed as many as sixty different brands. But I had become opposed to the concept of agglomeration. Bigness for bigness made no sense to me. When I decided a business was sufficiently developed, we'd spin it out into an independent entity. As we built up all these entities, I thought managing them centrally wasn't the best way. Once they achieved some scale they ought to stand on their own—make their own decisions with independence from the mother ship. We've done that now with ten separately traded public companies. We created a business model that is still unique to us—and as I write this we're contemplating our eleventh spin-off. I don't believe scale gets you anywhere other than sloppy governance. In so many cases consolidation is just an ego and organ-sizing competition. In today's world you don't need scale to compete, you just need a good idea—getting it noticed and distributed is at the touch of the send button on an iPhone. Good solid one-off ideas are a whole lot better than consolidating stuff just to be a bigger and more unwieldy enterprise.

Like almost everything in my life, iteration—*one dumb step in front of the other, course-correcting as you go*—is the only process I'm any good at. I'm best building things from scratch. I've learned I'm not a very good shepherd of things already built. I don't add much value to ongoing successful businesses and I wish I were a better manager who had training in dealing directly and effectively with the thirty thousand employees under our tents. I think I was most productive when I built the *Movie of the Week* up from just an idea, where I was the first employee and made every decision. Same as at Fox Broadcasting. I feel so much more able assembling all the pieces, where I can touch each of them directly. I'm much too much of a micromanager to be anything but frustrated hovering a superficial forty thousand feet above the day-to-day issues.

A few years ago I decided I didn't want to be on the ground, in the grind as much, so I ceded being the chief executive officer of our companies. I still remain chairman of our two principal publicly traded entities. This leaves me time to get in trouble elsewhere.

CHAPTER 29

And there's no trouble I enjoy more than building things, starting with a drafter's blank page. No process is more detailed, more precise, more potentially infuriating than a building project. Or more gratifying and exhilarating (usually said after completion).

When we outgrew our rented headquarters office space in midtown Manhattan, I thought we ought to have a place of our own. I like to be near water—actually I *need* to be near water—and I thought it would be great to convert one of the piers on the Hudson River into an office building. I found out that wasn't easy or practical, so I started to look for land we could acquire that at least looked out on the river. We found an available old warehouse that was being used as a garage for trucks on the Lower West Side. But what to build? I didn't want just a box with some snazzy glass coating.

I'd always admired Frank Gehry, who'd never done a building in New York. I'd gone to Bilbao some years before and marveled at his genius; I was dazzled by the museum he designed and by the effect it had not just on the city but worldwide. I had known him socially and went to see him at his office in Santa Monica—he wanted me to see his almost-finished Disney Concert Hall in downtown L.A. As we drove in my convertible we talked about our shared love of sailing and sailboats. At some point I said, "Wouldn't it be great to have a building that looked like sailcloth?" When we got there, he left me alone to wander around the dazzling Disney Hall. A while later Frank reappeared with one sheet of paper, a sketch he'd just made; it was a white structure that really looked like it was sailing along in a breeze. It was a pure Gehry original and I loved it at first sight, but he quickly said it probably couldn't be built because there was no current method of making glass that you could see through from inside but that looked white on the outside. Neither of us, though, are much daunted by practicality. Years later, after endless mock-ups and experiments, that building now sits on the bank of the Hudson River like a floating iceberg. At night it's a mesmerizing glass lantern, a Frank Gehry architectural masterpiece. I still have the original line drawing Frank made that astonishingly looks exactly like the building we built.

When we started digging the foundation we found so much toxic material that it took us almost a year to get it cleaned up enough to begin construction. As the skeleton rose, a shape like no other in the city, much less the world, I kept thinking back to my childhood when I took a bulldozer to clear away orange trees for my father's tract houses. When I came back after they were finished and saw the hope and optimism on the faces of the people lining up to buy these houses, it welded deep in me an ethical link between building and goodness. One of the few things that reliably depresses me is when I see buildings abandoned during construction. Seeing hope and optimism extinguished just kills me.

The Lower West Side of Manhattan has been Diane's and my territory now for thirty-five years. It started when she bought an old artist's lair as a combination design studio and home on West Twelfth Street. She was one of the uptown pioneers who colonized the very unruly Lower West Side. Some years later she moved to a classic landmarked building on the corner of Washington and Fourteenth Street, where she built a penthouse bedroom and terrace above four floors of offices. She settled into downtown life in the Meatpacking District—so called because the area was filled with meatpacking warehouses and trucks to transport their beef. Before it got dandified, prostitutes stood on the street corners as the trucks rumbled by at dawn. Diane's activism knows no bounds or territories, and she got drawn into the neighborhood's local affairs. There was this elevated train track, called the High Line, that snaked around the Lower West Side. It was originally part of the turn-of-the-century railroad system that made

New York the commerce capital of the country, but it was overgrown with weeds and had fallen into decay. Thirty feet up in the air, no train had run on it for decades. Local building owners and developers wanted to tear it down. It was seen as a barrier to building anything new, not that these owners had done much developing over the years; they mostly just sat on their real estate holdings waiting for them to appreciate in value while they hypocritically complained that the old railroad was standing in the way. In the waning days of the Giuliani administration, they got a demolition order, and the mayor signed it. Diane and her neighbor the restaurateur Florent hosted a fundraiser: Save the High Line. Two young men, Robert Hammond and Joshua David, had this idea to build an urban park alongside the old train track, and this vagabond group got the demolition order stayed for a few months until Michael Bloomberg became the mayor and backed their crazy idea. The city put up a lot of the money, as did our family foundation, and eight years later the High Line park opened, and everyone was suddenly agape as this old forgotten structure emerged as an airborne green ribbon, one of the most original public parks ever created. Emulated all over the world, now it is one of the must-see attractions in New York. Oh, and those builders who wanted the High Line torn down? They've now profited by erecting dozens of architecturally ambitious commercial buildings all around it.

"No, no, no," I said when Diana Taylor, my friend who was chair of the Hudson River Park, called to tell me, "I've got your next project." I told her I felt we'd done our part for the Lower West Side. She said Pier 54, the famous entertainment and part-time cruising pier, was falling apart and had to be torn down, and they needed a sponsor to help build a new one. She sent over a maquette of a slab of concrete with a few trees on it, and I took a short look and said rebuilding that old pier didn't interest me. Soon after I was flying in a helicopter to New Jersey and asked the pilot to cruise up the Hudson River as I looked down on all the piers along the river and wondered why they were all rebuilt as rectangles. I thought that didn't seem required, since boats were no longer going to tie up to either side. The Hudson River Park Trust had reclaimed many of these unused piers, and turned them into pocket parks jutting out from the bike and running paths that went all the way up to the George Washington Bridge. I admired what they'd done, but questioned why there hadn't been anything aspirational or original built on the mighty Hudson River. Why didn't we have something unique like the Sydney Opera House in Australia, an architectural icon for one of the great cities of the world? I couldn't get that ambition out of my mind, so I called Diana and asked if I might be able to dream up a park that wasn't just another rectangle. She said, "It's your money. If you want to fantasize, go ahead." We started to do just that. I could never have imagined it would take ten years and so much friction and conflict, but building a park that floats on a river wasn't going to be for the fainthearted.

The pier that was being torn down had historically hosted concerts, and I wanted ours to also have performance spaces. We began an informal architects' competition. I liked the work of Bjarke Ingels and Santiago Calatrava, and I remembered seeing a dazzling exhibit by the British designer Thomas Heatherwick. I asked each of the three to give ideas in whatever form they wished and said we'd pay their expenses. Bjarke Ingels from BIG came back with an intriguing, winding, snail-like concept that was just too radical and not enough of a park. Calatrava had ideas that looked too much like his bridges. Heatherwick, though, came back with a brass ark that was madly ambitious and incredible to look at, but even Noah would have been daunted trying to build it. Heatherwick had a pixieish, magician-like persona and endlessly spewed brilliant ideas, some totally off the wall, some artily odd, but all original and delightfully entertaining. I wanted that sensibility and asked him to come back with a design that was at least in the realm of practical. Shortly thereafter, he walked in with a concept that dazzled at first sight—it was square, not a rectangle, with a bowl-like structure held up by 267 concrete piles topped with 132 tulip-shaped bowls that looked like a floating tulip field. One of its four corners rose seventy-five feet above the water and had the most perfectly gorgeous views out to the Statue of Liberty. It was a geometrical masterpiece, whimsical and oh so devilishly original and iconic that I thought there's just no way we could build the thing. I was told driving that many piles into the porous Hudson River was a really bad idea and if we ever started the piledriving we'd end up with a bunch of concrete sticks waving in the wind. I wasn't being very practical and said this was just too good an idea to abandon, so let's find a way to do it. If you're willing to throw away practicality and you're lucky enough to have enough resources, there's always a way.

The original estimate to rebuild the pier was $70 million. The new current eyeball estimate was at least $150 million with no one confident it would hold. Everyone said, please just stop this nonsense and get a more sober-minded architect to come up with something doable. Nevertheless I plowed on, though I did blanch some when the estimate climbed to $250 million. Part of that escalation was our decision to add an amphitheater and other performance spaces. I don't remember one irrevocable moment when I was presented with the final budget and said "Yes." We just slid our way forward, and I never held up my hand to say "Stop." But I thought if I was right and this lived up to its potential, who would care twenty or fifty or five hundred years from now what it cost. But money was just the start of the troubles to come.

Just as we were making commitments to buy enormous amounts of concrete and to corral all the barges we'd need to start the work, we were besieged by various public interest groups that were hostile to the very idea of driving piles in the Hudson River. I'm not saying they weren't virtuous, but I thought it knee-jerk just to say, "Building anything in our wondrous Hudson River is by definition a bad idea." The Riverkeeper organization said we were going to pollute the Hudson, that we were going to deprive the American eel fish of its needed sunlight. I responded that there were 315 miles of the Hudson River, and couldn't the eels go a few blocks upriver for their sunlight? Another group said we would block kayakers from using this portion of the river, all three acres of it. They were mostly well-meaning, but many of the complaints were made more for political reasons. We received our first formal lawsuit in year three. It was backed by the Durst family, ostensibly because they, too, thought no one should build on the river, but really because they were resentful and angry about mistreatment by the trust that governs everything on the river. Years ago Durst had wanted to commercialize a pier and the trust turned him down. They had been seeking revenge ever since, and there we were, a fat target. I went to Mr. Durst and asked, "Can't you find another project to object to?" He replied, "You have my sympathy—but no."

We had already spent $45 million, and my family pleaded with me to just get out of this. Their attitude was *Let's not go where we're not wanted.*

Exasperated, I decided to abandon the project. But it wouldn't let me go. It took several months and the intercession of Governor Cuomo to get the lawsuits settled. I'll always be grateful to him—without his intervention we would have been toast. At even greater cost we started up again, planting those piles in the water, never knowing how deep we'd have to go because there's no bedrock in the Hudson. In they went, and up grew our tulip bowls, and the planting of 112 trees, 18,000 perennials, and 66,000 bulbs. Finally, ten years after it began mostly as a daydream, all the cranes and barges were gone, the trees planted, flowers were blooming, and we were finished.

Before we let anyone in, I walked it alone, stopping at every viewpoint and marveling at what we had wrought. Whenever I'm out and about watching people crossing that bridge, a bridge that connects a little island to a big one, seeing them so happy-faced both coming and going, I know for certain it was worth all the storm and strife we went through to create this oasis from city life. Two million people came that first year, and many more millions since. Someday, a hundred or more years from now, if there still is a New York, if there's still a United States that hasn't been blown to bits by internal or external conflicts, people might wonder how this ever got built, and I hope they'll marvel at it in the same way I do whenever I see something unique that wouldn't have happened if it hadn't been for one person's imagination and will (and yes, wealth). And, also . . . a little craziness.

There's no motivation other than the public good for public art and parks to exist, and that they do is something of a miracle, given how many obstacles get in the way of making them happen. They don't kill cancer, they're not going to solve world hunger or inequality, but one thing they do is give pleasure and sustenance—sometimes also just solace—to people living in or visiting big cities made mostly of cold concrete.

We came up with the name for the park because I kept reading comments that said it would or should be called Diller Island, and that made me shudder. One day toward the end of construction, a group of us were sitting around talking about all the wondrous experiences people would soon be having on the island, and someone remarked, "Let's don't get carried away with ourselves, after all—it's just a little island." *That's it*, I thought—*Little Island! We have our name!*

Since I left corporate life some thirty years ago, there's hardly an area of the internet that IAC hasn't touched. The number and pace of transactions and attempts at transactions are dizzying. Some weren't successful, but enough were to produce a combined value of more than $100 billion. Not bad for a company that started out on fumes with $40 million in revenue. That wasn't my goal, because the money has always been a by-product, but as a report card I am proud of it. Far better this late in life to have some pride compared with the shame I'd felt for most of my early years.

Having all this wealth, I want to be sure we conduct ourselves responsibly. Our family lives on such an elevated scale, and it would be beyond hypocritical for us to deny how much we enjoy all of it. Our appetites for living are large, but, without too much virtue signaling, so, too, is our obligation to fulfill all the responsibilities that come with wealth. That's mandatory, and while I don't think we should be prideful about our philanthropic and charitable contributions, we ought to transparently account for them as a standard for future generations of our family.

Thus far we've supported more than eight hundred separate organizations with more than $670 million. I also believe there's nothing wrong in passing wealth on. Our children were raised with it and so long as they are responsible citizens leading purposeful lives I see no reason to deprive them of our good fortune. Alexander is spending lots of time and many millions of his own funds to enact into law a Thrift Savings Plan that would help all working Americans who currently have no vested savings. Tatiana finds every way she can to help the weak and endangered in society. I've watched as they've grown into wonderfully unique adults with their own wondrously unique children, and yes, I know that everyone says this about their own children, but *everyone* says this about ours.

As for much of the rest, I've been able to play a part in the cultural landscape of the last fifty years as well as the beginnings of the internet revolution. I'm a little more wobbly, but I'm still plying the waters for new opportunities just as artificial intelligence is forging the next revolution. I'll only stop revolving and evolving when my heart stops and I stop moving altogether. I've been so lucky in this life. Serendipity has delivered me opportunities that were inexplicable otherwise, and while I certainly can't see around any new corners, I want to walk adventurous streets for as long as I can.

As I am writing this, I'm lying in bed on my sailboat, the three-masted schooner *Eos*—named for the mythological goddess of the sun. It's another project built from scratch. It took six years to complete, and, no surprise, I was engaged with the placement of every stitch and screw. This theme of building has dominated my life. As has my need to be close to water, either in sight of, on top of, or swimming through it. I'm an Aquarian, a Water Bearer, and while I'm not a great believer in astrology, I have swum from the back of *Eos* in all the warm waters in the world. While I can go a good length with friends, it is Diane who is the champ swimmer. For her it is a kind of meditation. She'll disappear for two hours without people or distractions as she mantras her way across often un-placid seas. Our boat life isn't an occasional thing. We spend months cruising around the world, sometimes with family or friends, but often just Diane and me and one of our cloned Jack Russell terriers.

We now have five, all from the same mother, Shannon, who I found twenty-five years ago abandoned on a country road while I was biking in Ireland. She was just nine months old and followed me around for a day until I picked up and took her back to the U.S., where she lived until she was sixteen on our farm in Connecticut. When she started to decline, I couldn't imagine not having her in our lives. I'd heard about the successful cloning of dogs in South Korea and decided to try. The results have been extraordinary. The pups, born from Shannon's DNA, do not have her exact coloring or sequence of spots, but I see in each of them the essence of Shannon's spirit and soul. And yes, I know it is controversial and an indication of how outrageously advantaged our lives are. I hold no illusions about that.

We live life as fully as possible in every arena we're able to. I don't feel guilty about it and guilt isn't the reason for our philanthropy. I've worked hard, helped make some beautiful things, tell some great stories, built companies, and created jobs. I believe Diane and I have earned our keep, but we surely know our keep is vastly different from most others. There is such disparity in this that *fairly earned* doesn't seem enough. Nothing really does. The wealth gap is far too great and unless better guardrails are put around our capitalistic system I doubt it will, or even should, survive.

On February 2, 2001, Diane and I got married, twenty-six years after our not-so-cute meeting. Alexander, Tatiana, and I are all Aquarians and Diane had been planning to give a big party for our three combined birthdays. Hundreds of people were coming to celebrate at her downtown studio. We knew we were now a couple for life, so we decided to surprise everyone by getting married that day. We went down to city hall and found a willing judge to do the vows, and that night we surprised everyone in announcing our marriage.

More than two decades have passed since then, and now we often smile, remembering a scene that took place in the early years of our romance. As we were driving back to the city one weekend, we saw two very old people huddled lovingly together in the cold, arm in arm crossing Madison Avenue. We said to each other, "Maybe someday that will be us."

Us it has been and continues to be.

I have had quite a long run, and I am still running. If I had to ask myself why, I'd say with certainty it's because I'm still curious. I never see a plane taking off that I don't want to be on. I still want and need to be engaged and part of things. I was there in the great days of television in the late 1960s, when there were still new formats to invent. I was in the movie business in the 1970s, when movies were in one of their greatest creative periods, and I got to make some that have stood the test of time. I was back in television to invent the fourth network in the 1980s, and in the 1990s left corporate life to become something of an entrepreneur. Early in the twenty-first century I got to play at the beginning of the internet. And yeah, I got rich and accomplished. But that truly was the least of it. The most of it was building, always building. And even better than that was being lucky enough to let a family build me into something resembling a person.

ACKNOWLEDGMENTS

I began writing this book fifteen years ago. It was the epic of an intermittent process, starting and stopping for months, putting it aside for a year or two as I was overengaged in business pursuits. Once I had a full manuscript, around year ten, I asked some close friends to read it and give me whatever thoughts they had about the work, and whether I should even continue. I wouldn't and couldn't have proceeded without their enthusiasm and their extraordinarily helpful notes, which had me rewriting draft after draft until the manuscript was reluctantly torn from my cold dead hands a few months ago. It's entirely true that their support gave me the energy to both finish and commit to publish, which at various times I thought would never happen. I thank them anonymously as I know that would be their preference. And do so with unreserved gratitude. I do have to specifically thank those in my personal office, particularly Patrick Shae and Suzanne Kennedy, who kept track of the endless drafts, picture retrieval and collation, and all the also endless details of getting ready for publication; and everyone at Simon & Schuster, particularly the copyeditors who had to put up with my revisions way past so many missed due dates.

All my life I've been engaged in almost every form of creating product. This is the first time I've ever been the product itself. It's an unnerving experience, but one that shows me how vital it is to have the support of others when you're vulnerable and in the barrel of making work. That's a lesson I hope to never unlearn when I'm back on the other side.

ABOUT THE AUTHOR

Barry Diller's business career has ranged from the end of the golden age of Hollywood to the frontiers of media and technology. He began his career at ABC in the 1960s, where he invented the Movie of the Week and the miniseries, revolutionizing television programming. Diller later became the CEO of Paramount Pictures from 1974 to 1984, where he oversaw the production of classic films such as *Saturday Night Fever*, *Raiders of the Lost Ark*, and *Grease*. In 1984, Diller joined 20th Century Fox, where he launched the Fox Broadcasting Company. In 1995, Diller founded IAC, a conglomerate focused on e-commerce, media, and internet companies. Under Diller's leadership, IAC has grown into a digital powerhouse, owning brands such as Vimeo, Angi, and the Match Group. Diller also chairs Expedia Group, one of the world's largest travel companies. He is married to Diane von Fürstenberg, fashion designer, author, and philanthropist.